WHITE
LIKE ME:

*Reflections on Race
from a Privileged Son*

revised and updated

TIM WISE

Soft Skull Press
Brooklyn

Cover design by Brett Yasko
Interior design by Gary Fogelson

Soft Skull Press
An Imprint of Counterpoint LLC
2117 Fourth Street
Suite D
Berkeley, CA 94710

www.softskull.com
www.counterpointpress.com

Distributed by Publishers Group West

Printed in the United States of America

The Library of Congress has cataloged the first edition as follows:

Wise, Tim J.
   White like me: reflections on race from a priviledged son / by Tim Wise.
      p. cm.
   ISBN 1-932360-68-9
1. Racism—United States, 2. United States—Race relations. 3. Wise Tim J.
4. Whites—United States—Social conditions. I. Title.

   E185.615.W565 2005
   305.8'00973—dc22

2005001052

2008 Edition: ISBN-13: 978-1-933368-99-3 ISBN-10: 1-933368-99-3

10 9 8 7 6 5 4 3

CONTENTS

PREFACE

TO THE NEW EDITION

IT IS RARE, if not altogether unheard of, for an author to be allowed a second opportunity to do their first works over. Once a book is published, it's done. For good or bad, and whether or not the author feels as though he or she has managed to make the points intended, it's out there. If you have more to say as a writer, fine, but you'll have to say it in another book, because it's too late to revisit the first one.

In the case of *White Like Me,* however, I have been given a second bite at the apple, so to speak. Soft Skull Press—now an imprint of Counterpoint—and its publisher, Richard Nash, in particular, felt as though it was important enough to not only rerelease the book, but to give it an entirely new season, as if it were essentially a new title. Herein one will find new stories, along with many from the first edition; an entirely new chapter; and an epilogue (in the form of an open letter) on Hurricane Katrina and the way in which that tragedy, still unfolding in New Orleans, relates to the subject matter of this book: racism and white privilege.

For all intents and purposes, this is a new book, and better than the original. I have grown in the three years since writing the first edition, both as a writer and as someone trying to understand racism and institutionalized white supremacy. So this will be a more mature volume, I think, with tighter analysis, far better style, and, I'm hoping, the ability to move the conversation even further than was accomplished the first time around.

That *White Like Me*, by virtue of this rerelease, has become a living document, and evolved into something smarter and stronger than before, is indicative of the way that our understandings of race, privilege, inequality, and our own lives evolve and change over time. As years go by, and with some effort on our parts, hopefully we get a bit smarter, a bit deeper in our levels of comprehension. So long as we draw breath we are never done growing. Just as I have tried to impart new knowledge in this edition of *White Like Me*, I hope we will all keep learning, keep growing, and remain open to the ways in which we can change and transform even a deeply broken society.

PREFACE

TO THE FIRST EDITION

"WHAT HAPPENED TO YOU?"

IT'S A QUESTION no one likes to hear, seeing as how it typically portends an assumption on the part of the questioner that something is terribly wrong, something that defies logic and calls for an explanation.

It's the kind of query one might get from former classmates on the occasion of one's twenty-year high school reunion: "Dear God, what the hell happened to you?" Generally, people don't ask this question of those whom they consider to have dramatically improved themselves in some way, be it physical, emotional, or professional. Instead, it is more often asked of those considered to be seriously damaged, as if the only possible answer would be, "Well, I was dropped on my head as a baby," to which the questioner would then reply, "Aha, I see."

So whenever I'm asked this, I naturally recoil for a moment, assuming that the persons inquiring "what happened" likely want an answer only in order to avoid, at whatever cost, having it (whatever "it" may be) happen to them. In my case, however, I'm usually lucky. Most of the persons who ask me "what happened" seem to be asking less for reasons of passing judgment than for reasons of confusion. They appear truly perplexed about how I turned out the way I did, especially when it comes to my views on the matter of race.

As a white man, born and reared in a society that has always bestowed upon me advantages that it has just as deliberately withheld from people of color, I am not expected to think the way I do. I am not supposed to speak against and agitate in opposition to racism and institutionalized white supremacy. Indeed, for people of color, it is often shocking to see white people even thinking about race, let alone challenging racism. After all, we don't have to spend much time contemplating the subject if we'd rather not, and historically white folks have made something of a pastime out of ignoring racism, or at least refusing to call it out as a social problem to be remedied.

But for me, and for the white folks whom I admire in history, ignoring race and racism has never been an option. Even when it would have been easier to turn away, there were too many forces, to say nothing of circumstances, pulling me back, compelling me to look at the matter, square in the face—in *my* face, truth be told.

Although white Americans often think we've had few first-hand experiences with race, because most of us are so isolated from people of color in our day-to-day lives, the reality is that this isolation *is* our experience with race. We are all experiencing race, because from the beginning of our lives we have been living in a racialized society, where the color of our skin means something socially, even while it remains largely a matter of biological and genetic irrelevance. Race may be a scientific fiction—and given the almost complete genetic overlap between persons of the various so-called races, it appears to be just that—but it is a social fact that none of us can escape no matter how much or how little we may speak of it. Just as there were no actual witches in Salem in 1692, and yet anti-witch persecution was frighteningly real, so too race can be a falsehood even as racism continues to destroy lives, to maim, to kill, and, on the flipside, to advantage those who are rarely its targets.

A few words about terminology: When I speak of "whites" or "white folks," I am referring to those persons, typically of European descent, who are able, by virtue of skin color or perhaps national origin and culture, to be perceived as "white," as members of the dominant group. I do not consider the white race to be a real thing, in biological terms, as modern science pretty well establishes that there are no truly distinct races, genetically speaking, within the human species. But the white race certainly has meaning in social terms, and it is in that social sense that I use the concept here.

As it turns out, this last point is more important than you might think. Almost immediately upon publication, this book's first edition came under fire from various white supremacists and neo-Nazis, who launched a fairly concerted effort to discredit it, and me as its' author. They sought to do this by jamming the review boards at Amazon.com with harsh critiques, none of which discussed the content—in all likelihood none of them had actually read the book—but which amounted, instead, to ad hominem attacks against me as a Jew. As several explained, being Jewish disqualifies me from being white, or writing about my experiences as a white person, since Jews are, to them, a distinct race of evildoers that seeks to eradicate Aryan stock from the face of the earth.

On the one hand (and ignoring for a second the Hitler-friendly histrionics) of course, it is absurd to think that uniquely "Jewish genes" render Jews separate from "real" whites, despite our recent European ancestry. And it's even more ridiculous to think that such genes from one-fourth of one's family, as with mine, on my paternal grandfather's line, can cancel out the three-quarters Anglo-Celtic contribution made by the rest of my ancestors. But in truth, the argument is completely irrelevant, given how I am using the concept of whiteness here. Even if there were something biologically distinct about Jews, this would hardly alter the fact that most Jews, especially in the United States, are sufficiently light skinned and assimilated so as to be fully functional as whites in the eyes of authority. This wasn't always the case but it is inarguably such now. American Jews are, by and large, able to reap the benefits of whiteness and white racial privilege, vis-à-vis people of color, in spite of our Jewishness, whether viewed in racial or cultural terms. My "claiming to be white," as one detractor put it, was not an attempt on my part to join the cool kids. I wasn't trying to fool anyone.

Whiteness is more about how you're likely to be viewed and treated in a white supremacist society than it is about what you *are,* in any meaningful sense. This is why even some very light-skinned folks of color have been able to access white privilege over the years by passing as white or being misperceived as white, much to their benefit. Whiteness is, however much clichéd the saying may be, largely a social construct. This is a book about that construct and how it plays out in the larger culture. It is not a scientific treatise, and because it is not, it is quite impervious to whatever science may or may not have to say about race, now or in the future.

As for the concept of privilege, here, too, clarification is in order. I am not claiming, nor do I believe, that all whites are wealthy and powerful. We live not only in a racialized society, but also in a class system, a patriarchal system, and one of straight supremacy/heterosexism, able-bodied supremacy, and Christian hegemony. These other forms of privilege, and the oppression experienced by those who can't manage to access them, mediate, but never fully eradicate, something like white privilege. So I realize that, socially rich whites are more powerful than poor ones, white men are more powerful than white women, able-bodied whites are more powerful than those with disabilities, and straight whites are more powerful than gay, lesbian, bisexual or transgendered whites.

But despite the fact that white privilege plays out differently for different folks, depending on these other identities, the fact remains that when all other factors are equal, whiteness matters and carries great advantage. So, for example, although whites are often poor, their poverty does not alter the fact that, relative to poor and working-class persons of color, they typically have a leg up. In fact, studies suggest that working-class whites are typically better off in terms of assets and net worth than even middle-class blacks with far higher incomes, due to past familial advantages. No one privilege system trumps all others every time, but no matter the ways in which individual whites may face obstacles on the basis of nonracial factors, our race continues to elevate us over similarly situated persons of color.

The notion of privilege is a relative concept as well as an absolute one, a point that is often misunderstood. This is why I can refer to myself as a "privileged son," despite coming from a family that was not even close to wealthy. In relative terms, compared to persons of color, whites receive certain head starts and advantages, none of which are canceled out because of factors like class, gender, or sexual orientation. Likewise, heterosexuals receive privileges relative to LGBT folks, none of which are canceled out by the poverty that many straight people experience. So too, rich folks have certain privileges on the basis of their wealth, none of which vanish like mist just because some of those wealthy persons are disabled.

While few of us are located only in privileged groups, and even fewer are located only in marginalized or oppressed groups—we are all privileged in some ways and targets in others—the fact remains that our status as occasional targets does not obviate the need for us to address the ways in which we receive unjust advantages at the expense of others.

There would be nothing wrong with someone writing a book like this and only dealing with male privilege, straight privilege, class privilege, Christian privilege, or able-bodied privilege. Likewise, those in other countries could write about privilege and oppression systems there: Japanese privilege vis-à-vis ethnic Koreans in Japan, upper-caste privilege in India and the oppression of the Dalits there, or Jewish privilege in Israel and the continued institutionalized mistreatment of the Palestinians. Those would all be illuminating, to be sure. But this book is about white privilege in the United States, because it is real and must be confronted. It is not necessarily more important than the other types of privilege, but it is important enough to merit its own examination.

I have divided the book into several sections reflecting the key lessons about whiteness that I am in the process of learning, and which lessons I hope to pass along to others.

The first of these is that to be white is to be "born to belonging." This is a term I first heard used by my friend and longtime antiracist white ally Mab Segrest, though she was using it in a different context. To be white is to be born into an environment where one's legitimacy is far less likely to be questioned than would be the legitimacy of a person of color, be it in terms of where one lives, where one works, or where one goes to school. To be white is, even more, to be born into a system that has been set up for the benefit of people like you (like us), and as such provides a head start to those who can claim membership in this, the dominant club.

Second, to be white not only that one will typically inherit certain advantages from the past, but also that one will continue to reap the benefits of ongoing racial privilege, which is itself the flipside of discrimination against persons of color. These privileges have both material components, such as better job opportunities, better schooling, and better housing availability, as well as psychological components, not the least of which is simply having one less thing to constantly worry about during the course of a day. To be white is to be free of the daily burden of constantly having to disprove negative stereotypes. It is to have one less thing to sweat, and in a competitive society such as ours, one less thing on your mind is no small boost.

Third (and this section is new to this edition), in the face of these privileges, whether derived from past injustice handed down or present injustice still actively practiced, to be white is typically to be in profound denial about the existence of these advantages and their consequences. I say denial here, rather than ignorance, because the term *ignorance* implies an involuntary lack of knowledge, a purity, an innocence of sorts, that lets white Americans off the hook, even if only linguistically. The fact is, whites' refusal to engage the issues of race and privilege is due largely to a *willed* ignorance, a voluntary evasion of reality, not unlike the alcoholic or drug addict who refuses to face their illness. How else but as the result of willed ignorance can we understand polls taken, not today, but in the early sixties, which demonstrated that even then—at a time of blatant racism and legally accepted discrimination against black people—the vast majority of whites believed that everyone had equal opportunity?

The only way that one can be completely ignorant of the racial truth in the United States, whether in the sixties or today, is to make the deliberate choice to think about something else, to turn away, to close one's ears, shut one's eyes, and bury one's head in the proverbial sand.

Oh sure, there are young people, perhaps of high school age or even younger, who might truly be ignorant in the strictest sense of the word when it comes to issues of racism and privilege. But if so, this is only because their teachers, preachers, parents, and the mass media to which they are daily subjected have made the choice to lie to them, either directly or by omission. So even the ignorance of the young is willed, albeit by their elders, much to their own detriment.

Fourth, whites can choose to resist a system of racism and unjust privilege, but doing so is never easy. In fact, the fear of alienating friends and family, and the relative lack of role models from whom we can take direction, renders resistance rare, and even when practiced, often ineffective, however important it may be. Learning how to develop our resistance muscles is of vital importance. Thinking about how and when to resist, and what to do (and not do) is critical.

Fifth, even when committed to resistance, and even while in the midst of practicing it, we sometimes collaborate with racism and reinforce racial domination and subordination. In other words, we must always be on guard against our own screwups and willing to confront our failings honestly.

Sixth, whites pay enormous costs in order to have access to the privileges that come from a system of racism—costs that are intensely personal and collective, and which should inspire us to fight racism *for our own sake.*

And finally, in the struggle against injustice, against racism, there is the possibility of redemption.

Belonging, privilege, denial, resistance, collaboration, loss, and redemption: the themes that define and delineate various aspects of the white experience. The trick is getting from privilege, collaboration, denial, and loss to resistance and redemption, so that we may begin to belong to a society more just and sustainable than what we have now.

Given my ten-year residency in New Orleans, from 1986–1996, I decided to conclude this edition of the book with an epilogue on the ongoing catastrophe known as Hurricane Katrina. Katrina was a tragedy that burst into our national consciousness nine months after the initial release of *White Like Me,* but which has since provided a unique opportunity to reflect on the themes herein and relate them to an ongoing news story, in the hopes that doing so can make the ideas discussed in this volume more real to readers. I have opted to address the subject matter of Katrina and its aftermath in the form of an "Open Letter to White America," since white America, two years after the fact, seems, by and large—with some exceptions duly noted—to have gone back to sleep when it comes to the way in which Katrina exposed the extent of institutional racism and white privilege in the United States.

As with the first edition, I wish to once again thank my loving and supportive wife, Kristy, who made several suggestions about ways I could improve the book. I also must thank our two wonderful daughters, Ashton and Rachel. I hope that in my desire for a better world for all, I haven't neglected the world that is closest to home and to my heart. In that regard, I will try to do better.

I also need to thank a number of other people, including my parents, Lucinda and Michael Wise, and grandparents, living and deceased: Mary Neely McLean, Ralph Carter McLean, Leo Wise, and Mabel Wise. I also must thank my friends, notably Albert Jones, my best friend for over three decades, for all of your support and wisdom, and for serving as a sounding board for my politics all these years; and everyone who has inspired, supported, and influenced my work as a writer, activist, and aspiring antiracist ally. These include, in no particular order: Bob Zellner, Dorothy Zellner, Anne Braden, Lance Hill, Larry Powell, Ron King, Ron Chisom, Barbara Major, David Billings, Diana Dunn, Marjorie Freeman, Sharon Martinas, Chris Crass, James Bernard, Francie Kendall, Michael Eric Dyson, Derrick Bell, "Coach" Jimmy Coit Jackson, Angela Davis, Ray Winbush, Molly Secours, Betita Martinez, Felicia Gustin, Jean Caiani, Lauren Parker-Kucera, Catherine Wong, Eddie Moore Jr., Victor Lewis, Hugh Vasquez, Joe Feagin, Ted Quandt, Kimberle Crenshaw, Peggy McIntosh, Jesse Villalobos, Judy Watts, Donna Johnigan, Olayeela Daste, Haunani Kay-Trask, Justin Podur, Brian Awehali, Richard Davis, Mab Segrest, Horace Seldon, Paul Marcus, Robert Jensen, Randall Robinson, Paul Kivel, Rev. Johnny Youngblood, and the entire St. Paul Community Baptist Church family in Brooklyn.

BORN

TO BELONGING

"*People who imagine that history flatters them (as it does, indeed, since they wrote it) are impaled on their history like a butterfly on a pin and become incapable of seeing or changing themselves, or the world. This is the place in which it seems to me, most white Americans find themselves. Impaled. They are dimly, or vividly, aware that the history they have fed themselves is mainly a lie, but they do not know how to release themselves from it, and they suffer enormously from the resulting personal incoherence.*"

JAMES BALDWIN, "THE WHITE MAN'S GUILT," *Ebony,* August 1965

IT IS NOTHING IF not difficult to know where to begin when you first sit down to trace the story of your life. Does your life begin on the day you came into this world, or does it begin before that, with the lives of your family members—your parents and grandparents and such—without whom you would never have existed?

For me, there is only one possible way in which to answer the question. My story has to begin before the day I entered the world, October 4, 1968, for I did not emerge onto a blank slate of neutral circumstance. My life was already a canvass upon which older paint had begun to dry, long before I arrived. My parents were already who they were, with their particular life experiences, and I was to inherit those experiences, for good or ill, whether I liked it or not.

What I'm trying to say is that when we first draw breath outside the womb, we inhale tiny particles of all that came before, both literally and figuratively. We are never merely individuals; we are never alone; we are always in the company, as uncomfortable as it sometimes can be, of others, the past, of history. We become part of that history just as surely as it becomes part of us. There is no escaping it, merely different levels of coping. It is how we bear the past that matters, and in many ways it is all that differentiates us.

I was born amidst great turmoil, none of which had been of my own making, but which I could hardly have escaped in any event. My mother had carried me throughout all of the great upheavals of that tumultuous year, 1968,- perhaps one of the most explosive and monumental years in twentieth century America. She had carried me through the Tet Offensive in Vietnam, through the assassinations of Martin Luther King Jr. and Robert Kennedy, through the decision by President Johnson not to seek reelection in the midst of the unfolding murderous quagmire in Southeast Asia, and through the upheaval in the streets of Chicago during that year's Democratic Party convention. I think that any child born in 1968 must, almost by definition, be especially affected by the history that surrounded him or her upon arrival—there was too much energy floating around, good and bad, not to have left a mark.

Once born, I inherited my family and all that came with it. I also inherited my nation and all that came with that. And I inherited my "race" and all that came with that, too. In all three cases, the inheritance was far from inconsequential.

More than that, all three inheritances were intimately connected, intertwined in ways I could not possibly have understood at the time, but which are all too clear today. To be the child of Michael Julius Wise and Lucinda Anne (McLean) Wise meant something; to be born in the richest and most powerful nation on earth meant something; and to be white, especially in the United States, most assuredly meant something—a lot of things, truth be told.

What those inheritances meant, and still mean, is the subject of this inquiry; it is the theme that will be revisited again and again in these pages, with special emphasis on the last issue: What does it mean to be white, especially in a nation created for the benefit of people like you?

We don't often ask this question, mostly because we don't have to. Being a member of the majority, the dominant group, allows one to ignore how race shapes one's life. For those of us called white, whiteness simply *is*. Whiteness becomes, for us, the unspoken, uninterrogated norm, taken for granted, much as water can be taken for granted by a fish.

In high school, whites are sometimes asked to think about race, but rarely about whiteness. In my case, we read John Howard Griffin's classic book, *Black Like Me,* in which the author recounts his experiences in the Jim Crow South in 1959, after taking a drug that turned his skin brown and allowed him to experience apartheid for a few months from the other side of the color line.

It was a good book, especially for its time. Yet I can't help but find it a bit disturbing that it remains one of the most assigned volumes on summer reading lists dealing with race. That it continues to prove so popular signifies the extent to which race is considered a problem of the past—the book, after all, is more than four decades old, and surely there are some more contemporary racial events students could discuss—not to mention the degree to which race is still viewed as something that can only be understood from the perspective of "the other." Whites are encouraged to think about race from the perspective of blacks, which is nice. Indeed, whites *should* listen to and learn from the stories of black and brown peoples—real black and brown peoples, not white men pretending to be black until the drugs wear off. But Black Like Me leaves another aspect of the discussion untouched: namely, the examination of the white experience.

Although whiteness may mean different things in different places and at different times, one thing I feel confident saying up front, without fear of contradiction, is that to be white in the United States, whether from the South, as I am, or from the North, West, or Midwest, whether one is rich or poor; male or female; Jew or Gentile; straight or gay, is to have certain common experiences based solely upon race. These experiences have to do with advantage, privilege (in the relative sense, vis-à-vis people of color), and belonging. We are, unlike people of color, *born* to belonging, and have rarely had to prove ourselves deserving of our presence here. At the very least we can say that our right to be here hasn't been questioned, in the most part, for a long time.

While some might insist that whites have a wide range of experiences, and so, presumably, it isn't fair to make generalizations about whites as a group, this is a dodge, and not a particularly artful one at that. Of course we're all different, sort of like snowflakes, which come to think of it are also white. None of us have led the exact same life. But irrespective of one's particular history, all whites were placed above all persons of color when it came to the economic, social, and political hierarchies that were to form in the United States, without exception. This formal system of racial preference was codified in law from the 1600s until at least 1964, at which time the Civil Rights Act was passed, if not 1965, with the passage of the Voting Rights Act, or 1968 (that year again), when our nation finally passed a law making racial housing discrimination illegal.

Prior to that time we didn't even pretend to be a nation based on equality. Or rather we did pretend, but not very well; at least not to the point where the rest of the world believed it, or to the point where people of color in this country ever did. Most white folks believed it, but that's simply more proof of our privileged status. Our ancestors had the luxury of believing those things that black and brown folks could never take as givens: all that stuff about life, liberty, and the pursuit of happiness. Several decades later, whites can, indeed *must,* still believe it, while people of color have little reason to join the celebration, knowing as they do that there is still a vast gulf between who we say we are as a nation and people, and who we really are.

In other words, there is enough commonality about the white experience to allow us to make some general statements about whiteness and never be too far from the mark. Returning to the snowflake analogy, although as with snowflakes, no two white people are exactly alike, it is also true that few snowflakes have radically different experiences from those of the average snowflake. Likewise, we know a snowflake when we see one, and in that recognition we intuit, almost always correctly, something about its life experience.

CLIMBING THE FAMILY TREE AND SURVEYING THE PRIVILEGED LAND BELOW

AT FIRST GLANCE, mine would not appear to have been a life of privilege. Nor would it seem that I had been born to any particularly impressive set of inherited advantages. Far from affluent, my father was an on-again, off-again stand-up comedian and actor, and my mother has worked for most of my life in marketing research. While I was growing up, my parents' income would have fallen somewhere in the range of what is politely considered working class, even though their jobs were not traditional working-class jobs. Had it not been for the financial help of my grandparents, it is altogether likely that we would have been forced, at certain points along the way, to rely on food stamps. Most certainly we would have qualified for them in several of my years as a child.

I spent the first eighteen years of my life in a perfectly acceptable but inadequately maintained 850-square-foot apartment with spotty plumbing, a leaky air conditioner, certainly no dishwasher or washing machine, and floorboards near the sliding glass door in my bedroom that were perpetually rotting, allowing roly-polies or slugs to occasionally find their way inside. The walls stand out in my mind as well: thin enough to hear every fight my parents ever had, and to cave in easily under the weight of my father's fists, whenever the mood struck him to ventilate the plaster.

But before the busted-up walls or the leaky faucets at the Royal Arms Apartments (funny how folks always try to make the most average places sound palatial), there had already been quite a bit of family water under the proverbial bridge. Examining the source of that stream provides substantial insight into

4

the workings of privilege, and the ways in which even whites who lived, as I did, in modest surroundings, had been born to belonging nonetheless.

Even if one does not directly inherit the material advantages of one's ancestry, there is something empowering about the ability to trace one's lineage back dozens of generations, as so many whites but so few persons of color can. In 1977, when my third grade teacher would encourage the students to trace our family trees—inspired by the miniseries *Roots,* and not cognizant of how injurious it might be for black students to make the effort, only to run head-first into the crime of slavery and its role in their family background—it was apparent that the white kids, who could go back much further and with less pain than the black kids, had gained a sense of pride, even *rootedness,* as a result.

Genealogy itself is something of a privilege, coming far more easily to those of us for whom enslavement, conquest, and dispossession of our land has not been our lot. Genealogy offers a sense of belonging and connectedness to others, with firm, identifiable pasts—pasts that directly trace the rise and fall of empires, and which correspond to the events we learned about in history classes, so focused were they on the narratives of European peoples. Even when we personally have no desire to affiliate ourselves with those in our past about whom we learn, simply knowing from whence you came has the effect of linking you in some great chain of mutuality. It is enabling, if far from ennobling. It offers a sense of psychological comfort, a sense that you belong in this story known as the history of the world. It is to make real the famous words, "This land is *my* land."

As I sat down recently to examine my various family histories, I have to admit to a sense of excitement as I peeled back layer upon layer, generation after generation. It was like a game, in which the object was to see how far back you could go before hitting a dead end.

Sure enough, on several branches of my family tree, I had no trouble going back hundreds, even thousands of years. In large measure this was because those branches extended through to royal lineage, where records were kept meticulously, so as to make sure everyone knew to whom the spoils of advantage were owed in each new generation.

Make no mistake, my claim to royal lineage here—including the Capets in France and the Stuarts in England, not to mention some random and assorted German princesses, and ultimately William the Conqueror, Julius Caesar, Cleopatra, and King Herod—means nothing. After all, since the number of grandparents doubles in each generation, by the time you trace your lineage back even five hundred years (assuming generations of roughly twenty-five years each), you will have had as many as one million grandparents at some remove. Even with pedigree collapse—the term for the inevitable overlap that comes when cousins marry cousins, as happened with all families if you go back far enough—the number of persons to whom you'd be connected by the time you got back a thousand years would still be several million.

That said, I can hardly deny that as I discovered those linkages, even though they were often quite remote—and despite the fact that the persons to whom I discovered a connection were often despicable characters who stole land, subjugated the masses, and slaughtered others in the name of nationalism or God—there was still something about the process that made me feel more *real,* more alive, and even more purposeful. To explore the passing of time as it relates to world history, and the history of your own people, however removed from you they may be, is like putting together a puzzle, several pieces of which had previously been missing. That is a gift, and one that cannot, should not, be underestimated.

And for those of us prepared to look at the less romantic side of it all, genealogy also makes it possible to uncover and then examine one's inherited advantages.

Going back a few generations on my mother's side, for instance, we have the Carter family, traceable to one John Carter, born in 1450 in Kempston, Bedfordshire, England. It would be his great-great-great-grandson, William, who would bring his family to the Virginia Colony in the early 1630s, just a few of 20,000 or so Puritans who came to America between 1629 and 1642, prior to the shutting down of emigration by King Charles I at the outset of the English Civil War.

The Carters would move inland after their arrival, able to take advantage in years to come of one of the New World's first affirmative action programs, known as the "headright" system, under which male heads of household willing to cross the Atlantic and come to Virginia were given fifty acres of land that had previously belonged to one of at least fourteen indigenous nations whose members had lived there, foremost among them the Powhatan.

Although the racial fault lines between those of European and African descent hadn't been that deep in the earliest years of the Virginia Colony—race-based slavery wasn't in place yet, and among indentured servants there were typically more Europeans than Africans—all that would begin to change in the middle of the seventeenth century. First, beginning in the 1640s, the colony began to assign blacks to permanent enslavement. Then in the 1660s, they declared that all children born of enslaved mothers would be slaves, in perpetuity, themselves. That same decade, Virginia announced that no longer would Africans converted to Christianity be immune to enslavement or servitude. Then, in the wake of Bacon's Rebellion in 1676, which witnessed both European and African laborers joining forces to overthrow the government of Governor Berkeley, elites began to pass a flurry of new laws intended to limit black freedom, elevate whites, and thus divide and conquer any emerging cross-racial alliances between the two groups.

In 1682, the colony codified in law that all whites, no matter their condition of temporary servitude, were to be seen as separate and apart from African slaves, and that they would enjoy certain rights and privileges off limits to the latter: among these, due process in disputes with their masters, and the right to redress if those masters in any way abused them. Furthermore, once released from terms of indenture, white servants would be able to claim up to fifty acres of land with which to begin their new lives as free laborers. Ultimately, indentured servitude would be abolished in the early eighteenth century, replaced by a dramatic upsurge in chattel slavery. Blacks, along with "mulattoes, Indians and criminals" would be banned from holding any public or ecclesiastical office after 1705, and the killing of a rebellious slave would no longer be deemed murder. Rather, according to Virginia law, the event would be treated "as if such accident had never happened."

The Carters, as with many of the Deans (another branch of my mother's family), lived in Virginia through all of this period—the period in which whiteness was being legally enshrined as a privileged space for the first time. And they were there in 1800, too—like my great-great-great-great-grandfather, William M. Carter—when a planned rebellion by Thomas Prosser's slave Gabriel, in Henrico County, was foiled thanks to other slaves exposing the plot. As a result, Gabriel was hanged, all free blacks in the state were forced to leave, or else face reenslavement, and all education or training of slaves (even hiring them out to persons other than their owners) was made illegal. Paranoia over the Prosser conspiracy, combined with the near-hysterical reaction to the Haitian revolution under way at that point, which would expel the French from the island just a few years later, led to new racist crackdowns and the extension of still more advantages and privileges to whites like those in my family.

Then there were the Neelys, the family of my maternal great-grandmother, who can be traced to Edward Neely, born in Scotland in 1745, who came to America sometime before the birth of his son, also named Edward, in 1770.

The Neelys would move from Ulster County, New York, in the Hudson Valley, to Kentucky, where Jason Neely, my great-great-great-grandfather was born in 1805. The land on which they would settle, though it had been the site of no permanent indigenous community by that time, had been hunting land used in common by the Shawnee and Cherokee. Although the Iroquois had signed away all rights to the land that would become Kentucky in the Treaty of Fort Stanwix in 1768, the Shawnee had been no party to the treaty, and rejected its terms. Not that their rejection would matter much, as ultimately the area came under the control of whites, and began to produce substantial profits for farmers like Jason Neely.

By 1860, three years after the Supreme Court, in its *Dred Scott* decision announced that blacks could never be citizens, even if free, and "had no rights which the white man was bound to respect," Jason had accumulated eleven slaves, ranging in age from forty down to two—a number that was quite significant by local and even regional standards for the "Upper South."

And then we have the two primary and parental branches of my family, the McLeans and the Wises.

The McLeans trace their lineage to around 1250, and apparently at one point were among the most prosperous Highland clans in Scotland, owning as many as five islands in the Hebrides. But having allied themselves with Charles Edward Stuart (claimant to the thrones of England, Ireland, and Scotland), they ultimately lost everything when Stuart (known as Bonnie Prince Charlie) was defeated at the Battle of Culloden in 1746. The McLeans, as with many of the Highlanders, supported the attempt to restore the Stuart family to the thrones from which it had been deposed in 1688. Once the royalists were defeated, and the Bonnie Prince had been forced to sneak out of Scotland dressed as an Irish maid, the writing began to appear on the wall for the McLeans, and many of the Highland Scots who had supported him.

With that, family patriarch Ephraim McLean (my great-great-great-great-great-grandfather) set out for America, settling in Philadelphia before moving south in 1759. Once there, Ephraim would ultimately be granted over 12,000 acres of land in North Carolina and Tennessee—land that had previously belonged to Catawba and Cherokee Indians, and much of which had been worked by persons of African descent for over a century, without the right of the latter to own so much as their names.

Although the family version of the story is that Ephraim received these grants deservedly, as payment for his service in the Revolutionary War, there is something more than a bit unsatisfying about this narrative. While Ephraim served with distinction—he was, in fact, wounded during the Battle of King's Mountain, recognized as among the war's most pivotal campaigns—it is also true that at least 5,000 blacks served the American Revolution, and virtually none of them, no matter the distinction with which they served, received land grants. Indeed, four out of five blacks who served failed to receive even their freedom from enslavement.

In fact, Ephraim's ability to fight for the revolution was itself, in large part, because of white privilege. Although the Continental Congress authorized the use of blacks in the army beginning in 1777, no southern militia with the exception of that in Maryland allowed them to serve. The Congress, cowed by the political strength of southern slaveowners and threats by leaders in South Carolina to leave the war if slaves were armed and allowed to fight, refused to press the issue. This meant that blacks would be kept from service, and denied whatever postwar land grants for which they might otherwise have been eligible.

In the early 1780s, Ephraim became one of the founding residents of Nashville, and served as a trustee and treasurer for the first college west of the Cumberland Mountains, Davidson Academy. On the board with him were several prominent residents of the area, including a young Andrew Jackson, in whose ranks Ephraim's grandson would later serve, during the 1815 Battle of New Orleans, and alongside whom his great-nephew, John, would serve during the massacre of Creek Indians at Horseshoe Bend.

Ephraim's son, Samuel (my fourth great-grandfather), was a substantial landowner, having inherited property from Ephraim. Although the records are unclear as to whether Ephraim had owned slaves (the odds, however, are good), Samuel most certainly did; he had at least a half-dozen by the time of his death in 1850.

Down through the generations the McLeans would pass on the land they had accumulated, and the good name and reputations that came along with it, taking full advantage of their whiteness and what it had come to mean over the years.

In contrast to this tale, in which European immigrants come to the new country and are almost immediately welcomed into the emerging club of whiteness, we have the story of the Wises (not our original name), whose patriarchal figure, Jacob, came to the United States from Russia escape the Czar's oppression of Jews. Theirs was similar to the immigrant stories of so many other American Jews from Eastern Europe. You've heard the drill: They came here with nothing but three dollars and a ball of lint in their pockets; saved and saved, worked and worked, and eventually climbed the ladder of success, achieving the American dream within a generation or two.

Whether or not it had really been as bleak as all that, it certainly hadn't been easy. Jacob's arrival in 1907 (or 1910, it's not clear which) was not actually his first time to make it to the United States. He had entered New York once before, in 1901, but had the misfortune of cruising into the harbor only ten days or so after an American of Eastern European descent, Leon Czolgosz, had made the fatal decision to assassinate President William McKinley. McKinley had lingered for a week after the shooting, and died just a few days before the arrival of my great-grandfather's boat. As the saying goes, timing is everything—a lesson Jacob would learn, sitting in steerage and coming to realize that he had been literally just a few days too late.

So back he went, along with the rest of his shipmates, turned away in the shadow of Lady Liberty by a wave of jingoistic panic, anti-immigrant nativism, hysteria born of bigotry, and a well-nurtured, carefully cultivated skill at scapegoating those who differed from the Anglo-Saxon norm. That Czolgosz claimed to be an anarchist, and thus his shooting of McKinley came to be seen as a political act, and not merely the lashing out of a madman, sealed Jacob's fate for sure. To the authorities, all Eastern Europeans were to be viewed for a time as anarchists, as criminals, and later as communists. Czolgosz was to be executed, and tens of thousands of Eastern Europeans and other "undesirable" ethnics would be viciously oppressed in the following years.

The mind of a well-fed twenty-first-century American is scarcely equipped to contemplate just how long the trip back to Russia must have been, not merely in terms of hours and days and weeks, but as measured in the beating of one's heart, the slow and subtle escape of all optimism from one's tightened lungs. How painful it must have been, how *omnicidal* for Jacob, meaning the evisceration of everything he was, of everything that mattered to him—the extermination of desire, of hope. Though not of the same depth, nor coupled with the same fear as that which characterized the journey of Africans in the hulls of slave ships (after all, he was still a free man, and his journey, however aborted, had been voluntary), there must have been points where the magnitude of his cynicism and despair was intense enough to make the distinction feel as though it were one without much meaning.

So he returned to Minsk, in modern-day Belarus, for nearly another decade, it taking that long for him to save up enough money to make the journey again. When he finally came back, with family in tow, it would be for keeps. His desire for America was that strong: borne of the belief that in the new world things would be different, that he would be able to make something of himself and give his family a better life. The Wise family continued to grow after his arrival, including, in 1919, the birth of Leon Wise, whose name was later shortened to Leo—my grandfather.

Jacob was the very definition of a hard worker. The stereotype of immigrants putting in eighteen hours a day is one that, although it did not begin with him in mind, surely was to be kept alive by him and others like him. There is little doubt that he toiled, and sacrificed, and in the end there was a great payoff indeed. His children all became moderately successful, at least comfortable—my grandfather would graduate from a prestigious university, Vanderbilt, in 1942; and the family liquor business would grow into something of a fixture in the Nashville, Tennessee, community that the Wise family would ultimately come to call home.

But lest we get carried away, perhaps it would do some good to remember a few things about Jacob Wise and his family. None of these things, it must be stressed, take away from the unshakeable work ethic that was a defining feature of his character. But they do suggest that a work ethic is rarely, if ever, enough on its own to make the difference.

After all, there had been millions of black folks with work ethics at least as good a as his; millions of peoples of color—black, brown, red, yellow, and all shades between—had lived and toiled in this land, typically for far longer than him, and yet with few exceptions, they could not say that within a mere decade they had become successful shop owners, or that one of their sons had gone on to graduate from one of the nation's finest colleges.

Jacob was able to move south and, even as a religious minority in the buckle of the Bible Belt, find opportunity that was off limits to anyone of color. He may have been a Jew, but his skin was the right shade, and he was from Europe, so all suspicions and religious and cultural biases aside, he had only to wait and keep his nose clean a while, and then eventually he and his family would become white. Assimilation was not merely a national project; for Jacob Wise, and for millions of other Jews, Italians, and Irish, it was an implicitly racial one as well.

Even before assimilation, in fact, he had been able to gain access to jobs and opportunities that were off limits to African Americans. His very arrival in the United States—as tortuous and circuitous as was the route that he had been forced to take in order to achieve it—was nonetheless made possible by immigration policies that at that moment (and for most of our nation's history) have favored those from Europe over those from anywhere else. The Naturalization Act of 1790, which was the very first law passed by the U.S. Congress after the ratification of the Constitution, made clear that all free white persons, and *only* free white persons, were to be considered citizens, almost as soon as they arrived. Meanwhile, during the period of both of Jacob's journeys—the one that was aborted and the one that finally delivered him to his new home—there had been draconian limits on, for example, Asian immigration. These restrictions would remain largely in place until 1965, the year his grandson, my father, would graduate from high school.

If that's not white privilege—if that's not affirmative action of a most profound and lasting kind—then I dare say neither concept has much meaning any longer. And if that isn't relevant to my own racialization, since it is the history into which I was born, then the notion of inheritance has lost all meaning as well.

THE MODERN LEGACY OF WHITE BELONGING

LOOKING BACKWARDS in time, it becomes possible to see whiteness playing out all along the way in the history of my family, dating back hundreds of years. The ability to come to America in the first place, the ability to procure land once here, and the ability to own other human beings while knowing that you would never be owned yourself, all depended on our European ancestry.

Nonetheless, one might deny that this legacy has anything to do with those of us in the modern day. Unless we have been the direct inheritors of that land and property that our families accumulated so long ago, then of what use has that privilege been to us? For persons like myself, growing up not on farmland passed down by various branches of my family, but rather, in a modest apartment, what did this past have to do with me? And by extension, what does your family's past have to do with you?

In my case, race and privilege were every bit as implicated in the time and place of my birth as they had been in the time and place of my forbears. I was born in a nation that had only recently thrown off the formal trappings of legal apartheid. I was born in a city, Nashville, that had, just eight years earlier, been the scene of some of the most pitched desegregation battles in the South, replete with sit-ins and boycotts and marches, and white backlash to all three.

Nashville was a city where, eleven years prior to my birth, opponents of desegregation had placed a bomb in the basement of one of the city's soon-to-be integrated schools. And although the bombers in that instance galvanized opposition to terrorist tactics, opposition to integration delayed any meaningful movement in that direction until 1971, when busing was finally ordered at the high-school level. It would be 1974, the year I began first grade, before busing would filter down to the elementary level. This means that the class of 1986, my graduating class, was the first that had been truly desegregated throughout its entire educational experience. That's how far the reach of so-called past racism extends, right into the life of someone like myself, not even forty years of age. It is not, in other words, ancient history.

But when it comes to understanding the centrality of race and racism in the society of my birth, perhaps this is the most important point of all: I was born just a few hours and half a state away from Memphis, where six months earlier, to the day, Dr. King had been murdered.

I experienced the King assassination in a real if indirect way, as I suppose is always the case when one is in utero at the moment of a national catastrophe. At thirteen weeks gestation, of course, I could hardly have known that the world was burning down around me, that the bonds of human community were being ripped apart even as I sucked my thumb and fed from the umbilical cord connecting me to my maternal host.

My mom had been working that evening (not early morning, as mistakenly claimed by Bono in the famous U2 song), when King stepped onto the balcony of the Lorraine Motel, only to be felled a few seconds later by an assassin's bullet. Upon hearing the news, the managers of the department store where she was employed decided to close up shop. Fear that black folks might come over to Green Hills, the mostly white and relatively affluent area where the Castner-Knott's store was located, so as to take out vicarious revenge on whitey (or at least whitey's shoe department), had sent them into a panic. A small riot had occurred in Nashville the year before, sparked by the infamous overreaction of the Nashville police, and particularly Captain John Sorace, to a visit by radical activist Stokely Carmichael (Kwame Ture). Although the violence had been limited to a very small part of the mostly black North Nashville community around Fisk University—and even then had been totally unrelated to Carmichael's presence, contrary to the claims of then-Governor Beverly Briley—by the time King was killed, white folks were on high alert for the first signs of trouble.

That I experienced my mother's bodily reaction to King's murder, as well as the killing of Bobby Kennedy two months later (at twenty-two weeks in utero) may or may not mean anything. Whether or not cell memory and the experiences of one's parent can be passed to the child as a result of trauma, thereby influencing the person that child is to become, is something that will likely never be proven one way or the other. Even the possibility of such a thing is purely speculative, and more than a bit romantic. But it makes for a good story.

Even discounting the role of cell memory, and even if we disregard the possibility that a mother may somehow transmit knowledge to a child during gestation, my experience with race predated my birth, if simply because being conceived into a white family meant certain things about the experiences I was likely to have once born: where I would live, what jobs and education my family was likely to have had, and where I would go to school.

On my third day of life I most certainly experienced race, however oblivious I was to it at the time, when my mother and father moved our family into an apartment complex in the above-mentioned Green Hills community. It was a complex that, four years after completion, had still never had tenant of color, and this was not by accident. This was by design, and for those same four years it had been perfectly legal, too, as there had been nothing unlawful until 1968 about discriminating, even blatantly, against persons of color looking to purchase or rent a place to live.

And so in we went, because it was affordable and it was a step up from the smaller apartment my folks had been living in prior to that time. More than that though, in we went because we could. Just as we could have gone into any other apartment complex anywhere in Nashville, subject only to our ability to put down a security deposit, which as it turns out was paid by my father's father anyway. At least as early as Monday, October 7, 1968, then, I was officially receiving white privilege.

The only reason you are reading this book right now, the only reason this book exists, the only reason this story is being told, is because of white privilege. You are not reading this book because I am a great writer or because I am particularly smart. There are lots of folks, especially persons of color, who know a lot more about racism than I do, people who have forgotten more about the subject since breakfast than I will likely ever know. But you're not reading their book right now; you're reading mine, and that has everything to do with privilege.

After all, how does one come to be taken seriously as an antiracist activist, writer, and lecturer by their midthirties, as I was, or even before then really, since I've been doing this work professionally, on a national level since I was twenty-one?

For one thing, it helps to know the right people.

When I graduated from college, my first job catapulted me into this work at a highly visible level. I was hired as a Youth Coordinator for the Louisiana Coalition Against Racism and Nazism, the largest and most prominent of the various groups formed to oppose the candidacy of neo-Nazi political candidate David Duke, who was running for the United States Senate. Over time, and during his bid for governor of Louisiana, I would move up the ranks of the organization, finally becoming associate director, and one of a handful of the public faces associated with the anti-Duke effort. I was, by the time Duke had fizzled and the coalition folded, all of twenty-three. Sweet work if you can get it, but most won't. I did though, which begs the question, How?

Well, I got it the old-fashioned way, which is to say that I knew the two guys who started the organization. One was a professor of mine at Tulane, Larry Powell, and the other was an activist ally and Tulane grad student at the time, Lance Hill. Even before I graduated, Larry had asked if I might want the job, and for several months I had said no. I honestly didn't think Duke was going to do all that well, and so I repeatedly turned him down, planning as I was to return home for the summer, spend whatever small amount of graduation money I would have, and then cast about for some kind of job, or possibly just float for a year, maybe going to grad school myself, or law school in a year or so.

But then as the summer dragged on and it became apparent that Duke was indeed a threat in the Senate race, I committed to returning to New Orleans and doing whatever I needed to do to insinuate myself into the anti-Duke campaign. I figured, and I was right in this, that since I knew the principals and they had offered me work before, I would probably have no problem landing a position even several months after the campaign had swung into high gear.

Had I not known Larry and Lance, there is no way I could have gotten that job, in which case I could never have built up a reputation for doing anti-racism work as I did, in which case I would never have been able to land on the lecture circuit, as I would a few years later, in which case no one would know who I am, and I surely wouldn't have been asked to write this book. But it goes deeper than that, because there is then the question of how I managed to know these two men, who were in a position to offer me such a job in the first place.

Well, I knew them, of course, because I had gone to school at Tulane; but how had I gotten there? After all, my family was far from wealthy, and even then Tulane was extremely expensive. Although its cost is far greater today, as with all colleges and universities, in 1986, with tuition at $12,950, and all costs combined coming in at around $20,000, it was far pricier than anything my folks could afford. Complicating things further, I am notorious for procrastination—something that can be confirmed by anyone who knows me (my wife, my parents, my teachers, former bosses, the editor of this book, everyone)—and so I screwed around and didn't get my financial aid forms in on time. Since being late with financial aid forms means that one won't get as much assistance as might otherwise have been offered, how does one get to go to a place like Tulane?

It helps—and this is surely an understatement of some significance—when one's mother is able to go down to the bank and take out a loan for $10,000 to fill the gap between what the school was offering in assistance and the overall costs for my freshman year.

But how does one's mother get such a loan? Especially when, as was true for mine, she has never owned a piece of property? When she (and by extension you) have been living paycheck to paycheck, driving cars until they stopped running, taking few if any vacations because you just can't afford them?

It helps (again an understatement) if one's mother's mother can cosign for the loan. After all, banks don't typically lend money to folks without collateral like my mom, but they are very willing to lend the same money to someone *with* it, like grandmother, who was able to use her house as collateral against the loan.

The house, in which she still lives, was the fourth house that she and my grandfather, Ralph Carter McLean (who had been dead for six years by then) had owned. Although they had been of merely middle-class income—my grandfather having been in the military and then civil service for his entire adult life—they nonetheless were able to afford several nice homes, in "nice" neighborhoods, all of which had been entirely white, and again, as with the apartment complex where I grew up, not by accident. Although the Supreme Court, in 1948, had outlawed restrictive covenants barring blacks from living in these neighborhoods, it remained legal to discriminate in other ways until the late sixties, and even then, there was little real enforcement of the Fair Housing Act until teeth were added to the law in 1988.

So in a very real sense, my grandmother's house—without which I could not have gone to Tulane, met Larry and Lance, gotten the job against Duke, built up a reputation as an antiracist, and gotten out on the lecture circuit—was there to be used as collateral because we were white. Not only did we have a house to use for this purpose, but it was a house in a "desirable" neighborhood, seen as a good investment by the bank, which would continue to appreciate each year. In other words, it was a good bet that we'd be able to make good on the loan, and if we defaulted, so what? The bank would have a nice piece of property, worth more than the ten bills they were giving my mom, so in a real sense they couldn't lose, and neither could I.

The upshot of all this is simple: I am where I am today, doing what I am doing today, in large part because I was born white. I say this not to detract from whatever genuine abilities I may have, nor to take away from the hard work that helped my family in previous generations afford certain homes, but simply to say that ability and hard work alone could not have paved the way for me, just as they have not paved the way for anyone in isolation. Just as they did not pave the way, in isolation, for the millions of white families that got FHA and VA loans for homes from the 1930s to the 1960s—over $120 billion in equity in fact—at a time when such loans were essentially off limits to persons of color. We always have help along the way, some of us a lot more than others. My help came color-coded, and that has made all the difference.

Although not every white person's story is the same as mine, any white person born before 1964, at least, was legally elevated above any person of color, and as such received directly the privileges, the head start, the advantages of whiteness as a matter of routine. This goes for all whites, not merely some, but all. Even poor whites received the benefit of being considered superior to black people, for example. Even the poor whites received the benefit of public sympathy, as with the mostly positive, heart-rending portrayals of farmers in the Dust Bowl drought years of the 1930s, or the Appalachian poor in the early sixties. This, in contrast to the equally hostile images of the black and brown poor presented for the past forty-five years, via print and broadcast media.

Even whites born after the passage of the various civil rights acts of the 1960s have reaped the benefits of our skin color, since parents and grandparents don't tend to bury their accumulated assets, or "cultural capital" (itself the residue of material advantage) in a big hole in the backyard. In other words, it doesn't matter that today's whites weren't around "back then." It doesn't matter that today's whites never owned slaves, never killed any Indians, and never stole land from Mexico. We are here now, and so are the black and brown descendants of those persons of color whose ability to accumulate assets, professional credentials, education, and homes, was restricted for so long.

We are all here now, and the past has come with us into the present, whether or not we put out a welcome mat. The past may be an unwanted guest, but just like those family members you'd rather not have over for the holidays, the past is coming in the front door anyway—mine, and yours. It finds a window if the door is closed, and although the past is quite capable of sucking one's blood, or, even worse, of draining one's self entirely, quite unlike a vampire, it doesn't need an invitation in order to enter. Pity, that.

PRIVILEGE

"I'm not interested in anybody's guilt. Guilt is a luxury that we can no longer afford. I know you didn't do it, and I didn't do it either, but I am responsible for it because I am a man and a citizen of this country and you are responsible for it, too, for the very same reason . . . Anyone who is trying to be conscious must begin . . . to dismiss the vocabulary which we've used so long to cover it up, to lie about the way things are."

JAMES BALDWIN, "WORDS OF A NATIVE SON," *Playboy,* 1964

ALTHOUGH THE INHERITED benefits of whiteness are certainly real, if that were all there were to the story perhaps we could understand the tendency of white folks in the present day to shrug their shoulders when the subjects of racism and white privilege are raised. After all, even if one accepts the premise laid out in the previous chapter—that to be white is to be born to certain advantages and privileges that have been generally inaccessible to others—it would still be possible to argue that, unfair as that may be, we should just move on. Such persons might argue that the past can't be undone, and anyway, the fact that white folks in previous generations created a system of racism and white supremacy is not the fault of whites living today. So why should whites today have to deal with the residue of other folks' actions?

There are a number of problems with a position such as this. To begin with, and at the most basic level, we <u>do have to deal with</u> the residue of past actions. We clean up the effects of past pollution. We remove asbestos from old buildings for the sake of public health, even when we didn't put the material there ourselves. We pay off government debts, even though much of the spending that created them happened long ago.

And of course, we have no problem reaping the benefits of past actions for which we weren't responsible. For instance, few people refuse to accept money or property from others who bequeath such things to them upon death, out of a concern that they wouldn't want to accept something they hadn't earned. We love to accept things we didn't earn, such as inheritance, but we have a problem taking responsibility for the things that have benefited us while harming others. Just as a house or farm left to you upon the death of a parent is an asset that you get to use, so too is racial privilege. And if you get to use an asset, you have to also pay the debt accumulated, which is what allowed the asset to exist in the first place.

If you think this to be unreasonable, try a little thought experiment. Imagine you were to become the chief executive officer of a multibillion dollar company. And imagine that on your first day you were to sit down in your nice, cushy, corner-office chair and begin to plan how you would lead the firm to even greater heights. In order to do your job effectively, you would obviously need to know the financial picture of the company: what are your assets, your liabilities, and your revenue stream?

So you call a meeting with your chief financial officer, so that you can be clear about the firm's financial health and future. The CFO comes to the meeting, armed with spreadsheets and a Power Point presentation, all of which show everything you'd ever want to know about the company's fiscal health.

You're excited. The company has billions in assets, hundreds of millions in annual revenues, and a healthy annual profit margin. Life is good. Now imagine that as your CFO gathers up her things to leave, you look at her and say "Oh, by the way, thanks again for all the information. But next time, don't bother with the figures on our outstanding debts. See, I wasn't here when you all borrowed all that money and took on all that debt. So, I don't see why I should have to deal with that. I intend to put the assets to work immediately, but the debts? Nope, that's not my problem."

Once the CFO finished laughing, security would likely come and usher you to your car. And for obvious reasons: the notion of utilizing assets but not paying debts is irresponsible, to say nothing of unethical. No corporate executive could stick around long if they tried it. Likewise, persons who reap the benefits of past actions—and the privileges that have come from whiteness are certainly among those—have an obligation to take responsibility for our use of those benefits.

But the past isn't really the point anyway. Even if slavery had never happened, even if segregation had never happened, even if the genocide of indigenous persons had never happened, even if the generations-long head starts for whites hadn't existed, we would still need to deal with the issue of racism and white privilege. And this is so because discrimination and privilege *today*, putting aside the past for a second, are big enough problems to require our immediate concern. My own life has been more than an adequate proof of this truism.

READIN', WRITIN', AND RACIAL PRIVILEGE

White privilege was so ingrained in my school experience that hardly a single thing about my education was untainted by it. Whether it was the racialized placement of students into advanced or remedial tracks irrespective of actual ability (which data suggests happens, still today, all over the country) or the way in which extracurricular opportunities like drama or debate were such "white spaces," with very little opportunity in practical terms for nonwhites to participate, the trend was obvious and persistent.

The curriculum was almost completely Eurocentric, by which I mean shot through with the perspectives of persons of European descent, to the exclusion of pretty much all others. Worse still was the implicit assumption that the white lens through which subject matter was to be viewed was not a narrowly focused, even myopic one, but rather a universally valid tool for observing reality. Although there has been progress in this regard in some schools and school districts around the country, when it comes to history textbooks and literature reading lists, much about them looks exactly as it did twenty years ago: they remain top heavy with white folks' narratives, with a smattering of "others" thrown in, but more as an add-on than as a central part of the nation's collective story.

Multiculturalism is, in most instances, being presented as mere "parsley on the plate," in the words of Joy Degruy-Leary—which is to say, something that feels thrown together as an afterthought. And as with that sprig of parsley next to your meal at the restaurant, mainstream multicultural efforts are there for one of two reasons: either for prettiness, or for a cover-up. Either way, neither the parsley nor the material about folks of color is understood to be all that important, whether to the meal or the classroom content. When it comes to the way in which nonwhite folks and cultures are presented and discussed in class, the typical arrangement tends to reduce them to "food, fabric, and festival." But learning what exoticized "others" wear, eat, and how they celebrate, hardly alters the fundamental dynamics at work in the schools—dynamics that continue to favor the dominant group by making that group's story the centerpiece of everything that one studies, and everything about which one is supposed to know, in order to be deemed educated.

When I was in school, white teachers were among the biggest problems, and sadly, they still are. While there are many dedicated and antiracist white educators out there, in my experience the vast majority of them, though dedicated, have no earthly idea what it means to be antiracist. Then, as now, they fronted as enlightened, open-minded people, but so many of them reinforced (and still reinforce) racism and white privilege every day: punishing kids of color disproportionately even when whites break the rules just as often (there have been fourteen studies on this matter, and they all say the same thing), or blaming poor performance by kids of color on their "dysfunctional" families or presumably defective cultural traits—anything but their own tired teaching methods.

On numerous occasions I've asked teachers, purely hypothetically of course, what would happen if we could hook up all prospective and current educators to a lie detector, in order to ascertain whether or not they believed that some students because of race or economic status were generally less capable than other students. We would ask them if they believed that, generally speaking, black students or Latino students were less capable of academic success than whites, or perhaps Asians. We would ask whether they believed that black families place less emphasis on the importance of education than whites. We would ask if they believed that poor kids were less capable of learning than middle-class or affluent children.

If they disavowed these inherently racist and classist views, and the polygrapher determined they were being truthful, they would be thanked for their time and returned to the classroom to continue in their chosen profession. If, on the other hand, they endorsed the notion that some groups were less capable than others, they would be immediately terminated, their continued employment viewed as too potentially damaging to the young minds entrusted to their care. And finally, if they claimed to reject the notion of group-based superiority and inferiority, but were deemed to be lying about their real views—in other words, if they merely told the investigators what they assumed to be the more palatable answer—they would also be fired, but first, they would be zapped by a low-level electrical shock, not strong enough to injure, but strong enough to make the point.

Aside from the natural aversion to torture that animates most reactions to my hypothetical, the most common response is one of sheer panic, followed by heartfelt concerns that if teachers who believed poor kids or kids of color were less capable were to be fired, there would be a teacher shortage! As if a shortage of race and class-biased educators would be *a bad thing*.

That teachers assume so many of their colleagues hold these sorts of biased views suggests that sacrificing black and brown potential and privileging white students continues unabated in American schools, no matter how much less blatant the process may appear today as opposed to twenty, thirty, forty, or fifty years ago.

Of course, few if any teachers will admit that they adhere to such beliefs themselves. Rather, the most commonly heard refrain from educators, in my experience with them, is something to the effect that they "treat all kids the same and don't even see color" when they look at them. Putting aside the absurdity of the claim itself—studies have long indicated that we tend to make very fine distinctions based on color, and that we notice color differences almost immediately—color blindness is, in fact, not the proper goal of fair-minded educators in the first place. The kids in those classrooms *do* have a race, and their race matters, because it says a lot about the kinds of challenges they are likely to face. To not see color is, as Julian Bond has noted, to not see the *consequences* of color; and if color has consequences, which it surely does, yet you've resolved not to notice the thing that brings about those consequences, the odds are pretty good that you'll underserve the needs of the students in question, every time.

To not see people for who they are is to miss the cue that some, but not all, of your students are dealing with racism. It is to privilege the norm, which of course is white, by assuming that "kids are kids," and then treating the kids the way you'd treat your own. But with nearly nine in ten teachers in the United States being white, the children in the care of teachers for eight hours a day often look very different from the kids to whom those teachers go home at night. To treat everyone the same, or like the white common denominator, is to miss the fact that children of color have all the same challenges white kids do, and then that one extra thing to deal with: racism. But if you've told yourself you are not to see race, you'll be pretty unlikely to notice discrimination *based* on race, let alone know how to respond to it.

The consequences of this artificial color blindness, which so often papers over real divisions in a school, and serves to validate the white perspective that everything is okay, can be dramatic. So at my school, Hillsboro, voted one of America's "best" public schools in the 1985–86 academic year, we had a small scale race riot involving about three-dozen students—not white against black, but white and black on one side, against Southeast Asian students on the other, most of whom had come to the states after 1975.

Had you asked teachers or the administration if there were any racial problems at Hillsboro at the beginning of that year, they would have assured you there were not. They would have pointed to the generally positive rela-tionships between people of different races and downplayed or ignored the extreme isolation of the Southeast Asian kids, much to the detriment of the institution, as we would later come to learn when we had to have cops in the halls for two or three days, just to "restore calm."

Having never been asked to think about how we viewed the newcomers among us (often quite negatively), or to consider how misunderstandings often flared because of language and cultural barriers, the school shut its eyes and pretended everything was fine. By stifling any discussion of racial and cultural bias—by avoiding getting everything out in the open and requiring whites and blacks to learn about Thai, Lao, Vietnamese and Hmong cultures and interrogate our own prejudices—Hillsboro's color-blind perspective cre-ated the conditions that gave rise to that riot. Though blacks as well as whites were protected in our ignorance by the administration, there is little doubt but that the color-blind paradigm implicated in that year's upheaval was mostly a boon for the whites. After all, every other day it would insulate us, but not the black kids, from having to think about race. And in so doing, it would help to maintain the racialized status quo.

As destructive as white privilege is for students of color, of course, it is equally beneficial for those who receive it.

For me, white privilege was critical to my actually making it through school at all. Whether it was my ability to gain access to theatre or debate, or whether it was not being suspended for getting caught skipping class (or for cheating in almost every class and getting caught repeatedly), I relied on my whiteness to mark me as a capable person with lots of potential, even when I wasn't demonstrating much of it.

When I got to college my whiteness would serve me well, too. In my freshman year I would screw up royally on two occasions: oversleeping for an exam, showing up an hour late into a three-hour test; then missing another final altogether, showing up in the afternoon for a test that had been given at ten in the morning. In the first instance I was allowed to enter the testing room, even though students weren't supposed to come in after the test had begun, and in the second case, despite the fact that missing the exam had been my own fault, I begged the teacher to let me make it up and he did, in his office, right then and there.

Although I can't know for sure if either of these lucky breaks had to do with being white, I can certainly imagine that had I been black, either or both of the professors might have taken a more skeptical view of my seriousness as a student. The first might well have looked at me as irresponsible and not allowed me to enter: that *was* the policy after all, and he could have enforced it without seeming to be racist had a black person showed up late for the exam. And the second professor could have viewed me as just not having what it took to be a successful Tulane student—a commonly held stereotype about black kids there, even when they did quite well. So I can't know for sure, but I also can't doubt that in a situation like either of those, I'd rather have been white than anything else.

But perhaps this is the most important point: no matter what my professors might have thought about my miscues, about oversleeping, or about missing an exam altogether, one thing I would never have been forced to consider was that they might take either of those things as evidence of some racial flaw on my part. In other words, I would not have to worry about being viewed through the lens of a racial stereotype, of having one or both of them say, if only to themselves, "Well, you know how *those* kinds of students are," where "*those* students" meant white students. I could rest assured that my failures would be my own and would never be attributed to racial inferiority or incompetence.

For people of color, the same experience would have been entirely different. They would not have been able to so easily assume that their race would be irrelevant to the evaluation given them by a white professor, just as students of color must always wonder if whites will view them through the lens of group defect if and when they answer a question incorrectly in class— something else I never had to sweat. So black or brown students in that situation would not only bear the pressure of having dropped the ball; they would further carry the burden of wondering whether they had dropped it, in the eyes of authority figures, on behalf of their entire group. If we understand nothing else, let us at least be clear that such a weight is not an inconsequential one to bear. By the same token, to be able to go through life without ever having to feel as though one were representing whites as a group is not an inconsequential privilege, either.

* * *

BLACK PEOPLE UNDERSTAND race long before white people do. They know how it shapes their lives—or at least that it *does* shape their lives, even if they remain a bit sketchy for a while on the details—before they finish elementary school in most cases. And for every ounce of racial wisdom contained in the mind of a black child barely ten years old, or even seven for that matter, there is a corresponding void in the mind of a similar white child, the latter having never had to contemplate his or her racial position or identity in most cases, and thus remaining gleefully ignorant of the role of race in the warp and woof of society.

It doesn't matter, by the way, if you're a white kid who grew up around black and brown folks. It doesn't matter if you had black friends—I mean *really* had them, and *really* friends, not just acquaintances. If you're white you simply will not, cannot, understand race, or even see that race matters at that age. There is no reason that you should; no experience would have forced the issue; and few parents would have sat you down to begin the lesson.

That's a luxury, a privilege. Not necessarily one that serves us well—after all, to be ignorant about the world in which one lives is never advisable—but a privilege nonetheless. Because the knowledge of black children (and other kids of color, too) when it comes to race, and how they must learn to navigate the color line in their daily lives, is a substantial burden to bear. When black mothers have to teach their sons to keep both hands on the wheel if stopped by a police officer, so as not to get shot—something I have never heard a white mother speak of doing with her white son—we know we're talking about more than a minor irritant.

I was in third grade when I received one of my earliest lessons about race, even if the meaning of that lesson didn't sink in for several years afterward. The persons who served as my instructors that day were not teachers, not professional educators, but two friends, Bobby and Vincent, whose understanding of the dynamics of race—their blackness and my whiteness in particular—was so deep that they were able to afford me a lesson spontaneously, during something as meaningless as afternoon recess.

One day on the playground, Bobby, Vince, and I were tossing a football back and forth. One of us would get between the other two, who stood at a distance of maybe ten yards from each other, and try to intercept the ball as it hurtled through the air from one passer to the next.

Football was never my game, really. Though I was athletic, and actually obsessed with sports throughout my youth, I was also pretty small as a kid and as such saw very little future in playing a game that involved running into people and being tackled. I preferred baseball, but that day had chosen to toss the pigskin around because it was there, and it was too cold for baseball, and I liked hanging out with Bobby and Vince.

In fact, that's something of an understatement: I treasured my time with my black friends, in part because already by third grade, and for several years after, it seemed as though teachers were doing their best to separate us, to channel us in different directions. At the time I didn't understand what any of that was about, but I knew that it made me covetous of whatever time I could carve out with the kids on the other side of the classroom.

Our game began innocently enough, with Bobby in the middle, usually picking off passes between Vince and me. Vince, I recall, had this strange throwing motion, not unlike his even stranger basketball jump shot—sort of a herky-jerky, behind the head kind of toss—that was so telegraphed in terms of where it was headed that intercepting it was never too difficult.

Next it was Vince's turn, and he too picked off several of the passes between Bobby and me, though the zip with which Bobby delivered them often made the ball bounce off Vince's hands, too hot to handle.

When it came time for me to be in the middle, I frankly had little expectation about how many passes I could intercept. My size alone at that age virtually ensured that if Vince and Bobby wanted to, they could simply lob the ball over my head, and so long as they did it high enough, and fast enough, there would be very little opportunity for me to pull the ball down.

But strangely, I caught every one. Each time they would pass just a bit beyond my reach and I would jump to one side or the other, hauling their efforts into my breast, never dropping a single one nor allowing even one pass in thirty to make it beyond me.

At first, I reveled in what I assumed must be my newfound speed and agility. What's more, I beamed with childish pride at the smiles on the faces of both Bobby and Vince, assuming that those smiles signaled how impressed they were with my effort, and perhaps even how amazed they were that they had been unable to slip anything by me. And I continued to interpret this series of events as evidence of my own abilities, even as they began, both of them, to repeat the same refrain after every pass, beginning with about the tenth throw of the series. As the ball left Bobby's throwing hand and whizzed toward its destination in Vince's outstretched arms, only to be thwarted in its journey time and again by my leaping effort, they would repeat, one and then the other, the same exclamation.

"*My nigger Tim!*"

Pop! The ball would once again reverberate as it hit my hands and was pulled in for another interception.

"*My nigger Tim!*"

I would toss it back, and we would repeat the dance, Bobby moving to his left, Vince to his right, me following their steps and the thrower's eyes, taking cues from their body language as to where the ball would be going next.

Pop! Another catch.

"*My nigger Tim!*"

After the first dozen times they said this, each time with more emphasis, and a bit of a chuckle, I began to sense that something was going on, the meaning of which I didn't quite understand. A strange feeling began to creep over me, punctuated by a voice in the back of my head saying something about being suckered. Not to mention, I instinctively felt odd about being called a "nigger" (and note, it was indeed that derivation of the term, and not the more relaxed, even amiable "nigga" which was being deployed) because it was a word I would never use, and which I knew to be a slur of the most vile nature, and also, let's face it, because I was white, and had never been called a nigger before.

Though I remained uncomfortable with the exchange for several minutes after it ended, I quickly put it behind me as the bell rang, recess ended, and we headed back to class, laughing and talking about something else unrelated to the little psychodrama that had been played out on the ball field. If I ever thought of the event in the days afterward, I probably contented myself with the thought that although their word choice seemed a bit odd, they were only signifying that I was, at that moment, one of the club so to speak—that I had proven myself to them.

Well, I was right about one thing: They were, without question, "signifying"—a term for the cultural practice of well-crafted verbal put-downs that have long been a form of street poetry in the black communities of this nation.

As it turns out, it would be almost twenty years before I finally understood the meaning of this day's events, and that understanding would come while watching television. It was there that I saw a black comedian doing a bit about making some white guy "his nigger" and getting him to do whatever he, the black comic, wanted: to jump when he said jump, to come running when he was told to come running. To 'step 'n' fetchit,' so to speak.

So there it was. On that day, one cold winter afternoon in 1977, Bobby and Vince had been able to flip the script on the racial dynamic that would, every other day, serve as the background noise for their lives. On that day they were able to make me not only a nigger, but *their* nigger. The irony couldn't have been more perfect, nor the satisfaction, I suppose, in having exacted a small (very small) measure of payback. Not payback of me, per se, since at that age I had surely done little to deserve the burden, but of my people, writ large. It was harmless, and for them it had been fun: a little cat and mouse routine with the white boy who doesn't realize he's being used. And not just used, but used in the way our people have been used, and are still being used every day.

Today Tim, *you* the nigger. Today, you will be the one who gets to jump and run, and huff and puff. Today *we* laugh, and not with you, but at you. We like you and all that, but today, you belong to us.

As I thought about it, however, I was overcome with a profound sadness. Not because I had been tricked or played for a fool. That's happened lots of times, usually at the hands of other white folks. Rather, I was saddened by what I realized in that moment. And what I realized was that even at the age of nine—which is how old both Bobby and Vince were at that time—they had known what it meant to be someone's nigger. They knew more than simply how to say the word, they knew how to use the word, when to use it, how to contextualize it, and how to fashion it into a weapon. And the only way they could have known any of this is because they had either been told of its history and meaning, had been called it before, or had seen or heard a loved one called it before, none of which options are much better than the others.

Even as the school system we shared was every day treating Bobby and Vince as that thing they now called me—disciplining them more harshly or placing them in remedial level groups no matter their abilities—on the playground they could turn it around, and claim for themselves the power to define reality, *my* reality, and thereby gain a brief respite from what they surely knew was happening in class. Yet the joke was on them in the end. Because once recess was over, and the ball was back in the hands of the teachers, there were none prepared to make *me* the nigger. I would not be among the students made to dance, to shuck and jive, to follow orders, or to obey.

It had been the reality of white privilege and black oppression that had made the joke funny in the first place, or even decipherable; and it would likewise be white privilege and black oppression that would ultimately make it irrelevant and even a bit pathetic. But folks take their victories where they can find them, I suppose. I know I always did, and I found them more often than not.

A LIFE RAFT CALLED PRIVILEGE
(Or How Whiteness Saved My Life and Secured My Future)

IT WAS PREDICTABLE, I suppose, that I would develop a love for live theatre. My father, though a comedian by trade, actually always made more of a living as an actor than as a comic, and although I only saw his comedy act a few times, I saw him perform in plays dozens of times growing up. So when I got the chance to act in school, I naturally took it. Growing up in a home where my father was always on stage, even when he wasn't, had provided me with a keen sense of timing, of delivery, of what was funny and what wasn't, of how to move onstage, of how to "do nothing well," as my theatre teacher in high school would put it.

I grew up memorizing lines to plays I would never perform, simply because my dad had saved all the scripts from shows he had done in the past. They were crammed into a small brown-lacquered paperback book cabinet that hung in the living room of our apartment—one after another, with tattered and dog-eared pages, compliments of Samuel French, the company that owns distribution rights for most of the stage play scripts in the United States, or at least did at that time.

I would pick them up and read them, out loud in my room even, alternating voices for different characters. The plays dealt with adult themes, many of which I didn't understand in the least, but which I pretended to, just in case anyone ever needed a ten-year-old to play the part of Paul Bratter in *Barefoot in the Park*.

When my dad was about to head back on the road to do another play, I would run lines with him, as much for myself as for his own benefit. I would deliver the lines as if I were playing opposite him, and secretly hoped that one day we would get the chance to do a play together. We even spoke about making that happen, much to my mother's chagrin. Specifically, we talked about doing *A Thousand Clowns*, perhaps at some dinner theatre, or on the road. The play—which deals with a young man being raised by his socially dysfunctional and financially irresponsible uncle—would have been perfect for us, if a bit too close to home.

Having grown up in a theatrical household, I jumped at the chance to perform once I got into middle school, where drama class was offered for the first time as an elective. My drama teacher, Susan Moore, was among the most eccentric persons I have ever met. Had I been older I would have probably appreciated her eccentricity, but at the age of ten and eleven, eccentric is not seen as endearing but weird, and that's how the students, including myself, viewed her. She was the strange fat lady (we weren't too sensitive on issues of body type, as I'm sure won't surprise you), who had a dozen cats and whose clothes always smelled like cat litter, and whose car smelled even worse. One of my friends, Bobby Bell, who was not in the drama club, but who once got a ride from Ms. Moore for some reason, dubbed her wheels the "douche 'n' push," which we all thought was hilarious, even though I doubt any of us really knew what a douche was. In fact, once I learned the meaning of the word, calling her car a douche 'n' push seemed less funny than just gross. It sorta took away the fun of saying it, which thinking back had been substantial.

I don't know whether or not Ms. Moore even got paid for the work she did at the school, putting on plays and working with students after classes ended and for one period a day during the academic year. We didn't study much in terms of theatre technique. For good or bad, Susan thought it best to just throw us into the process of doing theatre, learning as we went. So she would pick a play, and we would work on it for the better part of a year: reading it, learning it, trying to understand it, and then finally producing it, acting in it, building the sets, and performing.

The good thing about this process was that it led to fairly sophisticated outcomes, at least for fifth and sixth graders. When you have ten- and eleven-year-olds pulling off Shakespeare's *Taming of the Shrew* and never dropping a single line, you know you're doing something special. As the lead character, Petruchio, in that production, I can attest to feeling significantly older and wiser than my years for having done it, for having taken on a Shakespearian comedy at such a tender age and succeeded.

On the downside, unless you got one of the coveted roles in the play chosen for that year by Ms. Moore, your participation in the lifeblood of the drama club would be circumscribed. Occasionally, Susan would write in characters and create a few lines for them, so that as many kids as possible could get a chance to be onstage, but this hardly flattened the hierarchy of the drama club. There were the actors, and then there was everyone else: the students who would work the lights, paint the sets, pull the curtains, or just hang out and perhaps help the actors run lines, or maybe just quit the drama club and find something else to do.

Of course, having a father who was an actor gave me a leg up and assured me of a prominent role in whatever production was chosen as our annual play. Ms. Moore could presume my talent, and although that talent may have been genuine, there were certainly no cold readings or auditions for anything. A few of us would pretty much rotate: I would be the male lead in one play, and in the next production that honor would go to my best friend, Albert. The female leads would also pretty much rotate between two of the girls in our class, Stacey and Shannon. It was a fairly closed circle.

In sixth grade we would switch from Shakespeare to *You're a Good Man, Charlie Brown*, which, given that it's a musical and neither Albert nor I could sing, should have guaranteed that it would be our turn to pull curtains or some such thing. But despite our lack of ability we were cast as Charlie and Linus, respectively, and in my case Ms. Moore actually agreed to take the song "My Blanket and Me" out of the play altogether, because I made clear that I was terrified to sing a solo in public.

My ability to force script changes was not, itself, about race—at least not directly. But my ability to be in the position I was, and therefore to make that kind of demand, and to gain the director's acquiescence, most assuredly was about race, at least in part. Had I been anything but white it would have been impossible to land the parts I landed in any of the productions done at that or any other school. These were roles written, after all, for white actors. Shakespeare's work is not, to be sure, replete with black characters, and there are only so many times a school can do *Othello*. Likewise, *Charlie Brown* was written before the introduction of the comic strip's one black character, Franklin, and although Ms. Moore added a few lines to the script and had a black kid deliver them in the person of Franklin, this hardly altered the racial dynamic at work.

To be white at that school, as in most schools, was to have a whole world of extracurricular opportunity opened to oneself—a world where if you were a mediocre student (as I definitely was), you could still find a niche, an outlet for your talents, passions, and interests in the form of theatre. To be black or brown at that same school was to ensure that no matter how good an actor or actress you were, or were capable of becoming, you were unlikely to be in a position to avail yourself of this same outlet for your creativity. Unless the drama teacher is prepared to violate the aesthetic sensibilities of the audience, which is rare, and cast a person of color in a role that is traditionally played by a white person (like Romeo or Juliet, or Hamlet, or Snoopy even), black, Latino, and Asian kids are just out of luck.

Although things may have changed a bit, and maybe even a lot at certain schools, please note that even today, even when a cast is racially mixed, white perspectives have a way of creeping into the material performed in a way that most probably don't even realize.

This past month, my wife, our two daughters, and I attended a performance of the musical *Schoolhouse Rock Live* by a cast of ninety or so kids in fifth through eighth grade at the same school attended by our kindergartener. Although the performance was wonderful, it was more than a little disconcerting to hear students singing songs like "The Great American Melting Pot" and "Elbow Room," both of which reflect troubling, even borderline racist views. So, in "Melting Pot" the children (about a third of whom were kids of color) sang the line, "America was the new world and Europe was the old," in one stroke eradicating the narratives of indigenous persons for whom America was hardly new, and any nonwhite kid whose old worlds had been in Africa or Asia, not Europe. And in "Elbow Room," the cast sings the glories of westward expansion in the United States, which involved the murder of native peoples and the violent conquest of half of Mexico. Among the lines in the song is one that intones, "There were plenty of fights /To win land rights /But the West was meant to be /It was our manifest destiny!" Let it suffice to say that happily belting out a tune in which one merrily praises genocide is always easier for those whose ancestors weren't on the receiving end of the deal.

Getting back to the point about my own involvement in theatre, and so you won't misunderstand how important this story really is, please know that theater was a life raft for me in middle school, without which I might well have gone under altogether. My ability to access it, and the whiteness that granted me that ability, was no minor consideration.

My family life was in crisis, with my father's alcoholism having reached its zenith. Things got so bad that at one point I began to keep track with hash marks on a page the number of days in a row that he had been drunk: twenty-one on the day I stopped counting, or, having been pressed down upon the page too hard out of childhood anguish, my pencil tip broke, I can't remember which. Only by escaping into the world of acting (a strangely ironic choice, I realize) was I able to make it through those grades at all. It was my refuge.

I could lock myself in my room with a play script, avoid my father, escape the smell of Canadian whiskey or bad vodka on his breath, and avoid the verbal battles that were the hallmark of his relationship with my mother. The only times I would come out of my room were in those moments when I honestly felt that if I didn't he might kill her. Although my home was not one characterized by physical abuse—thankfully, my dad only struck my mom once (which of course was one time too many) by pushing her into a wall outside my room—when you're ten and eleven years old your mind has a hard time processing the distinction between verbal and physical violence, and knowing where that line is, and just how much it might take for the abuser to cross the metaphorical Rubicon.

No matter the infrequency of physical abuse, in my mind the threat always seemed to hang like a pall over our home. At one point, I was so sure he would kill her that I began planning an escape route. If I could intervene and save her I would, but if it became apparent that I wouldn't be able to do much good, I knew how to get my bedroom window open fast, and exactly where I would run to get help, or to borrow the weapon with which I would end my father's life that very night.

That my father was not going to kill my mother was hardly the point. When you hear him say that he's going to, even purely rhetorically, and you're a child, you are in no position, intellectually speaking, to deconstruct the context of his words. All you can do is spend precious moments of your youth trying to figure out ways to save your mom's life, or at least your own, on that day when your father has one drink too many and burns dinner because he wasn't paying close enough attention, or can't find his keys and flies into a rage and reaches into the utensil drawer—and not for a spoon or salad fork.

So when I say that theatre was a life raft, I am not engaging in idle hyperbole. I mean it all too literally; without it, I would have had no refuge. While my physical existence may have continued—after all, my father never killed anyone in the end, and had he meant to, it's doubtful I could have dissuaded him with a sonnet—my emotional well-being, already teetering on the edge, would likely have taken a nosedive, with dire consequences in years to come. Drama was how I released my frustrations, my demons; it was how I avoided falling into clinical depression; it was how I got my mind off other things, like killing my father before he could harm my mom, which I actually did contemplate in my more panicked moments.

So let me spell it out: Without theatre, which I was only able to access in the way I did because I was white, it is a very open question how my life would have gone. If all the other variables had been the same, but I had been black, or anything other than white, and thereby bereft of the diversion offered by acting, I feel confident that things would have gone down differently than they did. As for my father, he should be very grateful that we were white, and that I had an outlet. That's all I'm saying.

* * *

GIVEN MY MEDIOCRE grades and subpar SAT score, it's a good thing I was an accomplished debater in high school. Otherwise, I would never have gotten into Tulane, or any other selective college for that matter.

Debate was for me in high school what drama had been in middle school: a place to put my energy and also an escape from the craziness that was my home life. The idea of throwing myself into an activity that allowed me to travel, to get away from home at least two weekends a month, was more than a little appealing. I was sure by now that my father was not going to kill my mother, so I didn't fear leaving them alone, and mostly I just needed a break from the fighting and the drinking.

There have always been debaters of color, and indeed, my high school's top debater when I arrived was a black senior, James Bernard, who taught me a lot about debate as well as activism. Still, the activity is very white, not merely in terms of its demographic, but also in terms of its style, its form, and its content at the most competitive levels. Debate literally exudes whiteness, and privileges white participants in a number of ways.

On the one hand, there is the issue of money. Debaters, in order to be nationally competitive, require funding: either a school with a huge budget to pay for trips to national tournaments, or families that can swing the cost of sending their kids away for three days at a time, often by plane, for the purpose of competing. I had neither, but somehow my folks managed to afford my debate habit, perhaps by borrowing money from my grandparents or just cutting back on other things and never telling me.

Then there are the summer debate camps, which even in the 1980s cost about $1,500, and which run for three to four weeks. Those who can afford to go to these get a huge jump on the competition. In fact, I don't know of any nationally competitive team whose members didn't attend at least one camp during the summer before. The one year that I couldn't afford to go set me back considerably in terms of my own skills, for several months at the beginning of my junior year. Not going to debate camp that summer put me at a decided disadvantage in terms of understanding the ins and outs of the topic for that year—ins and outs that those who had attended workshops had spent twelve hours a day researching for at least three solid weeks, with all the resources of college libraries and coaches to help them.

Obviously, given the interplay of race and socioeconomic status in this country, blacks, Latinos, American Indians, and Southeast Asians (all of which groups have much higher poverty rates than whites) are woefully underrepresented in the activity, relative to their numbers in the student population. But the cost of debate is hardly the only thing that causes the activity to be so white. The substance of the arguments made and the way in which the arguments are delivered also tend to appeal to whites far more readily than to people of color, for whom the style and substance are often too abstract to be of much practical value.

Those who haven't seen a competitive debate may be inclined to think that such a thing is a deep discussion of some pressing issue. But if that is what you expected, and you then happened into a debate at one of the nation's top tournaments and watched any of the elimination rounds (those involving the top sixteen or thirty-two teams, typically), you would think you had walked into a world of make believe. Even if you could understand a single word being said, which is unlikely since the "best" debaters typically speak at lightning speed—and I was among the biggest offenders here, able to rattle off five hundred words a minute—you still wouldn't really understand what was going on.

The terminology is arcane and only of use in the activity itself, including terms like *topicality, hypo-testing, counterplan, permutation, infinite regression,* and *kritik*. The purpose of competitive debate is essentially, a) to speak faster than your opponents so they will "drop" one of your arguments, which you will then insist to the judge is the most important issue in the round, and which warrants an immediate ballot in your favor; b) to make sure that whatever the topic, your argument for or against a particular policy can be linked to nuclear war or ecological catastrophe, no matter how absurd the linkage (so, for example, claim that your opponent's plan to extend the retirement age will contribute to global warming); and c) to find the most obscure reference, source, or argument on a given subject, and no matter how ridiculous, use it, because if it's obscure enough, the other team won't know how to respond.

Though one can theoretically learn quite a bit from debate, especially during the research phase of the operation, the fact remains that superficiality, speed, and mass extinction scenarios typically take the place of nuanced policy analysis, such that one has to wonder how much the debaters really come to know about the issues they debate at the end of the day. Learning is always secondary to winning. And for the sake of winning, debaters will say virtually anything.

My own debate experience serves as vulgar confirmation of this maxim. On the one hand, I ran cases (which in debate terms means the primary position taken by the affirmative team upholding the year's formal resolution) calling for the cutting off of weapons sales to Venezuela, and also for the restoration of voting rights to ex-felons: positions with which I agreed. On the other hand, I also ran cases calling for a program that would employ all poor folks who were out of work to build a missile defense system (possibly the dumbest idea ever advocated in a debate round), and for reinforcing the nation's water reservoirs against poisoning by terrorists. Although the idea of protecting soft targets from terrorism might make sense, the evidence we used to make our case was almost exclusively from the most disgusting of anti-Muslim, right-wing sources (and this was in 1985 and 1986 mind you, long before 9/11). I am still taking extra baths to wash off the ideological stench of having read evidence in debate rounds from people like Michael Ledeen or Daniel Pipes (the latter of whom posted something attacking me on his Campus Watch Web site a few years back, so I guess the feeling is mutual).

When we were on the negative side, I would argue, among other things, that poverty should be allowed to continue because it would eventually trigger a glorious socialist revolution (which isn't even good Marxist theory, let alone a morally acceptable position to put forward), or that civil liberties should be eradicated so the United States could transition to a society in which resource use was limited by force, family size was strictly controlled, and thus planetary destruction was averted.

The reason I call this process a white one is because whites (and especially affluent ones), much more so than folks of color, have the luxury of looking at life or death issues of war, peace, famine, unemployment, or criminal justice as a game, as a mere exercise in intellectual and rhetorical banter. For me to get up and debate, for example, whether or not full employment is a good idea, presupposes that my folks are not likely out of work as I go about the task. To debate whether racial profiling is legitimate likewise presupposes that I, the debater, am not likely to be someone who was confronted by the practice as my team drove to the debate tournament that day, or as we passed through security at the airport. In this way, competitive debate reinforces whiteness and affluence as normative conditions, and makes the process far more attractive to affluent white students. Kids of color and working-class youth of all colors are simply not as likely to gravitate to an activity where pretty much half the time they'll be forced to take positions that, if implemented in the real world, might devastate their families and communities.

Because debaters are encouraged to think about life or death matters as if they had little consequence beyond a given debate round, the fact that those who have come through the activity go on to hold a disproportionate share of powerful political and legal positions—something about which the National Forensics League has long bragged—is a matter that should concern us all. Being primed to think of serious issues as abstractions increases the risk that the person who has been so primed will reduce everything to a brutal cost-benefit analysis, which rarely prioritizes the needs and interests of

society's less powerful. Rather, it becomes easier at that point to support policies that benefit the haves at the expense of the have-nots, because the
damage will be felt by others whom the ex-debaters never met and never had
to take seriously.

Unless debate is fundamentally transformed—and at this point the only
forces for real change are the squads from Urban Debate Leagues who are
clamoring for different styles of argumentation and different evidentiary
standards—it will continue to serve as a staging ground for those whose interests are mostly the interests of the powerful. Until the voices of economically
and racially marginalized persons are given equal weight in debate rounds
with those of affluent white experts (whose expertise is only presumed
because other whites published what they had to say in the first place), the
ideas that shape our world will continue to be those of the elite, no matter
how destructive these ideas have proven to be for the vast majority of the
planet's inhabitants.

Until debate is substantially diversified, so that previously ignored voices
will have a chance to be heard on their own terms, and in their own styles,
little will change. What debate needs most is an infusion of persons who
because of their life experiences are almost guaranteed to be less naïve;
people who know full well that the system is anything but fair. Such persons
have a right to be heard, and white, upper-middle-class, and affluent debaters
need to hear them. They need to know how power works, and they will never
gain an understanding of that by listening over and over to the voices of
others like themselves.

But debate will never change in this way unless the gatekeepers of the
activity are prepared to step up and demand it, not just with their words but
with their actions, their money, their judging criteria, and even their ballots.
Folks of color and working-class folks won't join an activity if they feel their
wisdom isn't going to be taken seriously. If they wanted to be ignored, they
would hardly need to get dressed up and travel to debate tournaments in a
hot van to do it. They could stay home and be ignored, because the powerful
ignore them every day anyway.

Understand, this is no mere ethical plea for inclusion. Continuing to
ignore the voices of the marginalized carries great risks for us all, because it
is precisely such persons who so often view the world differently and far more
accurately than the privileged. As a case in point, the polls taken right before
the U.S. invasion of Iraq in March 2003 indicated broad white support for
going to war, but almost nonexistent support among blacks. Most white folks
were convinced not only of the war's moral legitimacy, but were sure that
everything would go swimmingly, because other white people like Rumsfeld
and Cheney said so. But black folks knew better. Those with privilege had the

luxury of thinking they would be greeted as liberators. But black folks know that invaders rarely bring true freedom—they've been there, done that. For the sake of us all, and to slow down the rate at which blood is spilled across the globe, we desperately need to listen to those who live without the luxury of blinders.

Privilege makes its recipients oblivious to certain things, and debate, as an activity, is one of its many transmission belts—one that I was able to access, to great effect in my life. Lucky for me that I went to a school that offered it, that I had parents who somehow managed to afford it, and that its game-playing format wasn't yet a problem for me, ethically speaking. Lucky for me, in other words, that I was white.

AFFIRMATIVE INACTION:
Living on the White Side of the Law

THAT I HAVE somehow avoided a criminal record is nothing short of a miracle. Actually, that's not quite true. Far more important to maintaining my status as a free man has been the rather nondivine intervention of white privilege. In fact it may be in this arena that I, like so many other whites, have been the most fortunate. Though I am hardly proud of it, the simple fact is, I've broken plenty of laws, including some that would easily, if detected, have resulted in my long-term incarceration and sent my life in a fundamentally different direction. And among the most important reasons I wasn't caught, wasn't punished, and am here to write about it today is because of the color of my skin.

I can't even remember, because there are simply too many to recall, the number of parties I attended in high school, at which hundreds of underage kids, including myself, were drinking and taking various types of drugs. I'm talking parties with ten kegs of beer and open bars, where guys were taking cover charges at the end of the driveway and stamping people's hands, right on the road, in plain view of everyone, including the police cars that would occasionally cruise by to make sure the noise wasn't getting out of hand.

Occasionally, the cops would even come onto the property, in response to a noise complaint from neighbors, and tell us to cut the music down. There is simply no chance that the officers didn't know alcohol was being served. Likewise, they had to have been able to detect the smell of marijuana in the air. Yet not once did they arrest anyone, or even tell us to get rid of the booze and the weed, so as to warn us that next time we wouldn't be so lucky. Indeed next time we *would* be that lucky, and the next time, and the next time, and the time after that, always.

These parties were at the homes of white people, surrounded by other homes lived in by white people, and attended almost exclusively by white people. There would always be a few people of color around, but for the most part, these were white spaces: something that immediately gave law enforcement officials reason to cut us slack. And this was true even though violence often broke out at these functions, typically because one or another good old boy from the Catholic school across town (that's right, good-old-boy, truck-drivin' Catholics, named Bubba come to think of it—three of 'em, all named Bubba) would barge in, shotguns in hand, and proceed to beat the crap out of anyone they didn't like.

Had these house parties been in black neighborhoods they would never have been allowed to go on at all, as large as they were, even without a single illegal substance on the premises, and without a single weapon in sight. But for whites, in white neighborhoods, everything was different. Our illegality was looked at with a wink and a nod.

So too was criminal activity overlooked on the debate circuit. When debaters at Nashville's Montgomery Bell Academy were caught destroying law journals at Vanderbilt University's law school in 1984, by using razor blades to cut out important evidence, rather than take the time or spend the money to make Xerox copies, nothing happened to them. Oh, they probably had to have their parents repay the school for the damage. Or perhaps MBA paid the bill, just to keep the activities of their elite team quiet. But whatever the case, no one ended up with a criminal record, and MBA, as an institution, meted out no punishment either: no grounding their teams from competition, no public mea culpa. With the exception of those of us in the Nashville area who knew the MBA debaters and considered some of them friends, most folks on the national circuit probably knew little of what had happened. Needless to say, if an urban debate team made up of black or Latino kids went into the library of their local college and defaced private property, things would go just a tad bit differently.

When it came to drugs, the debate circuit was probably the best place to score, as drugs were every bit as prevalent there as wing-tipped shoes, diet cokes, ill-fitting suits, and socially awkward teens. So (and since we're speaking of MBA), everyone knew what the noise was, when the briefcase of one of their top debaters accidentally opened up in the auditorium at Emory University, in 1985, spilling its contents in front of five hundred students waiting to hear which teams had advanced to elimination rounds. The clinking of dozens of nitrous oxide canisters upon the stage—canisters used for doing "whippets," an inhalant with a nasty habit of causing seizures and heart attacks, even the first time they're used—was hard to mistake for anything else. Everyone knew what the noise signified, and no one did anything, except laugh, as the debaters from the prestigious boy's prep school scrambled to put the evidence of their recreational activity away.

That summer, I attended debate camp at American University in Washington, D.C. Upon arriving, I checked in, dropped my bags off in my dorm room, and then spent the next two hours in the room of arguably the best debater in the history of the activity (who also, interestingly enough, went to MBA—I'm sensing a trend here) getting baked into oblivion. Everyone knew what was going on in that room, yet no one did a thing. Even if you couldn't smell the pot, you couldn't miss the aroma of burning cologne—entire bottles of it—that had been poured out just inside the door and set on fire to cover up the real action that was taking place inside. No seventeen-year-old kid wears that much frickin' Polo.

And then there was alcohol.

When it came to drinking, I would venture to guess that pretty much every white student at my school who wanted a fake ID had one, many of them because of my own entrepreneurial efforts.

Tennessee, lucky for us, had at that time what was probably the easiest driver's license in the country to fake. The state had only switched to a photo ID in 1984, so many of my classmates were able to use their paper licenses—the alteration of which took all of about fifteen minutes, a razor blade, and some glue—until their expiration dates; but even when the picture IDs came in, they were simple to replicate. All you needed was a poster board, some black art-supply-store letters for the wording, an orange marker for the TEN-NESSEE background at the top, a light blue piece of paper for the subject to stand in front of, off to the side of the board, and a clear piece of acetate (like for an overhead projector) onto which you could stencil the state seal, copying it from the encyclopedia. You would then place half of the seal on the bottom-left side of the board, and stand with your shoulder just behind the other half, hanging off the board, giving the appearance that the seal had been computer generated and stamped onto the picture. Although the methods and materials were crude, they worked.

I began my fake ID business out of my home, shuttling people in and out of my parents' apartment, with their knowledge I should add, occasionally a dozen in one afternoon. The process was simple: You brought a package of instant film, along with $20. I would take an entire roll. However many seemed usable were yours to keep, but you had to let them sit for twenty-four hours before cutting them to license size, so that the chemicals in the paper would dry—otherwise, the paper would separate and the ID would fall apart. Then you had only to apply a plain white sticker to the back of the otherwise black instant camera film, so as to mimic the plain white backing on a real license. Simple.

Tennessee didn't laminate licenses back in those days, so all you had to do was pop your fake into the little plastic holder that the state had provided you for your real driver's license, and you were pretty much able to get into any club you wanted, and drink at most bars.

My fake ID business provided me with a modest but welcome stream of revenue, and of course every one that I made was punishable by a $500 fine and up to sixty days in jail. Likewise, every occasion when I used one myself—which would have been probably three hundred times between the age of sixteen and the time I was finally able to drink legally in my senior year of college—was similarly punishable. That I thought I could get away with such an enterprise had everything to do with the cavalier way in which white youth view law enforcement in most cases. Because we know we can get away with drinking, and drinking and driving so long as we aren't hammered, and passing fake ID, we do it without so much as a second thought.

The worst that's going to happen, we figure (usually correctly), is that we're going to get turned down by someone who knows that we're passing a phony. But they aren't going to call the cops. It's like the guy for whom I made an ID right before he left to go to college (he of the whippet canisters mentioned above), who tried to pass off my artwork at the door of some club, and had the misfortune of having the bouncer take the picture out of its plastic sleeve and bend it back and forth. It fell apart within seconds, owing not to my own shoddy work I should point out, but to the unfortunately crappy quality of instant film. The bouncer laughed and told him to get lost, but my client knew he wasn't going to jail that night, a freshly branded outlaw (this is an inside joke, which will be understood by perhaps fifty people). We both laughed about it in fact, when he had the occasion to tell me what happened a year later.

I even showed my fake ID to cops, on two different occasions, as did plenty of other folks I knew. Now, we wouldn't have done this if we'd been pulled over for speeding or something. Being high on privilege doesn't make you a complete idiot, after all. But if we were out on the street, or at a club, after curfew, drunk, and a cop wanted to see our ID to check how old we were? Passed a fake twice in those situations. Never got busted, even when I showed a phony Iowa license to a cop who was originally from Iowa, and had to know the ID was phony, since I had just made up the template off the top of my head and it looked like crap. That was the same night that another of my friends, also white, showed the same cop an ID that was real, for what that was worth, but belonged to a thirty-one-year-old guy (my friend was eighteen) with red hair (his was brown), and a beard (he was clean shaven). Not even close, but close enough for white boys I guess.

When I got to college, the fake ID thing wasn't that important, since pretty much everyone could get away with drinking in New Orleans. But the drugs, well, that was a different story altogether, because drugs are every bit as illegal in New Orleans as anywhere else—at least, if you're black and poor, and have the misfortune of doing your drugs somewhere *other* than the dorms at Tulane University. But if you are lucky enough to be living at Tulane, which is a pretty white place, especially contrasted with the city where it's located (which was two-thirds black before Katrina), then you are absolutely set.

My freshman year, I lived on the eighth floor of Monroe Hall, next door to the biggest pot dealer on campus, and by reputation one of the biggest in the city. He would drop quarter-ounce bags in the hallway and not miss them. And being a dealer who, unlike most, liked to smoke his own shit, he would just write it off to being high, *really high,* and never got too mad about it. I should say that I very much liked living next door to him, for obvious reasons.

There were two black guys on our hall, both on the football team. One of them smoked weed and the other didn't, but even the one who did looked at us like we were nuts. The sheer volume of grass being consumed dwarfed anything he was used to, and the way we were smoking it—out of three-foot bongs, because two feet just wouldn't have gotten us nearly messed up enough—he likewise found bizarre. "Can't y'all just roll a joint, man?" he would ask, not realizing that no, we couldn't just roll a joint. Privileged people like to overindulge. It comes with the territory. We weren't afraid of getting caught, as he was—since, after all, things would probably turn out differently if he were busted, on a lot of levels—so concealing our habits wasn't foremost on our minds.

Without question, I saw far more drugs, drug use, and drug dealing going on at Tulane, on my dorm floor alone, in any given week, than I ever saw in public housing projects, where I would work as a community organizer many years later. And as with the drinking and drug use in high school, it was overwhelmingly a white person's game, meaning either that white people have some genetic predisposition to substance abuse, which I have a hard time believing and for which there's no evidence in any event, or there's something about being white in this country that allows one, even encourages one, to take a lot of stupid risks, knowing that nine times out of ten everything will work out; you won't get busted and you won't go to jail, neither of which black or brown folks can take for granted in the least.

Perhaps this is why national studies have found that next to having a large Division I sports program, the single most highly correlated factor with alcohol and substance abuse on college campuses is the percentage of students who are white: the whiter the school, the bigger the problem. Not because there's something wrong with white people, per se, but because privilege encourages and makes more likely all kinds of self-destructive behaviors, and allows those who enjoy the privileges to remain cavalier about their activities all the while.

* * *

IT WAS CERTAINLY a cavalier attitude about drug use, and the prospects of getting in trouble, that white folks brought to Grateful Dead concerts for nearly forty years, and that I carried with me in the summer of 1990, when my girlfriend at the time and I went to see two shows, one outside of Kansas City, the other in Louisville.

Anyone who ever went to a Dead show will know exactly how brazen was the illegal activity taking place in the parking lot, inside the show—everywhere you turned, in fact. Nothing like a stadium filled with aging hippies and their younger-generation wannabes to bring out the patchouli, falafel, and tofu burgers, not to mention, of course, plenty of weed and assorted hallucinogens.

Drugs had always been part of the Dead scene, dating back to the band's days in San Francisco in the mid-to-late sixties, and became more or less permanently linked with the group after 1970, when they were the targets of an infamous drug bust in New Orleans. Dead shows, known for extended guitar jams that seemed to go on for longer than you were in high school, provided the perfect environment for experimenting with acid, psilocybin (mushrooms), and pretty much any other mind-altering substance you could get your hands on. And because the scene was overwhelmingly white, those who indulged their habits at concerts could usually take for granted that they would get away with it; this, in marked contrast to the way in which black concertgoers, at a hip-hop show, would likely feel.

The numbers of police at concerts, it seems, is almost always inversely proportional to the number of whites in attendance. If it's Woodstock '99, with 200,000 people in the crowd, almost all of them white, then there are no uniformed officers at all, and an inadequate number of security guards—as became evident when some of those white folks decided to set fire to the venue in Rome, New York, loot ATM machines, commit several dozen sexual assaults in the mosh pit, and burn down the lighting scaffolds around the staging area. On the other hand, if it's a hip-hop concert, put on by Hot 97 in New York, and a simple fight breaks out because more tickets were sold than there were seats, cops from a half-dozen surrounding jurisdictions get called in to restore calm and support the NYPD forces that had been on the scene from the beginning.

So when Debbie and I pulled up to the Louisville show, fresh out of party supplies, I simply walked around the parking lot *asking* people where I could make a buy, knowing it would be about as easy as buying a bag of popcorn at a movie theatre. Though I was nervous about purchasing drugs from a stranger, I never really thought I was likely to come upon a cop and end up going to jail that night. And sure enough, within three minutes I was sitting in the front seat of somebody's VW bus (as stereotypical as you're likely envisioning it to be), buying a half-ounce of 'shrooms, exiting the bus, walking into the stadium without fear of being searched, and proceeding to enjoy the show for the next four hours.

For the record, the 'shrooms were awful: so weak that I barely got a buzz the entire time. Hell, I may have been eating dried-up shiitake for all I know. But that was hardly the point. I could have walked into the stadium at the University of Louisville that afternoon with a half-pound of grass or twenty sheets of acid, and nothing would have happened to me. Because no matter the crime being committed, *I am not the stereotype.*

I know this because cops have told me. On those rare occasions when I've conducted trainings with law enforcement officers, I've asked them straight out: "What's the first thing you think when you see a young black or Latino male, driving around in a nice car in your neighborhood?" And without hesitation or exception they will reply, "Drug dealer." I then ask, "What's the first thing you think when you see a young white male, driving around in a nice car in your neighborhood?" And without hesitation or exception they will reply, "Spoiled little rich kid, daddy bought him a car." This, despite the fact that young whites are more likely to use, and just as likely to deal drugs as their black and brown counterparts, according to all available research.

In other words, within the first few minutes of our session, two questions are able to elicit clear evidence of racial bias from cops who have been sworn to protect and serve, and to do so equitably. And we're supposed to believe that they can put aside those biases and do their jobs fairly? We're supposed to trust them? We're supposed to call on them for help? For the privileged such a thing might make sense, but it doesn't take much to see why, for people of color, interacting with police is an entirely different kind of experience.

* * *

FOR PEOPLE OF color, they certainly know that they can't wantonly give police a hard time or mouth off to them and expect to get away with it. But that's something I've done before, quite secure in the knowledge that my privilege would likely insulate me from mistreatment as a result.

For instance, there was the time in October 1993 when I was driving down Napoleon Avenue in New Orleans, having just passed Claiborne, and within about an eighth of a mile was pulled over by two of the city's finest (which phrase I should point out has no literal meaning—it's sorta like saying you just drank two of the best wines made in Arizona). I had watched them swing around at a U-turn in the median (or what New Orleanians call the neutral ground), pull in behind me, and then follow me for a few seconds before turning on the lights.

I had committed no moving violation, of this I was certain. I was wearing my seatbelt, though it wasn't even mandated by law yet. I hadn't made any lane changes for which I might have failed to signal. Yet I knew why I had been stopped. It was the same reason for which I had been stopped three previous times in the past year, despite breaking no laws: namely, I was driving a beat-up car (though fully functioning) with tinted windows (though not illegally tinted) and an anti–David Duke sticker on the back bumper. As such, the cops quite logically assumed I was black (after all, Duke did get between fifty-five and sixty percent of the white vote in his 1990 and '91 campaigns, so this wasn't a bad bet on their parts). And if you think I'm exaggerating or perhaps mistaken about what the cops were thinking when they stopped me, then perhaps you can interpret for me the meaning of the officer's one-word comment when I rolled down the window and he got a look at my face: "Oh."

In other words, they thought they were going to pull over a black guy, maybe find some violation on his part, maybe search his car for drugs, or just give him a hard time. But now they had to manufacture something, because I, in the throes of white privilege, had the temerity to say what damn near no black person ever would, namely, "Why'd you stop me when you know I haven't done anything?"

Not only did the cop not pull me out of the car and sprawl me over the hood, which is likely what he'd have done to any twenty-five-year-old of color who had smarted off to him that way, but he stumbled around for a minute, went back to his partner in the police cruiser, and then came back a few minutes later to say that they had pulled me over because my license tags said 1993—which was true, but then again, it *was* 1993, and my tags weren't going to expire until December 31. I mentioned this to the officer, who then stumbled around some more, and then finally said that they couldn't tell that the expiration month was December until they stopped me, which was absurd, and which then prompted me to ask (again, still pumping the white privilege here) that if that had been the case, why hadn't he hopped back in his car once he got out, looked at the tag, and saw it was still valid? Indeed, if that was the reason he had stopped me, what were we still doing, there?

As it turns out, my insurance had lapsed two weeks earlier, which he then discovered much to his relief when he asked to see my proof of the same. Now he would be able to write me a ticket. But because he was apparently still thrown off by my lack of melanin, he did proceed to tell me how to beat the ticket at the courthouse by pleading a section something-or-other, which for first-time offenders would result in the ticket being thrown out. And I *was* a first-time offender since on the previous three occasions I'd been stopped the police had let me go with a warning (for what, I never did figure out).

I paid the ticket. It had been worth it just to learn the value of my white skin.

Of course I know there are whites who sometimes get in real trouble with the law. In fact I know a guy who got busted in college, at the University of Mississippi, for selling acid—a lot of it. And he did go to prison and he did some hard time, despite being white and from an affluent family. But before I forget, I should mention that the guy I'm speaking of got out a few years back, and since gaining his freedom has become the president of his own company, with a little help from his family of course.

So even in the exceptions one sometimes finds the rule.

* * *

CASE IN POINT: the father of a friend of mine, whom I'll call William.

William is, by his own accounting, the epitome of the self-made man. Indeed, in some ways I would hardly argue with him. Having grown up very poor, and under conditions that give meaning to the term dysfunctional, it is nothing short of amazing that years later he would work his way up in one industry and then become a successful entrepreneur in his own right within another. By the time I came to know him, he was a millionaire, and has since only added to his wealth by way of several successful real-estate ventures.

It will come as no surprise that William is of a political mindset that is quite literally eons away from my own. I doubt he'll read this book, and if he does it will only be because of our history, and even then he'll hate it. And he won't appreciate at all my including this story within its pages. For his sake and that of his family, I have changed his name. But for the sake of making an extremely important point, I must tell at least a portion of his story, because it so completely demonstrates the way in which white privilege operates even for those whites who have suffered tremendously under the weight of economic marginality and familial abuse.

William was once what those given to understatement used to call rambunctious. He hung out with what those same persons once called a "tough crowd," and like a lot of folks with such a cadre of friends, he would, from time to time, get into a bit of trouble. Most often the trouble was minor: a scuffle here and there, perhaps some minor-league vandalism or petty pranks, but nothing that would really signify serious juvenile or young adult delinquency. At least this was true until one point in the late 1950s, when William was arrested for rape.

As it turns out, William had raped no one. He had been out drinking and partying with his buddies, and after having his fill of the festivities, got dropped off back at home. Unfortunately for William, however—and more to the point, unfortunately for some young woman—his friends weren't done for the evening, and several of them would that very night commit the sexual assault for which they would then blame William. Having no one to back up his alibi, and the girl's word apparently counting for very little, William found himself sitting in jail for a crime he didn't commit.

It's been several years since I heard this story, so I can't recall whether or not he was actually convicted before the truth emerged, or whether he was merely sitting in jail awaiting trial, but in any event it hardly matters to the point of this story, as you'll soon see.

What I do recall is that eventually William went free and had his record expunged. This happy ending was the culmination of a long and concerted effort on the part of the woman who was to become his wife (or maybe they were already married—again, a minor detail which hardly matters), as well as the eventual admission of wrongdoing on the part of at least one of his former friends, and the willingness of a judge to make right a terrible wrong. Justice, thankfully, was done, and William was free to get on with his life. As I've already told you, he did so to great effect, as is made all too clear by a look at his current investment portfolio. Indeed, the experience of being unjustly incarcerated was likely a huge motivator for William's success, since few things can better prove how precious liberty is than to have that freedom taken away.

Once free, William committed himself to hard work and self-discipline. He had been "scared straight," so to speak, and would remain on the legal up and up for the rest of his life, as far as I know. In fact, I can't imagine him breaking the law today for almost any reason. He is far from a perfect person—given to anger, hardheadedness, and a bottling up of emotion, all of which are somewhat typical of men of his generation—but all in all he is a decent if flawed man, who has spent the better part of the last forty-five years trying to do things on the straight tip, aware, no doubt, of just how easy it would have been for him to have gone the other way.

But there is one aspect of the story that I doubt he has ever considered. Not because he isn't a bright guy, but because even extremely bright people are unlikely to see that which their society hides from them by way of its social arrangements.

See, all of this happened in the South. I won't specify which state because it really doesn't matter, and I'm trying to maintain this individual's anonymity, but the point is, it was the South and it was the late fifties and early sixties when all of this was happening, and William was accused of raping a white woman.

If I have to say anything more about this episode in order to make my point to you, then it may be that this isn't the book you should be reading. You may need to put it down and do some homework on the history of this country, of the South in particular, of what happened routinely to black men who were accused, falsely or otherwise, of raping a white woman. Once you've read that history—and feel free to start with the work of Ida B. Wells Barnett—come back to this page and start again.

William is, very simply, alive because he is white. And if there is one thing I figure all can agree on it's that getting rich when you're dead, when you've been hauled out of jail and strung up from a tree by thugs who saw no need to wait for a guilty verdict before meting out your punishment, is, well, shall we say, difficult. Without his white skin, and having been accused of sexually assaulting a fair maiden of the Jim Crow South, our dear William would, at best, have rotted for years in prison, seeing how few if any judges at that time would have taken seriously his protestations of innocence. At worst, he would have joined the long list of black men—"Strange Fruit," as Billie Holiday called them—that for so many generations had been hung from a high limb with a short rope.

Nothing about this truth takes away from his hard work or character, and none of it makes him a bad person. But it does indicate that he is implicated in a larger system of racism as a recipient of white privilege, whether he likes it or not—and in the case of this particular story, how can he not like it, very, very much? Parental abuse aside, poverty aside, hardship aside, he was a member of the club. And even if that membership had never provided William with another single solitary thing, not a single solitary job, loan, or anything else, it had provided him with his life, and without that none of the rest would have mattered because none of the rest would have happened.

NEVER OUT OF PLACE:
Whiteness and the Presumption of Belonging

WILLIAM, OF COURSE, is hardly the only one who might have missed a few things in terms of the value and benefit of his white skin. There is so much that white folks never think about, things that go completely over our heads, but which have much to do with privilege. Even when we should see them for what they are, we don't.

When I went away to college I considered myself a hip liberal, aware of racism and committed to fighting it. And yet within just a few weeks of my arrival there, I had largely missed the meaning of two different incidents— one of them fairly minor, the other pretty significant—and thereby missed an opportunity to respond to them in a forthright manner.

The first took place during freshman orientation, when all the bright young seventeen- and eighteen-year-olds who had come to Tulane sat in a very hot auditorium in late August, and listened to the typical "welcome to our school" shtick given to all students at all colleges in the country. There were the expected platitudes about the grandeur and history of the university, and about the importance of adjusting to life away from home, and of course warnings about the pitfalls of going to school in New Orleans. Among these snares, of course, was the ubiquitous problem of heavy drinking—the drinking age had just been raised to twenty-one, but most students (though not me) had birthdays that fell within the grandfathering period. But we were also warned to stay away from certain neighborhoods, and to travel in groups as well, because not all of New Orleans was as safe as Uptown, where the university was located.

At first glance this may seem like nothing more than good advice, but to the extent the warnings were all in regard to mostly black and poor neighborhoods, it was highly racialized and selective in a way that prioritized the well-being of whites to the exclusion of persons of color—since after all, the latter might also have been at risk in certain white spaces. This was made all the more obvious by the second thing that happened, within a month or so of the beginning of school: namely, the announcement by the sheriff of neighboring Jefferson Parish that he had instructed his deputies to stop any and all black males driving in the Parish in "rinky-dink" automobiles on suspicion of being up to no good, as he put it.

What's important here is that at no point had Tulane officials suggested that students, even black ones, stay away from Jefferson Parish, even though it was understood to be less than hospitable to black folks. The truth was, Sheriff Harry Lee—a Chinese American loved by good old boys from the white flight suburb in large part because of his antiblack biases—had been profiling African American males for a long time before he ever went public with his law enforcement techniques; and Tulane had thought nothing of it. School officials had sought to make sure that we didn't make the mistake of straying into the black and mostly poor parts of town, out of a concern that we might become victims of random street crime; but at no point did they warn students of color of the many areas in the metropolitan vicinity where they (and they quite alone) might have been endangered.

This was yet another way in which whiteness was privileged at Tulane, another way in which the interests and concerns of whites were implicitly catered to, in ways no persons of color could expect when it came to their own concerns regarding racism.

Despite thinking that Harry Lee was a real asshole, especially when he went on *The Today Show* and tried to justify his racist policies to the nation, I did absolutely nothing to protest those policies. I said nothing and did nothing, even as those policies privileged me, by signaling that I (and persons like me) would be allowed to come and go as we pleased, in and out of any part of the metropolitan area we felt like visiting. I had failed miserably to recognize just how personal this system of privilege was, no matter how hip I fashioned myself.

Who was I kidding? My very presence at Tulane had been related to whiteness. During my time there I would come to learn that the same school that had recruited me, and traveled 540 miles to pluck me out of Nashville, had not been recruiting for several years at Fortier High, the basically all-black high school located approximately 350 yards from the entrance to campus on Freret Street. There was a clear presumption that Fortier students, as well as those from several other New Orleans–area high schools, were incapable of being successful at Tulane, and so the attempt to recruit them simply wasn't made. Meanwhile, there I was, with an SAT score roughly 200 points below the median then (and 300 or more below it now), being admitted without hesitation and given substantial financial aid. Better to spend money and resources, I suppose, on hard-drinking white co-eds from Long Island, or Boston, or Miami, or Northbrook, or Winnetka, or Manhattan, than to spend some of the same on local blacks, whose parents were good enough for cooking Tulane food, and cleaning Tulane toilets, and picking up Tulane garbage, but not for raising Tulane graduates.

Whiteness, as these stories in part demonstrate, is about never being really out of place, of having access, and, more to the point, the sense that wherever you are, you belong, and won't be likely to encounter much resistance to your presence. Despite my lousy test scores and mediocre grades, no one ever thought to suggest, for example, that I had somehow gotten into Tulane because of some form of "preferential treatment," or as a result of standards being lowered. Students of color, though, with similar grades and scores, had to regularly contend with this sort of thing, since they were presumed to be the less-qualified beneficiaries of affirmative action.

But what kind of affirmative action had I enjoyed? What preference had I received? Of course it wasn't race directly. It's not as if Tulane had admitted me because I was white. It was because I had been on one of the top-ten debate teams in the nation—and that, as we've already discussed, was related to whiteness in many ways—my academic credentials were overlooked. Standards were lowered, but no one seemed to care.

Similarly, I lecture around the country in defense of affirmative action and find it amazing how whites resent the so-called lowering of standards for students of color but swallow without comment the lowering of standards for the children of alumni. Each year, there are thousands of white students who get "bumped," in effect, from the school of their choice, to make way for *other* whites whose daddies happen to be better connected than their own. Yet rarely do the critics of affirmative action seem to mind this form of preferential treatment.

Most everyone I met at Tulane who was truly stupid—I mean, wouldn't know to come out of the rain stupid—was white and rich. Like the one guy who thought he was still supposed to start every research paper with a thesis statement, the way he'd been taught to do it in seventh grade, or the young woman on my hall sophomore year who was stunned when she received an overdraft notice from her bank—after all, there were still checks in her checkbook.

I never heard anyone lament the overrepresentation of the cerebrally challenged white elite at Tulane, and I doubt anyone is challenging the latest round of similarly mediocre members of the ruling class now. That's what it means to be privileged: wherever you are, it's taken for granted that you must deserve to be there. You never seem to spoil the décor, or trigger suspicions of any kind. And it's not only the case with colleges.

* * *

HERE'S WHAT I mean.

I was already thirty minutes late for dinner, and I had absolutely no idea where I was. Despite the fact that I'd driven the road once before—the route from Spokane, Washington, to Moscow, Idaho, passing through Pullman on the way—I was utterly lost. What's worse, the fog had rolled in so quickly and so thick that I couldn't see a thing in front of me. I was in farm country, after all, and anything from a cow to a horse, to some chickens or goats, could have been up ahead, and had they been, they would have died that night, because I certainly wouldn't have seen them coming.

My cell phone rang, and although the last thing I needed at that point was another distraction, I answered it, knowing it would be the welcoming committee, waiting for me at the restaurant—the one I felt certain was not up ahead in the fog, but down some other road, the turn for which I had missed a few miles back. My hosts, who had brought me in for a speech the next morning to commemorate Martin Luther King Day in Moscow, were worried about me, but glad to know I was okay. They gave me directions out of the fog, and eventually I found my way to my destination more than an hour after I was supposed to arrive.

It's a good thing I had just gotten a cell phone, I thought to myself; otherwise I would have been forced to pull over to the side of the road, or perhaps walk up to one of the farmhouses (provided I could have found one in that fog), and ask for help.

Of course I could have done that, and wouldn't have hesitated to do so, had it been necessary. And thinking about that, it dawned on me that out in the middle of nowhere, with not another car on the road, under a star-filled Idaho sky, my whiteness had once again been of value.

Had I needed to walk up to some house off the side of the road and ask for directions or to use the phone, there would have been no reason that I wouldn't have done either or both of those things. I could have waltzed right up, even on a night as foggy as that one, knocked on the door or rung the bell, smiled, and known that when the door opened there would be no reason to fear that my presence would have prompted the owners to call the police or reach for a gun. Indeed, I could have counted on their opening the door in the first place. My face would not have signaled a threat.

But what if the Moscow, Idaho, MLK Day Committee had invited a black speaker to give the next day's talk? And what if that black speaker had also driven from Spokane and gotten lost in the fog, having missed the turnoff? Would such a person have been able to get out of his or her car, walk up to the same house, and knock on the same door? While in the simplest terms such a person would surely have been *able* to do so, the question is whether that person would have been able to take for granted that his or her doing so would be met with the same kind of response that I could assume would meet me? Could a person of color in that situation simply assume that their knock would result in a warm and generous offer to come inside and use the phone?

Don't get me wrong, the odds are that the white folks (and they are white, let's be clear about that) who live along the highway from Pullman to Colfax are all fine people, none of whom would harm a black person, or any person of color were they to knock on their door. But no person of color could afford to take the chance that such optimism might be misplaced. I, on the other hand, could have taken that chance, had it been necessary, without having to worry about whatever cues might be given off by my skin color.

That I would have been able to find my way out of the fog, one way or the other, without having to think about my race is what white privilege is all about. It's that one less thing to sweat; and when you're already sweating the fog, a dying cell phone battery, and no map to guide you, having one less thing to worry about means a lot.

To be white is to rarely find oneself feeling "out of place," the way a person of color would likely have felt in Idaho that evening. And no, being white in an urban, mostly black and brown community is hardly equivalent.

First off, how many times do whites find ourselves in such places, unless by choice? How often do we simply forget where the so-called ghetto is? Hell, most of us know exactly where it is, and how to avoid it, and we do damn near everything possible to make sure we never have to drive through it. In other words, even if our lives would be endangered and our whiteness of negative value in such places (and really, that's a huge if), that kind of scenario is rare, precisely because we have the privilege of living where we want for the most part, of being able to avoid such places, to move away, to work elsewhere, to shop elsewhere, or whatever—a privilege people of color often don't have.

On the other hand, people of color are far more likely to find themselves in places where *they* are the ones out of place than we ever are. People of color can't really avoid white spaces, and if they do it's probably because they live in the poorest areas and are the most destitute persons of color around. After all, to have much opportunity in the job market, or success in education, typically requires a fairly high level of interaction with white folks, since so much of the power within either setting resides in white hands.

But even more to the point, I have been in those very places where, to hear some tell it, my whiteness would work against me, and have found that if anything, the opposite is true. I worked as a community organizer in public housing, among other places, for a little more than a year in New Orleans, and during that time—a period when the projects there were among the most "dangerous" and run down in the nation—although I was usually the only white person around, I never experienced any real fear (discomfort at standing out like a sore thumb, yes, but not fear), nor was I given any reason to feel that afraid. If anything, people avoided me, because the only white folks they were used to seeing in their neighborhood were either cops or social workers, neither of which they were likely to mess with, since doing so with the first could get you shot and doing so with the latter could get your kids taken away.

In other words, my whiteness conferred authority upon me, and power, even in the place where I was completely alone in the racial sense. Surrounded by black folks, most of them poor, and no doubt some who weren't real fond of whites, my whiteness nonetheless insulated me in large measure from any mistreatment.

Being white also meant that I wasn't likely to be perceived by any truly dangerous character in the 'hood as a rival drug dealer or gang member, for example. Since the dealers these folks knew were all black, and the gang members they dealt with were, too, there was little likelihood that I might be mistaken for someone trying to muscle in on their turf. Had I been black though, and a community organizer, I might have had to worry about just that possibility—being mistaken as a criminal associate by folks who looked like me. So on that level, too, being white was a source of protection.

Whether in Idaho or in the Desire Housing Projects, whiteness was of benefit, in relative and absolute terms. It is that one less thing to worry about. It bestows advantage, no matter how much fog we may try and use to cover up that simple fact.

THE COLOR OF SUSPICION:
Race, Whiteness, and Danger

CONSIDER HOW QUICK we've been—especially whites, it seems—to jump on the bandwagon of profiling when it comes to Arabs, Muslims, or anyone perceived as either, since 9/11. Immediately after that tragic day, it seemed as though you couldn't find anyone other than Arab and Muslim advocacy groups willing to speak out against the notion that anyone matching the description of a Middle Eastern male should be subjected to extra scrutiny at airports, for example.

To point out the civil liberties implications, or even to make the argument that profiling might be flawed as a law enforcement tactic—since surely terrorists would know the profile and find ways to beat it—was guaranteed to bring down the wrath of reactionary sentiment, perhaps even to be thought of as an enemy of the state who secretly harbored pro-terrorist sympathies. So most folks kept quiet.

Almost immediately I could notice the difference during my travels. Any flight on which there was someone who looked as though he might be even a distant relative of hijacker Mohammed Atta was searched more intently than anyone else. Sadly, for most of us—myself included—this presumption of guilt when it came to perceived Arabs and Muslims made us feel safer.

Of course it didn't actually *make* us safer, and when Richard Reid—of mixed British and Afro-Caribbean ancestry—got on a plane in France and tried to bring it down with a shoe bomb shortly after 9/11, the world got a glimpse at how flawed profiling can be. Reid, despite his alarming behavior, was not stopped at the airport because he had a proper British name and accent, and didn't look the part of an al-Qaeda terrorist. Luckily, his skills as a shoe bomber were woefully inadequate so he was stopped, but the point is that no one suspected him. They were too busy enforcing the profile.

That Arabs are being treated with suspicion since 9/11, while white men were not treated that way after Tim McVeigh's bombing of the Federal Building in Oklahoma City (or for that matter, after the crimes of the Unabomber, the Olympic Park bomber, or the hundreds of white men who have bombed or burned abortion clinics since the mid-1980s) is entirely about white privilege. After all, the nineteen men who hijacked the four planes on that fateful day are no more representative of 1.5 billion Muslims on the planet than McVeigh, Terry Nichols, Ted Kaczynski, or Eric Rudolph are of the 100 million or so white men in this country. Yet in the case of the former we act as if profiling is a moral and practical imperative, while we would never have stood for the same treatment in the latter case.

Roughly a year after the Oklahoma City bombing, I was packing to move from New Orleans back to my hometown of Nashville, and needed a truck to transport all of my stuff from one place to the other. The closest moving truck company to my home happened to be a Ryder Truck franchise (the same company used by McVeigh), so when I was ready to load boxes and furniture I headed down to the Ryder location and asked for a truck that just happened to be the same size and model as the one Tim McVeigh had used to bring down the Murrah building.

I walked in, put my license and credit card on the counter, and within fifteen minutes I was headed back to my house to load up. I am white. I am male. I have short hair. At the time I was clean shaven—and my name, in case you've forgotten, is Tim. Yet no one at Ryder thought to ask for an additional security deposit, just in case I decided to fill their truck with explosives and take out a city block. No one looked at me funny, ran a background check, or said anything at all, other than, "Mr. Wise, will you be needing a map?" That was it. They could tell the difference, or thought they could, between that Timothy and this Timothy.

That's what it means to be white: the murderous actions of one white person do not cause every other white person to be viewed in the same light, just as the incompetence or criminality of a white person in a corporation does not result in other whites being viewed with suspicion as probable incompetents or crooks. Whites can take it for granted that we'll likely be viewed as individuals, representing nothing greater than our solitary selves. Would that persons of color could say the same, even before September 11, let alone after?

And yes, it's true that I have been searched in airports since 9/11, as have millions of whites. Statistically, the odds are good that such a thing is going to happen, even if certain folks of color are the ones being examined most intently. I've been hauled over to the side of security, made to put my arms out and spread my legs for "wanding" and full-body pat-downs. But despite having had the same *physical* experience as so many Muslims, or Arabs (or for that matter simply persons of indeterminate, but clearly nonwhite ancestry, to whom suspicion so often attaches), the *emotional* experience of being searched is, for me and any other white person, entirely different. As I stand there, legs spread, being merely inconvenienced by a search, I am not worried that anyone is looking at me and thinking, "Damn, *I hope he's not on my plane!*"

But what traveler of Arab, Persian, Kurdish, Afghan, or North African descent, or of discernable Muslim or even Sikh faith could presume the non-chalance of those witnessing *their* searches by security officials? To ask the question is essentially to answer it, and to understand, if one is willing, both the psychic tax of color in this culture and the psychic subsidy that is whiteness.

THE COLOR OF DIVINITY:
Race, Whiteness and Euro-Jesus

ON THE OPPOSITE END of the spectrum from presumed deviance and criminality, one finds virtue, goodness, even holiness. And so, as we ponder the way in which color has been effectively criminalized in the minds of so many, we should probably also consider the way in which whiteness is constructed as synonymous with virtue at its ultimate level—that of divinity itself.

I remember the first time I openly questioned the color of Jesus in front of white Christians. As you can probably imagine, an incident like that can be hard to forget, if for no other reason than the response such a thing brings forth.

In 1997, while speaking at a Catholic college, I broached this subject by asking what it meant that we had grown accustomed in this culture to seeing a Jesus who had been so thoroughly Europeanized, and why no one seemed to think anything of it. How had this happened and why? After all, no anthropologist or archaeologist familiar with the time and place in which Jesus lived would believe he was as pale as churches in the West have portrayed him to be—to say nothing of the absurdly blue eyes or blondish-brown hair. Not to mention the earliest representations of Jesus, found on catacomb walls dating to the third century, picture him as a man of brown skin, and the earliest representations of his mother, Mary, with whom my Catholic hosts that evening certainly have more than a passing familiarity, also picture her as a woman of color.

Immediately after my presentation, the questions and comments poured in, the first of which came from a young man who clearly thought I was missing the point when it came to the color of Jesus.

"But Tim," he calmly assured me, "what you're forgetting is that it really doesn't matter what color Jesus was; it only matters what he did."

Yes, it's what Jesus *did,* another young woman explained, and what he had done, was of course, to die for our sins. Another young man, trying to be kind, but sounding like a real ass in the process, explained that perhaps I, being a Jew, really couldn't understand that, but Christians did, so they tended not to dwell on such things as the race of their messiah.

Well that's all fine, I said, but if it really doesn't matter what color Jesus was, then why is he always portrayed in white churches, and even some black ones, and at this school, as a white man? If the temporal, bodily Jesus is not the point, then why choose to represent him visually at all? Why represent Jesus, or Mary, or the disciples, or any other Biblical figure if these things don't matter? Why represent God himself as a white man with a white beard? Why represent Adam and Eve as if they had spent their days in the Garden of Sweden, rather than the Garden of Eden? After all, that's what they look like in the infamous Arthur Maxwell Bible Story books for kids, which, at least in my experience, seem to be available in pretty much every pediatrician's office in the South, if not the country. And if you have to represent these folks for some reason, why not make them *black?*

Not getting my point, several students shot back in exasperation, "No, no, no, you don't understand; it doesn't matter what color any of them were, it's what they did that matters!"

And again, I replied, "Cool, I get that, that's great. But if that's true—as opposed to something you say because it sounds nice—then why are none of these people ever represented in your churches and in this school as anything other than white? Why not make Jesus black just for a year? Then you could change him back, but just make him black right now and for the next 365 days. Why don't you ever do that? If it really doesn't matter?"

We went round and round like this for a while, until finally someone admitted that it was just easier to keep Jesus white, and presumably God and everyone else, because that's what folks were used to, and to change it would just confuse people, or even make people mad at the idea that religious symbols were being forced to change for the sake of political correctness.

This person's honesty, though no one else had been willing to offer it, was met almost immediately with agreement by everyone assembled. So apparently it wasn't just about being irrelevant or not the point; it was also very much about image, about keeping people (white people one presumes) happy, and not upsetting the proverbial apple cart. In other words, to present Jesus or God as anything other than white would make white people upset, and even to simply refrain from presenting any images of them at all, as Muslims and Jews typically refuse to do with God, would be seen as cause for great alarm. It was easier to keep lying; easier to continue bearing false witness, which last time I checked is a violation of one of those Commandments that God gave to a most-certainly nonwhite Moses (who was married to a very nonwhite Ethiopian woman at one point).

What does that say, I asked, about privilege? About the power that whites have? After all, people of color might just as badly want to make Jesus and God look like them, and while they may well be able to do so in their own churches or in their homes, it's pretty unlikely that their renderings of either would catch on and become the norm, become of the reference, the standard, the mainstream image that the rest of us would have in mind. What does it say about institutional white power that whites are able to visually represent the creator of the universe, and the one many of them consider to be his son, and their savior, as if they were no more distant from one another than first cousins? And what kind of comfort does that fraud give to little white children who get to believe, because their Bible Story books tells them so, that they are closer to God, physically speaking, than 90 percent of the planet's inhabitants? And how might the entire world change if white people were forced to deal with the truth, and see the truth hanging on their church walls every Sunday?

I have not been invited back to that school for a speech. And I'm not holding my breath.

FAMILY REUNIONS, FAMILY DELUSIONS

AS WITH RELIGION, I grew up with a keen awareness of the need to avoid political discussions if at all possible when attending the annual McLean family reunion. Although the family matriarch, Isabel, was a lifelong Democrat, former schoolteacher, and pretty liberal as southern women of her generation go, she was one of only a very few in my mom's dad's family with whom my mother or myself would ever seek to discuss the events of the day.

It was Isabel, for example, who, knowing everything there was to know about the family's past, would speak of an abolitionist in our family tree who had stood up against her family and convinced them to free their own slaves. This vignette had strangely been left out of the official family histories put together by others, who opted instead to speak of the family slave owners as loving, caring men and women who took good care of their darkies.

Since the McLean men—my grandfather and his brothers—had been in the military, it was especially dangerous to get into discussions of U.S. foreign policy, which in my teenage years had been the arena in which my political interest had blossomed, and which would become my academic focus at Tulane as well. So it was a potentially volatile family reunion in 1987, when several members of the family gathered around to watch the Congressional testimony of Oliver North, who had helped to cover up the Reagan administration's arms-for-hostages deal with Iran and the siphoning of money to the contra thugs we were supporting in Nicaragua, who by that point had murdered some thirty thousand civilians.

I had been watching the Iran-Contra hearings with a mixture of disgust and amazement—amazement that the likes of North were being let off so easily by the committee members—that was clearly different from the way in which many of the McLean brood were viewing the spectacle. When one of them asked what I thought about "Old Ollie," I replied that it would probably be best to leave it alone and that they likely wouldn't appreciate my opinion. They continued to press though, so that finally it became impossible to resist offering what was on my mind.

"I think he's a war criminal—him, Reagan, the whole bunch of them—and if there were any justice in the world they would all spend the rest of their lives behind bars," I noted.

I am nothing if not skilled at shutting down a conversation, and it was about that time that everyone started turning to the snack tray sitting on a table in the hospitality suite of whatever hotel we were staying in, hoping I suppose that if we just all went back to eating, we could get off the unpleasant business about war criminals and my bad attitude.

After that, I pretty much kept my views to myself at reunions, unless speaking to one of the few family members who I knew was open to what I had to say. With the exception of the one time I had to verbally lash a cousin for using the n-word, there were very few occasions when anything remotely controversial came up. Except for once more.

In the early nineties, the family decided to move the annual reunion permanently to Memphis, so long as Isabel remained alive, since this was where she lived. In 1993, during some free time on the second day of the trip, family members started splitting up, heading out in different directions to enjoy the city: some went shopping, some went to the zoo, others went to Graceland, the former home of Elvis Presley, while my mother and I chose to make the trek to the Lorraine Motel, where Dr. King had been assassinated. Given her personal reverence for the movement, the choice was hardly a surprising one for her, but the truth is, even if my mother had wanted to go to Graceland, she would probably not have been allowed in because she had gone with my grandmother some years before, only to say, loudly and well within earshot of employees in the gift shop, "I never liked him when he was alive, I don't know why the hell I'd want to buy any of his music now that he's dead."

So it was to the Lorraine we went, where after a moving if somewhat simplistic account of the civil rights era, tourists are led into a hallway that has been created, with glass windows on either side, between the two rooms rented by the King entourage that April. To the right is King's room, exactly as he left it before stepping out onto the balcony that fateful evening, and in front of you is the balcony itself, where a wreath marks the spot of King's death. It is a moving, almost overpowering moment. Sadly, the moment was to be utterly ruined when, upon turning to leave, we ran headlong into a "Don Sundquist for Governor" table, leading into an auditorium in the museum that was being used that day for a campaign rally for the very conservative Republican congressman who was running for the state's highest office. That such a solemn place should be off limits to all partisan politics might seem obvious to you, but it had not apparently occurred to the folks who operated the museum.

After leaving the Lorraine, we headed back uptown and went to have lunch at a café, where we were joined by one of my great-aunts, Jean, who was the widow of Walter McLean, my late grandfather's brother. Jean and Walter had lived, and Jean still did, in the same tiny Birmingham house for what seemed like forever. Over the years the neighborhood had changed from one that was nearly all white to one that was now virtually all black. Although Jean had never moved, had never run away as so many whites who lived around her had, this didn't necessarily signify that she was comfortable with the transition. As we were talking about the Lorraine and the museum, Jean interrupted to ask whether or not I thought there was ever going to be a "race war."

She said it just like that. "Well tell me this Tim, do you think we're ever going to have a race war?"

Honestly, I had never been asked such a thing before. It seemed so odd, such an old-white-person thing to say, like the kind of thing you can imagine whites sitting around asking themselves back during the Watts rebellion of 1965, or during any of the long, hot summers of the late 1960s, during which so many urban areas went up in flames, the almost inevitable result of institutionalized race and class inequities and injustices.

I wasn't sure how to answer such a question, because I wasn't sure exactly what was meant by it. Was Jean merely wondering whether a racial conflagration might take place because the problems that had sparked the riots of the sixties, or even a few years earlier in L.A. in 1992, hadn't yet been addressed? In other words, was she merely implying the inevitably of violence in the face of ongoing institutional racism? Or was she wondering whether or not black people were going to rise up and slaughter whitey as an act of revenge for the past four-hundred-plus years of white supremacy?

Initially, I simply answered no. No, I did not think there was going to be a race war, a view that she took to be terribly naïve. She could see the way her black neighbors looked at her every day, she said. She was convinced, beyond any doubt, that someday, mass violence between whites and blacks would erupt.

I suggested to her that maybe her neighbors were simply looking at her in amazement, surprised that she hadn't done like pretty much all the other white folks and moved out of the neighborhood a long time ago. Maybe it wasn't a look that hid some insatiable desire to harm her, but rather signified something as simple and benign as genuine confusion and bemusement. No, that wasn't it, she insisted.

Wanting to be kind, but at the same time to make a point, I decided to take another direction.

"Actually," I said, "we're already in a race war. It started several hundred years ago when white folks decided to exterminate Indian folk, and import slaves from Africa, ripping people from their homes, their cultures, their religions, their continent and bringing them to the land we were now on, so as to make Europeans wealthier."

This was not what my aunt had in mind, needless to say, when she thought of a race war.

"No," she interjected, "I don't mean all that."

All that is the term whites tend to use instead of other, more descriptive and far more accurate ones, like genocide, for instance. *All that* pretty well sums up, in two little words, what most whites think of the extermination or enslavement of nonwhite peoples, as in, "Why are you bringing up all that?" or "All that happened a long time ago; why can't they just let it go?"

Well you might not mean all that, I noted, but from the perspective of black folks, which appeared to be the group about which she was so nervous, *all that* is the only logical starting point for any discussion about a race war. Fact is, the war is on, we started it, and the only problem most whites seem to be having is that the targets have long since decided to fight back. They apparently had forgotten or never learned the rules: the ones that said we were always supposed to win, to get our way, to run the show.

Once again the conversation was halted in its tracks, to no avail I'm certain so far as she was concerned. Silence is how we as whites so often greet any evidence that the world as we have long perceived it might not be the world as perceived and experienced by others. My great-aunt Jean saw the issue as most whites probably would: race war is something *they* would do to us, that *they* would initiate, and for no reason, since history has no role to play in the understanding of anything, even the anger about which whites are so petrified.

It's much like the way whites responded after 9/11, in a way that was nothing if not bizarre to people of color, by saying things like, "Now we know what it's like to be attacked for who we are." Or, "9/11 was the worst act of terrorism in our nation's history." Or, "Why do they hate us?"

That most whites would have no idea why these kinds of comments are ludicrous, indeed evidence of a disconnection from the real world so profound as to boggle the mind, is precisely my point. For most whites, we *haven't* been attacked for who we are, and 9/11 *was* the worst act of terrorism, and hating the United States makes no sense, because in *our* America, we are the beacon of democratic light in a world of tyranny. That almost no one else in the world experiences the United States this way escapes us altogether. That lots of folks who aren't white know exactly what it means to be attacked for who they are, what it's like to be terrorized, goes entirely without comment.

Consider what a young white woman in the audience of *The Phil Donahue Show* said, the night that Professor Michael Eric Dyson and I were on, and the subject of 9/11 came up. Dyson made the rather obvious yet critical point that although 9/11 had been a tragedy of great magnitude, his people, black folks, had known about terrorism for a long time. As he put it: "I know a lot of you here in New York were running for your lives on 9/11, and that was terrible, but my people have been running for four hundred years, so what else is new?"

The young lady in the third row blew up as if Mike had called her momma a name.

"How dare you compare the experience of black America with 9/11," she exclaimed.

How dare *he?* Oh no, Dyson patiently explained, "How dare *you* compare the events of 9/11 with four hundred years of oppression." Don't get it twisted.

The ability of whites to deny nonwhite reality, and indeed to not even comprehend that there *is* a nonwhite reality (or several different ones), is as strong as any other evidence of just how pervasive white privilege is in this society. It determines the frame, the lens, through which the nation will come to view itself and the events that take place within it. It allows the dominant perspective to become *perspectivism,* by which I mean the elevation of the majority viewpoint to the status of unquestioned and unquestionable truth.

So I am reminded of the white man in his midthirties who, after the not-guilty verdict in the 1995 criminal trial of O. J. Simpson, stood crying his eyes out on CNN, rambling on about how, and I'm quoting him here, "I now realize that everything I was taught in the third grade about this nation having the most wonderful justice system imaginable was all a *lie!*"

Now he realized it! He had lived several decades in la-la land, having swallowed the pep-rally propaganda of his teachers, preachers, parents, Boy Scout leaders, and whomever else, and *now,* because of O. J., he had concluded that the system might not be fair after all. How nice for him. Had he grown up around people of color, they could have set him straight on how not-so-wonderful the American system of justice was a long time ago, like at least by the time he was eleven. But he had the luxury of believing the bullshit, see, and then assuming that only the O. J. case demonstrated a crack in the system. Everything in his world had been fine until O. J. walked. Then, and only then, was it as if the world was about to stop spinning on its axis.

By allowing white America to remain in this bubble of unreality, white privilege ultimately distorts our vision, and makes it difficult for us to function as fully rational beings. It protects us from some of life's cruelties, and allows us to wander around, largely oblivious to the fires that, for others, burn all around them. In the end, as we'll see later, this bubble of unreality can be a dangerous place to reside. But before we can understand why this is so, we need to examine the contours of the bubble itself. It is to that subject we now turn.

DENIAL

I HAVE THIS bad habit, whenever I go to an ATM to withdraw money from my checking account. It's a habit I developed back when I was broke, and which I've yet to conquer, even now that my money's straight—well, at least straighter than it was. Namely, after getting my cash and the receipt that comes along with it, I refuse to look at my balance, opting instead to stuff the unread piece of paper in my pocket. It's as if I think that if I don't *see* how broke I am, maybe I'm not really that broke after all. Pretty silly, but no more so than letting unopened bills sit on your kitchen table for a few extra days before looking at them and dealing with the bad news. Both are ways of putting off the inevitable, if only for a few hours. They allow us to remain in our much more comfortable bubbles, or beyond our veils of fiscal ignorance, for just a bit longer. And sometimes, a few extra hours of denial can go a long way.

Unfortunately, speaking again now of the broke days, I would always end up taking the crumpled receipt and throwing it in a drawer. Then a few weeks later, when cleaning out the drawer, I would come across it, and not remembering what bad news lay within the folds and creases of the now forgotten item, open it, only to react with shock and horror at how bad my financial picture really was.

In many ways, my strategy for dealing with those receipts mirrored almost perfectly the way that white America, writ large, deals with (or fails to deal with) the issues of racism and our own racial privileges. At some level, after all, we know exactly what has happened and continues to happen in this country when it comes to race. Our ignorance is only occasionally of the pure and involuntary type. More often than not, we *choose* not to see things, even when they are staring us in the face. We stuff the truth deep down in our proverbial pockets, in a safe place where we can, if only for a while, forget about it. But as with the ATM receipts, eventually we find ourselves confronted by the reality of the thing, and just as I would upon learning of my bank balance, feign utter shock, amazement really, that things could be *that bad*. We know, in other words, but we choose to avert our gaze for as long as we can, not that doing so ever makes things better in the long run. It neither puts more money magically in our accounts, nor erases the history of racial oppression.

Ultimately, burying our heads in the sand when it comes to the issue of racism doesn't change what's going on above ground. Of course, given the way in which young people are taught about the history of racism in the United States, you can almost understand—not forgive, but understand— such folks, especially if they're white, being under the impression that everything is fine nowadays. Since we teach history as an uninterrupted string of linear progress, where things were really bad, but slowly got better, and are always improving when it comes to race, students can easily be misled into thinking that the issue of racism is *so* yesterday's news. What can you expect from folks who are shown pretty much nothing but old, grainy black-and-white television footage from Birmingham, circa 1963, or Selma in 1965, or the March on Washington, when discussing the issue of race in America?

But white denial isn't only for those who came of age in the post–civil rights era. In fact, even before the civil rights acts of the sixties were passed— and at a time when in retrospect all would now agree that the United States was a formally racist and even apartheid state—whites were under the impression that there was no real problem. In 1962, more than nine in ten whites told pollsters from Gallup that blacks had just as good a chance as they did to get a good education. And in 1963, over three-quarters of whites said that, generally speaking, blacks were treated equally in their communities.

Indeed, if you go back and listen to what whites were saying in the thirties, it wasn't much different. And in the 1890s, newspaper editors in the South were quick to proclaim, "We were all gettin' along fine down here, till you Yankees started meddlin' in our business!" In the 1850s, white denial took on academic qualities, when Dr. Samuel Cartwright, a well-respected physician of his day, postulated the theory that not only was slavery not bad, but slaves who ran away from their masters were clearly suffering from a mental illness—drapetomania he called it—and needed to be whipped, ever so mildly, so as to be kept in line.

White denial, in other words, has been nothing if not an intergenerational phenomenon. In each generation white folks have essentially said, in the main, that there was no problem. And in each generation we were wrong. Folks of color, on the other hand, have, in each generation, been quite insistent that there was a problem, and in each generation they were right. The question then for us is simple: What are the odds that white cluelessness has suddenly converted to insight, and black and brown insight has suddenly become cluelessness?

Understanding the depths of white denial is important, if we are going to find our way out of the morass of racism in this country. You can't solve a problem, after all, if you refuse to acknowledge that it exists. And even if you do acknowledge racism, there is still the pesky little part about privilege that one can seek to deny. In other words, one might say, "Oh yes, racism is terrible," and yet not seek to address one's own level of implication in the thing, as the recipient of unearned advantages that come as the inevitable flipside of oppression and subordination. History has been taught as if racism were something done to people of color, with *no beneficiaries* at all; as if there could be a down without an up; as if one can have an "underprivileged" (a word we dearly love in this culture, and often audibilize with great sympathy), and yet not an overprivileged. Our denial, then, extends even so far as our lexicon, so that if there is no word for the phenomenon, the phenomenon conveniently fails to exist.

In order to understand how denial shapes the white understanding of racism, we must examine the way in which it has manifested, past and present. We need to peek under the veil of ignorance behind which white America has long hidden, and confront the deniers, even when they are our loved ones, our friends, our colleagues, or even ourselves. In the next chapter, methods of resistance will be examined, but before we can put any of those methods into practice, it would help to know what we're up against.

LONG TIME COMING, LONG TIME GONE:
Denial as a Cultural Imperative

WHITE DENIAL DIDN'T just happen, and it manifests not because whites are stupid or insensitive, or uncaring as a group. Rather, in a nation where racism was woven into the fabric of the culture, yet the national ethos was always one of equality and freedom, the contradiction required something that could paper over the hypocrisy.

If you've been told that everyone has equal opportunity, and yet, you see profound inequities between whites on the one hand and folks of color on the other, how do you resolve the apparent gap between promise and reality? You can either conclude that the ethos is a myth, that things aren't as equal as you've been told—which requires a rare willingness to rethink everything you've been taught—or you can decide that there must be something *wrong* with the people at the bottom. They must be inferior, they must not work as hard, or they must be less intelligent. Their genes or their cultures must be defective.

If you conclude that the problem is with the system, then you are compelled, as a fair-minded person, to do something about it. But that takes time and energy, and often seems too big a burden. Not to mention, if you're white and are willing to concede that the system is stacked against people of color, that means it must be stacked in your favor, and to admit that is to open oneself up to all kinds of unproductive guilt and self-recrimination. Plus, people aren't usually keen on changing a set of social arrangements that benefit them. Although there are any number of reasons why even the privileged should seek to challenge inequities (and we'll explore why in a later chapter), it clearly isn't the first thing a person is likely to do when they become aware of injustice.

If, on the other hand, you accept the second possibility—that the problem is with *them,* with those who are different than you—then you have no obligations to change anything. Whew! Much better.

It is precisely the collision between the rhetoric of equality and the crushing evidence of inequality and injustice that has, in other words, necessitated white denial. Whites, in order to maintain a sense of ourselves as good and decent people, living in a good and decent society, have been compelled to deny, deny, deny when it comes to racism.

The denial can be direct, or indirect, but in either case, it requires that white Americans pay no attention to the man behind the curtain, so to speak, and refuse to acknowledge the things that, in our hearts, we likely know to be true. In my own family, evidence of this process was painful to uncover, but impossible to miss.

Given some of the facts laid out earlier as regards the McLeans—my mother's dad's people—it goes without saying that in discussing the family history, ignoring the ownership of other human beings on the part of our ancestors wasn't really an option. But that doesn't mean that, once the crime is acknowledged, it can't be minimized, smoothed over, essentially made to be *no big deal.*

And so, in the McLean family history, compiled by a cousin of mine several years ago, slave-ownership is discussed, but in terms that strive mightily to normalize the activity and thereby prevent the reader (who in this case would be family, since this volume was never intended for mass consumption) from feeling even a momentary discomfort with this ignoble detour in an otherwise straightforward narrative of decency and upright moral behavior.

So we learn, for example, that Samuel McLean, my great-great-great-great-grandfather, "owned much land and slaves, and was a man of considerable means." This is stated with neither an inordinate amount of pride nor regret, but merely in the matter-of-fact style befitting those who are trying to be honest without confronting the implications of their honesty. Say it quickly, say it simply, and move on to something more appetizing: sort of like acknowledging the passing of gas in a crowded room, but failing to admit that you were the author.

A few pages later, the reader is then treated to a reproduction of Samuel McLean's will, which reads, among other things:

> I give and bequeath unto my loving wife, Elizabeth, my Negro woman, named Dicey, to dispose of at her death as she may think proper, all my household and kitchen furniture, wagons, horses, cattle, hogs, sheep and stock of every kind *except as may be necessary to defray the expense of the first item above.*

In other words, Elizabeth should sell whatever must be sold in order to hold on to the slave woman, for how would she possibly survive without her? But there is more:

> I also give the use and possession of, during her natural life, my two Negroes, Jerry and Silvey. To my daughter Sarah Amanda her choice of horses and two cows and calves, and if she marry in the lifetime of my wife she is to enjoy and receive an equal share of the property from the tillage, rent and use of the aforesaid 106 acres of land and Negroes Jerry and Silvey, that she may be the more certain of a more comfortable existence.

Furthermore, if Sarah were to marry before the death of her mother, she and her husband were to remain on the property with Elizabeth so as to continue to benefit "from the land and Negroes." If, on the other hand, Mom were to die before the wedding of Sarah, then the daughter was instructed to sell either the land or the slaves and split the proceeds among her siblings. Either way, Dicey, Jerry, and Silvey would remain commodities to be sure. Choosing freedom for them was never an option, for in that case, the McLeans might have to learn to do things for themselves; they might have to work. They might have to wash their own clothes, grow their own food, nurse their own wounds, make their own beds, suckle their own babies, and chop their own wood. And that would make them less "certain of a more comfortable existence," so of course it was out of the question.

To his son, Samuel D. McLean, Sam Senior bequeathed "a Negro boy named Sim," who would then be handed down, not unlike an armoire to his son John, my great-great-grandfather. Then, according to family legend and in what can only be considered the Margaret Mitchell version of the McLean's history, Sim went happily off to the Civil War with his master. What's more, we even have *dialogue* for this convenient plot twist, as Sim exclaims (and I'm sure this is a *direct* quote), "I've taken care of Mr. John all his life and I'm not going to let him go off to war without me." Cue the violins.

For his loyalty, "Sim got a little farm to retire on because they (the McLeans) knew he would not get a pension of any kind." No indeed, as property rarely receives the benefit of a 401(k) plan.

To his daughters, Sam McLean gave the slave woman Jenny and her child, and the slave woman Manerva and her child, and in both cases "any further increase," which is an interesting and chillingly dehumanizing way to refer to future children. But we are to think nothing of this subterfuge in the case of the children of Manerva or Jenny. We are to keep telling ourselves that they *are not people*; and we are to keep repeating this mantra, no matter how much they *look* like people. No matter that they share 99.9 percent of their genes with us, and us with them. Pay no attention to such small and trivial details.

For any family to look back fondly at ancestors who, without apparent compunction, trafficked in human flesh, is to engage in the most profound mental contortions imaginable. Indeed, the only psychological gymnastics more disturbing than those necessary to remember fondly such persons would be those engaged in by the slaveowners themselves, who had to become inured to the suffering of others of the human family in such a way as to call into question their ability to feel anything at all.

Let us be clear on this point, too: Their acts are neither excused by the times in which they lived, nor the passage of time since. Some will seek to make it so, by insisting that "everyone back then felt that way," but in so doing they insult history and every possible definition of human decency.

After all, the slaves themselves were certainly under no illusion that the conditions under which they toiled, lived, and died were just. They knew better. As such, and assuming that the slave owner had the capacity for rational and moral thought on par with his property, there is no excuse for whites, any whites, to not understand this basic truth as well. Furthermore, even if we were only to consider the views of whites to be important—a fundamentally racist position but one we may indulge for the sake of argument—the fact would remain that even many whites opposed slavery, and not only on practical but also on moral grounds. Among those who gave the lie to the notion of white unanimity—which has only served to rationalize and minimize the individual culpability of slaveowners—we find the Grimke sisters, John Fee, Ellsberry Ambrose, John Brown (and his entire family), and literally thousands more whose names are lost to history. No excuses, no time-bound rationalizations, no paeans to our ancestors' kind and generous natures, or how they "loved their slaves as though they were family" can make it right.

Our unwillingness to hold our people and ourselves to a higher moral standard—a standard in place at least since the time of Moses, for it was he to whom God supposedly gave those commandments including the two about stealing and killing—brings shame to us today. It compounds the crime, by constituting a new one.

The shame, it should be noted, does not only belong to those who, like my family, bought and sold other human beings. It extends to the white community more broadly, for it was the larger white public that allowed the system to continue, that rationalized it, that profited from the wealth created by slave labor. Even those whites who didn't own slaves benefited from the economic growth generated by the slaves of others. Even those whites who didn't own slaves benefited from the knowledge that there was a class of laborers below them, upon whom they could look down, condescendingly, as if to say, "I may be poor, but at least I'm not black." Collaboration, as we'll see in a later chapter, is every bit as morally compromising as perpetration of the deed itself. And collaboration has always been the name of the game for the vast majority of white Americans.

DENIAL AS STRUCTURED AND CULTIVATED STUPIDITY

WE BEGIN THE PROCESS of cultivating denial early on. More than that, we encourage young people to develop such an absurd conception of the country in which they live, that it's really rather miraculous when anyone breaks free from the propaganda to which they have been subjected.

I learned to read at a very early age, when I was only two years old. Born on October 4, 1968, I read my first book, without help, on May 5 1971. That's the good news. The bad news is that the book was *Meet Andrew Jackson*, an eighty-seven page tribute to the nation's seventh president, intended to make children proud, one supposes, of the nation in which they live.

Therein, I learned that Jackson's mom admonished him never to lie or "take what is not your own" (an admonition he apparently felt free to disregard as he got older, at least as it might have regarded native peoples), and that when Jackson, as a young man, headed west, he encountered Indians who "did not want white people in their hunting grounds," and "often killed white travelers." This part, of course, is true: people whose land has been invaded and is in the process of being stolen often become agitated, and sometimes even kill those who are trying to destroy them. Hard to imagine, I know, but true.

On page forty-six, I was told that although "some people in the North were saying it was not right to own slaves . . . Jackson felt the way most other Southerners did. He felt it was right to own slaves. He called his slaves his 'family.'" Sweet.

Ten pages later, I learned that Jackson fought the Creek Indians to preserve America and save innocent lives, though oddly there was no mention that in order to get an accurate count of the dead they slaughtered at Horseshoe Bend, soldiers in Jackson's command cut off the tips of Creek noses and sliced strips of flesh from their bodies for use as bridal reins for their horses. Must have been a last-minute editorial oversight, I guess.

At the end of the book, after recounting Jackson's rise to the presidency, *Meet Andrew Jackson* concludes by noting that when Jackson died, in 1845, his slaves cried and "sang a sad old song."

Looking at the pages of this, my first book, I find myself almost speechless at the mendacity of the white people who write this kind of tripe, and who seek to minimize the crimes of slavery and genocide. To insert the flourish about the slaves singing "Go Down Moses," or whatever, upon Jackson's death, is beyond contemptible. There is no scholarly record of such sad songs being sung by slaves as Jackson lay dying. This kind of detail, even if it were true—and it likely isn't—has no probative value or historical purpose in terms of letting us understand who Andrew Jackson was. It exists for the same reason the old fairy tale about George Washington cutting down the cherry tree and telling his dad because he "couldn't tell a lie" exists: because no fabrication is too extreme in the service of patriotism and national self-love. Anything that makes us feel proud can be said, facts notwithstanding. Anything that reminds us of the not-so-noble pursuits of our forefathers, and indeed our national heroes, gets dumped down the memory hole. And if you bring those kinds of things up, you'll be accused of hating America.

The way in which we place murderers and rogues like Andrew Jackson on a pedestal, while telling people of color to "get over it" (meaning the past) whenever slavery or Indian genocide is brought up, has always struck me as the most precious of ironies. We want folks of color to move past the past, even as we very much seek to dwell in that place a while. We dwell there every July 4, every Columbus Day, every time a child is given a book like *Meet Andrew Jackson* to read. We love the past so long as it venerates us. We want to be stuck there, and many would even like to go back. It is only when those who were the targets for slaughter and destruction in that past insist on having their voices heard that suddenly the past becomes conveniently irrelevant.

This is how denial is transmitted, via the normalized workings of a national propaganda machine. It cultivates ignorance the way a farmer cultivates corn or wheat. The end result, if this kind of thing is allowed to continue, is a public neutered of intellectual curiosity or the capacity for critical thought. If racism is ever to be finally undone—and that remains a very open question indeed—we will have to first and foremost stop lying to ourselves.

THE OPRAH EFFECT:
Looking for Exceptions and Missing the Rules

WHEN THE FIRST EDITION of this book was released, I was fortunate to get a bit of press traction on it. An interview on an NPR affiliate in New York City attracted the attention of an AP reporter, who then called, interviewed me, and put together an article, which was released and picked up by several papers across the nation a few months after the book hit the streets.

In order to make the piece balanced, the reporter felt it necessary to seek out critics—critics of my book, critics of my analysis, or critics of me, personally. He told me he was going to do it. I said that was fine, and only fair. I even gave him suggestions as to the persons he might wish to call. He called David Horowitz, current right-wing gadfly, former left-wing gadfly, and all-around windbag, who had neither read my book, nor read more than a few of my columns from what I can tell.

David and I had gotten into it a few years earlier. He had attacked me for supporting affirmative action, I had fired back with evidence to support my views, he then said that statistics didn't matter, to which I said it had been fun, but really, he was a silly, silly man. The full exchange is on my Web site (but notably, not his), and is not worth recounting here.

Anyway, when asked what he thought of my book, having not read it, he had nothing to say. But he couldn't resist letting the reporter know what he thought of my analysis and me more broadly. And what he said was that my theories about racism and white privilege were full of holes, and that all the evidence he needed to demonstrate their weakness was Oprah Winfrey.

When Justin, the reporter, called me to get my reaction to David's remarks, I remember sitting in stunned silence. I was amazed, and frankly a little embarrassed that such an answer had been all that David was able to muster. I mean, it's one thing to get the "what about Oprah?" line from a fifteen-year-old (and frankly, even most fifteen-year-olds are savvy enough to see how weak that kind of argument is), but coming from someone who fashions himself quite the conservative intellectual (no joke intended here), it was a little sad.

My response to Horowitz, offered to the reporter, and published in the article, was the one I give to people when they ask the "what about Oprah?" question after a speech, which is fairly often. Namely, I asked, "What about Madame C. J. Walker?"

If you're scratching your head, unsure as to who I'm talking about, don't worry, that's just more privilege—the privilege of not having to know nothin' about nobody who isn't white. Walker, as it turns out, was among the first African American millionaires (if not *the* first), who made a fortune developing and selling beauty products for black women, at a time when white cosmetics firms had no interest in doing so.

In other words, I explained, to use individual success stories, like that of Oprah, or anyone else—Bill Cosby, Colin Powell, Condoleezza Rice, Robert Johnson, or whomever—as proof that racism and white privilege don't exist, or at least aren't significant problems, is nonsensical. After all, Walker became a millionaire in 1911, even in the midst of what everyone—even David Horowitz—would admit was a racist, white supremacist, and viciously fascist society as regards black people. But so what? Did that mean that folks shouldn't have been fighting for an end to racism, simply because a few individuals had been able to "make it?" In other words, what do individual success stories have to do with larger social realities?

It was the same point I tried to make to John Stossel, on *20/20*, when he insisted that since many immigrants of color have come to the United States and become successful, anyone can make it, and white privilege can't really be that big a deal. The two have nothing to do with each other; the real question is, how much *more* successful would such persons be (and for that matter how many more Oprahs would there be, figuratively speaking), if racism and white privilege weren't such problems? Neither Horowitz nor Stossel's form of denial—known as an argument from exception—actually negates anything I have said or am saying now. They are tantamount to saying that since lots of Jews survived the World War II era, the Holocaust wasn't really that bad.

But that's the way denial works. It doesn't have to make sense.

So on that same *20/20* episode (which was to my knowledge the first time the term "white privilege" had even been uttered on primetime network television, let alone examined, albeit briefly), Stossel brought on Shelby Steele, one of the nation's leading black conservatives, to share his views. Although Stossel had taped Steele several months earlier—and so, in no way could Steele be said to be responding to my arguments—he and his producers edited the piece in a way that certainly made it *seem* as if Steele was being responsive.

And what did Steele argue? What he always argues, which is that blacks need to take personal responsibility for whatever problems they face, and not blame white folks any longer. Oh, and that whites need to let go of our guilt.

Stossel asked me about this argument, on camera, and for ten minutes I explained why the position was irrelevant, even if one accepted that it were true. In other words, the idea that blacks should take personal responsibility for their lives, as with all of us, is a good idea, and one that says absolutely nothing about whether or not we also need to take collective responsibility for eradicating the unfair barriers and unearned advantages that continue to skew equal opportunity. Since when have personal and collective responsibility been mutually exclusive? Blacks have always believed in self-help, and more than believe in it, they've always practiced it, precisely because they knew there was no point waiting for white folks to lend a hand. I spent over a year in New Orleans public housing as a community organizer and almost never heard black folks there talking about whitey. They were talking about trying to solve their own problems. But they also understood the role of racism in their lives. And they knew that self-help is always a lot easier when you don't have someone's boot on your neck.

Not to mention, I explained to a glassy-eyed Stossel, personal responsibility has to be for everyone, not just blacks. In fact, my whole argument is *about* personal responsibility, and specifically, whites taking personal responsibility for the receipt of unjust advantages. After all, if blacks are supposed to address their own problems, irrespective of white racism, then isn't there an equivalent obligation on our parts, as whites, to address our problems (like our racial biases or the privileges we receive and which are clearly a problem for others), irrespective of whatever we may think of black folks? My problem with Steele and others like him, I explained, is that they aren't consistent; they want blacks to take personal responsibility, while being content to let whites go on our merry way. Worse than that, they seem perfectly okay with having whites sit on the sidelines, *also* lecturing black and brown folks about how *they* (the folks of color) need to shape up. That is the epitome of not taking personal responsibility, since if I'm pointing my finger at you, I'm not dealing with my own mess.

ABC aired none of that footage. Indeed, of all the forms of privilege they dealt with on the two-hour special within which the white privilege piece appeared—and there were twelve different types they examined in all—the *only* one they felt the need to take issue with, and to present "both sides" on, as if to suggest that maybe the phenomenon wasn't real, was white privilege. And of all the authors interviewed for the special who had books out, I was the only one whose book was neither mentioned by name, nor shown on the air. So much for the liberal media. With such a distorted and incomplete presentation of an important subject, is it any wonder that denial remains so common?

Oh, and one last thing regarding Oprah, since she is so regularly conjured by those seeking to dismiss the notion of racism as a salient social phenomenon.

Perhaps you'll recall a few summers ago, when it made the news that Oprah had been in Paris, and had attempted to purchase a gift for Tina Turner at the closest Hermes boutique. According to the reports from Oprah herself, her friend Gail, and everyone close to her, she was denied entry by the high-end retailer, just a few minutes after the store had closed, even though she had called ahead and said she was on her way. As Oprah put it at the time, she felt as though she were having a "crash moment," referring to the Oscar-winning film, which had been released just that year, and which addressed the issue of racism in various everyday encounters. In other words, Oprah was suggesting that she had been treated differently on the basis of race. According to the store, they were setting up for a private party, couldn't let her in after closing time, and the snub was neither personal, nor racial.

Although there is likely no way to know whether the store's explanation was valid, let us assume for a moment that it was. Let us assume that it was nothing more than a big misunderstanding, and that there had been no intention to treat Oprah badly because of her race. Let us assume that the store was entirely innocent of any wrongdoing and that Oprah was completely wrong to assume otherwise. Here's the problem: *It doesn't matter.*

Don't misunderstand. It matters in terms of whether or not you should boycott Hermes. It matters in terms of whether they should be viewed as racist. But that's not what I mean. What strikes me as the most important issue here is that even Oprah Winfrey, with all her money, and all her power, and all her influence, *still* had to wonder, even if only for a moment, whether her race had trumped all of that in the eyes of someone else. *Even Oprah Winfrey,* who could buy every single item in Hermes and give them out, two hundred times over, to every last member of her audience, can't escape the possibility, can't be free of the fear, can't get past the insecurity generated by racism.

No white person, turned away after a store had closed, or given bad customer service, would *ever* have to consider that perhaps we had been treated that way because of our race. That is a privilege, and a deep and abiding psychological comfort. That even Oprah can't enjoy that peace of mind, that even she has to worry that *today* might be the day that someone pulls her card, speaks volumes. And it suggests that she might want to be the last person you conjure the next time you're looking to deny that racism continues to haunt black and brown America.

THE OCCASIONAL (AND MILDLY HUMOROUS) ABSURDITY OF WHITE DENIAL

ON A LIGHTER NOTE, if white denial wasn't so dangerous, even deadly, it might be funny.

Take Ralph Papitto (no, seriously, take him somewhere, preferably far, far away), formerly a trustee of Roger Williams University, who just a few months ago resigned after it was revealed that he had used the n-word in a board meeting. When being pressed about the lack of diversity on the board, the very wealthy and very aged white man lost it, saying that it was just too much of a burden to find black people, who he sadly noted he couldn't call "niggers" anymore, because it might get him in trouble.

Once his outburst was exposed, and he was confronted about it, he actually denied that the remark had been racist. In fact, he insisted that not only had he never used the word before that day, but indeed, he had never even *heard it*, until he heard it used in a rap song. Uh-huh. Reports that Papitto, who's like 107 or something, said "fo shizzle" as he left the building are apparently an embellishment.

Yes indeed, white folks can be creative when we're looking to deny the specter of racism. My senior year at Tulane offered up two prime illustrations of the lengths to which some folks will go in order to deny the obvious, no matter how ridiculous the denial might sound.

Case in point number one: A cross gets burned on the lawn of a fraternity house, the very night that that fraternity offers a bid to a black student for the first time. Quick: Act of racism or not? Well, *of course not.* Oh sure, it might be to *you*, but that's because you're either an oversensitive black person with a victim mentality or a bleeding heart white liberal, who hates himself and sees racism *every* time a cross gets burned. We can't be sure it was about race—this is actually what many claimed at the time, including some of the fraternity members themselves—because (drum roll please) the cross was only two feet tall.

Case in point number two: A cross gets burned on Martin Luther King day, in the backyard of a fraternity house whose members profess a bond with the confederacy as part of their tradition and secret rituals (oops, not so secret now, boys). Quick: Is it a coincidence? *Well, hell yeah* it's a coincidence! What are ya, a stupid Yankee? Shucks, that wasn't even a cross—this again is what the perpetrators said—it was just a couple of pieces of wood that we tossed in a bonfire, and which fell in a *cross like position.* And yeah, there was an MLK Boulevard sign attached to the crossbar, but we don't know how that got in there.

While cross-burnings on campuses are thankfully rare, other blatantly racist acts seem to be happening every few months, like white students wearing blackface, or throwing "ghetto parties," or "tacos and tequila" bashes, in which the participants dress up like pregnant Latina teens, maids, and gardeners, and get really drunk while making fun of Mexicans. But to hear a lot of white folks tell it, there's nothing racist about these things either.

"It's all in fun," people insist. "We were just dressing up as rappers!" explain others. A year or so ago, one young woman at a large Midwestern university even said she was trying to honor her hero, Oprah Winfrey, when she went to apply for a campus job wearing blackface paint.

On the one hand, it is certainly true that most whites are unaware of the way that blackface has been used historically to denigrate the intellect and humanity of blacks. Few of us were taught about the way that white working-class folks (many of them recent immigrants) initially adopted blackface as a way to make fun of black people, and to elevate themselves, if only psychologically, above the black persons from whom they felt competition in the workforce. And most people probably know little about the history of how ghetto communities were created by government and economic elites, to the detriment of those who live there. How many were taught, for example, that one-fifth of all black housing in the United States was destroyed in the middle of the twentieth century to make way for interstates, office buildings, malls, and parking lots, even as white housing was being subsidized by tax breaks and low-interest, government-guaranteed loans in the suburbs? Given the levels of historical ignorance, perhaps we shouldn't be surprised when folks feel it appropriate to hold ghetto parties, or wear greasepaint on their faces, since they lack the context to understand just how hurtful these kinds of things can be.

But then again, at some level, most of those engaged in these activities had to know they were treading on offensive ground. After all, *never* have the sponsors of these parties (and they've happened dozens and dozens of times) made the mistake of inviting *real* black people to the ghetto celebration. They knew better, apparently, than to approach their campus's black student associations and ask them to cosponsor the events. They didn't ask Latino students to come to "tacos and tequila" parties so as to lend authenticity to the fun. Had they been acting out of pure ignorance, they wouldn't have hesitated to try and make the events into multicultural funfests. But they never made this mistake, suggesting that even if only subconsciously, they had to know something was wrong.

At some level, we know, but haven't been taught to care. We've been taught to hide behind our proclamations of innocent intent, and then we get angry with folks of color for calling us on our behavior. When these events have happened at colleges, not only do the folks who did the deed feel that there was no harm done, but other whites rush to their defense as well, insisting that people of color need to lighten up (apparently in more ways then one).

Only when whites start challenging other whites, and begin to break the wall of silence that so often enables racist behavior, is anything likely to change.

THE MYTH OF REVERSE RACISM

SOMETIMES, SIMPLY DENYING that racism is a problem for people of color isn't enough. Increasingly, white denial has taken on new and more aggressive forms, as with the ubiquitous claims that it is *we* and not black and brown folks who are really being victimized. In other words, not only is white privilege a myth, but reverse racism, or reverse discrimination, is the real problem.

If I had a dollar for every white person who told me that their friend, uncle, or cousin didn't get into so-and-so school, or didn't get so-and-so job, or didn't get the city contract because the school/employer/city had to give the slot/job/contract to a black person, I'd be, well, let's just say, debt free. And so would black folks, having received all these supposed opportunities. Indeed, my own father, despite his progressive views about race, once said something like this when he failed to get a job for which he had applied. Despite not having a background in video camera work, when he failed to land a job as a videographer at a studio in town he was convinced, and proclaimed openly, that the only reason he hadn't gotten it had been because of his race: they had been forced to give it to a black guy, he insisted. Perhaps someone told him this, but if so, they lied. No law requires, encourages, or even allows any employer to simply hire blacks because they're black, or reject whites because they're white. That is not how affirmative action works in the real world, but rather, only in the fevered imaginations of whites who can't quite imagine that any black person would be more qualified than they were.

So whites think the reason they didn't get into Yale, or wherever, is because the school was busy giving away prized slots to folks of color; and this they believe, even though folks of color make up a pitifully small percentage of most entering classes at schools like that. This they believe, even though they have no idea what the overall qualifications of a given applicant might have been.

At the University of Michigan, Jennifer Gratz decided to sue the school (and ultimately won) because the year she was rejected, around a hundred blacks, Latinos, and American Indian students were admitted, despite having lower test scores and grades than her. Putting aside whether or not grades and scores should be the end-all-be-all when it comes to admissions, the bigger issue was that the very same year, there were well over a thousand whites who got in ahead of Gratz, despite having lower grades and scores. So why do whites like Gratz get upset about so-called less qualified black and brown folks, but pay no attention to the far larger group of whites, who are (according to the standards we claim are important) less qualified as well?

This would be like me going to the mall, looking for a parking space, not finding one, seeing lots of unused spaces for persons with disabilities, or pregnant moms, and then getting pissed at disabled folks or pregnant women, as if *they* had somehow kept me from getting a slot! Indeed, it would be more logical (though still pretty silly) to be upset about set-aside parking spots than affirmative action, since the latter involves no set-asides whatsoever. The truth is, if I'd gotten to the mall earlier, I'd be parked. I wasn't bumped to make way for certain groups, so much as beaten to the punch by hundreds of other shoppers, most of whom are able-bodied and very unpregnant, just like me. And in college admissions, if I didn't get in somewhere, the odds are good that there were dozens of whites who beat me out for every black or brown kid who did.

To get a sense for why the notion of reverse racism is so flawed however, perhaps two stories will serve to make the case best.

A few years ago, a headline in my hometown paper caught my eye. Turns out, a doctor at St. Thomas Hospital, just a few minutes from where I was living (and the hospital in which I had been born, albeit at a prior and different location at the time) had landed in some hot water. A patient had been brought in by her husband, desperately needing heart surgery. But rather than prioritizing the life and well-being of his wife, the husband insisted that no black men be allowed in the operating room, be they doctors, nurses, or orderlies, because he didn't want a black man to see his wife naked.

The man had already gone to two other hospitals in Nashville, only to have his request for a black-free OR rejected. Unsatisfied, he was intent on continuing to look, even if it delayed (or, one assumes, prevented) the necessary surgery from being performed on his wife.

At St. Thomas, though the request was also seen as racist and offensive, the white doctor to whom the request was made ultimately capitulated, worried about any further delay and the effect such a delay might have on the sick woman, who was in no shape to argue with her husband.

The surgery was performed, and indeed a black surgeon who would have been in the OR that night was kept from participating so as to satisfy the unhinged bigotry of the patient's husband. But once the decision to exclude the African American physician was made public, the hospital came under intense criticism, as well it should have, and the doctor who made the call was forced to apologize and acknowledge the violation of hospital policy, as well as his own moral and legal obligations.

But what was most interesting to me about the story was what *wasn't* said. After all, here was a white man, of modest economic means, able to get another white man, of professional stature and substantial means, to accede to his racism—more than accede to it actually, but rather to help enforce it—in a way that set limits on a man of color who was both more educated and more affluent than himself. Yet one could not imagine a black man, of whatever economic status or professional stature, walking into a hospital, demanding that white doctors be excluded from the operating room, and actually having his demand taken seriously, let alone agreed to.

The doctor in this case went along with the demand to exclude blacks from the operating room because he *could*. Given the history of discrimination in access to the medical profession, including medical schools, and the barriers to professional practice faced by people of color over the years, there exists today a limited number of such professionals from which to draw. As such, excluding them from a particular hospital or procedure is hardly a huge burden for the institution in question.

But if the situation had been reversed, and a bigoted black man had demanded the exclusion of whites from the operating room, there is simply no chance that his wishes would have been granted. Even if there were a doctor willing to agree to such conditions, it would be virtually impossible for him or her to follow through, because whites, having received the opportunities needed to enter the medical profession in large numbers, are hard to work around. "No whites" policies would result in a lot of empty operating rooms, whereas "No blacks" policies require only a small administrative headache at best, so few and far between are such professionals in the first place.

In other words, institutional racism is akin to the gasoline, allowing the otherwise stationary combustion engine of individual racism to function: The former gives the latter life, and the ability to impact others in a meaningful and detrimental way. Without the power to enforce one's racism, or to expect it to be enforced or enforceable by others, that racism is largely sterile. That's what makes the discourse about "reverse racism" so fraudulent. Yes, it is possible that in individual cases, persons of color in positions of authority may abuse that authority vis-à-vis white people. But as a general rule, the power to do such a thing is virtually monopolized by whites, in a way that makes the victimization of white people a rarity indeed.

* * *

IN FACT, SOMETIMES, even when people of color hold positions of power, their ability to oppress or in any way impinge upon the lives of whites is negligible.

To understand the extent to which this is true, let us travel now beyond the borders of the United States and examine race in another country with a history of white domination, but in which political leadership has recently the hands of blacks, and in which the demographic majority is also ~~black~~. Surely, one might think, if reverse discrimination were going to manifest—if reverse racism and white victimhood were going to have a fertile ground from which to grow—it would be in a place such as this. So let us journey now to Bermuda.

I visited this crown jewel of the dying but never fully deceased British Empire in the fall of 2005, invited in to discuss race and racism—issues that permeate much of what goes on in Bermuda, however much whites on the island may not always readily recognize this to be the case. To hear many white Bermudians tell it—and one must be clear that white Bermudians are often not *really* Bermudian, in that they are actually British expatriates, or their American equivalents—race is not an issue in Bermuda. In this island paradise, one is assured, Bermudians have conquered the demons that still bedevil we lesser intellects in the states, or in other lands around the globe. Bermuda, they say, is different. Indeed, in some ways it is: no two nations, after all, are exactly alike.

But in other ways, Bermuda is all-too similar to the United States, and its history is intimately intertwined with that of the United States, especially as regards the history of white racial supremacy in the hemisphere. It was, after all, Captain Christopher Newport who sailed the largest of the ships carrying whites to what became Jamestown, Virginia, in 1607, and who then shipwrecked on Bermuda with Admiral George Somers in 1609, while bringing supplies to the Virginia colony from England. Newport (who I recently discovered is my seventeenth great-grandfather), by virtue of his seamanship, ultimately contributed directly to the initiation of North American genocide and white conquest, beginning at Jamestown. And his accidental landing on Bermuda began the process by which Great Britain would come to hold the tiny Atlantic island as property of the empire.

Newport—who had made his name as a pirate, raiding ships of other nations and delivering their riches to wealthy investors back home—carried with him on the shipwrecked vessel John Rolfe, who would later introduce export tobacco to the Americas, which development would then lead to the enslavement of Africans for the purpose of cultivating the cash crop. That neither Rolfe nor Newport died in the wreck has proven to be among the lynchpin moments in history. Had they done so—rather than remaining alive, repairing their ship, and sailing on to Jamestown—the colonists would likely have perished, and with them the hopes for permanent colonization of the Americas. Having failed to plant adequate crops, and without the arrival of the supplies expected from England thanks to the shipwreck in Bermuda, the colonists in Jamestown were starving and dying in droves. Only Newport's arrival in 1610, almost a year after he was anticipated, allowed for colonization to be sustained. Although I suppose I must be grateful for Newport's having survived, since, as a direct contributor to the genetic line from which I derive, I would literally not exist without him, the fact remains that his survival has been decidedly a mixed bag so far as persons of color are concerned.

In any event, and getting back to Bermuda, it is not only a place divided by race demographically—about 54 percent of the 65,000 persons there are black, about 43 percent are white, including white expatriates, and the rest are a mix of other groups of color, including a growing number of Asians— but it is also divided by a vast gulf of perceptions. Blacks there believe race to be among the island's most vexing issues, while whites generally do not. And as with the United States, it is blacks who have a firmer grasp on reality, to say nothing of the history that has brought them to the place where they find themselves today.

As with the United States, Bermuda was a nation whose early economy was built largely on the backs of slave labor. And although slavery there was abolished in 1834, immediately upon emancipation, blacks were confronted with new laws restricting voting to those who didn't own sufficient amounts of property. As a result, less than five percent of votes for a century after the end of slavery would be cast by blacks, despite blacks being a majority on the island for this entire period.

Among the methods employed to dilute the black vote and reinforce white racist rule was plural voting, whereby rich whites could buy up property in each precinct of the island and then vote in each place where they owned land, as well as syndicate voting, whereby groups of rich whites could buy up property and then get however many votes in a precinct as there were owners on the piece of property. If fifty whites went in together on a piece of land (which none of them alone could have afforded), they would suddenly find themselves possessing fifty votes in the given precinct, whether or not they lived there. So although blacks were the majority of eligible voters in Bermuda, even by the early 1900s these various schemes intended to allow multiple votes by whites meant that the clear majority of votes being cast on the island would remain white votes, well into the late-twentieth century.

Even today, black political strength is diluted in the nation's parliament, by way of an electoral apportionment system that guarantees equal representation to each district of the island, irrespective of population. Parishes on the island have wildly different population sizes, with mostly white areas more sparsely populated and mostly black communities much more crowded. Yet, representation in Parliament is the same for all parishes. As such, whites end up with more representation, and thus, more power, than their numbers would otherwise dictate. Such a scheme, though it appears to violate Section 12 of the nation's constitution, which reads, "No law shall make any provision which is discriminatory either of itself or in effect," few whites seem too concerned about it.

Getting back to the historical context, as in the United States, hospitals, schools, churches, the civil service, the military officer corps, theatres, restaurants, neighborhoods, hotels, and even graveyards were segregated by race for most of the nation's history. For most of these forms of formal institutional racism, the ending came only within the last forty-five years.

As in the U.S., it was common practice throughout the twentieth century for land to be confiscated from black owners and communities to make way for commercial development benefiting whites, or even so as to develop a country club, or private community, which would then practice racial exclusivity in terms of membership or residency.

Electorally, universal suffrage has only existed in Bermuda since the late sixties, suggesting that white Bermuda long viewed blacks there as incapable of self-government. Indeed, the founder of the United Bermuda Party (which ruled the island from the sixties until 1998, when it was defeated by the majority-black Progressive Labour Party) famously argued against universal suffrage by claiming that it would be disastrous for the island until black Bermudians had become sufficiently educated and "disciplined." That the gentleman in question, Sir Henry Tucker, was also the manager of the Bank of Bermuda (whose lending practices hardly helped empower the black community), and was opposed to the equalization of educational resources, makes the venality of his argument all the more apparent.

Equally troubling for black opportunity in Bermuda has been a long-standing preference for foreign guest workers (who are overwhelmingly white), in housing and employment. Guest workers are given housing subsidies unavailable to locals, and often procure jobs that are all but off-limits to local blacks as well. These preferences not only push black Bermudians out of job opportunities, but drive up the price of housing and other goods and services, by distorting market rates for land especially, thereby making Bermuda an extremely expensive place to live.

Black Bermudians are especially resentful of guest worker preferences, since their purpose has always been seen, understandably so, as a way to whiten the island. Though white elites there insist guest workers are needed to fill certain professional positions for which locals are unqualified, the claim fails to withstand even a moment's scrutiny. Most foreigners working on the island do *not* work in professional positions requiring a particularly intense level of education or skills, and less than two in ten have management level positions. That most foreign workers are filling medium- and semiskilled jobs calls into question the extent to which worker importation is really about filling skills gaps and economic necessity, as opposed to the purpose of achieving a whiter Bermuda.

Interestingly, the largest opportunity gaps on the island actually appear between natives, either black or white, and not between black natives and white foreigners. So, for example, although black Bermudians with college degrees are roughly as likely to have management-level jobs as white foreigners in the country, relative to white Bermudians, blacks are not doing nearly as well. Forty-three percent of white Bermudians with college degrees have management level jobs, as opposed to only 28 percent of similarly educated black Bermudians.

Black Bermudians are 54 percent of all natives with college degrees, while whites are only 38 percent of similarly educated natives. Yet 60 percent of natives with top-level management jobs are white and slightly less than a third are black. While 38 percent of white Bermudians with college-level educations have positions in senior or executive management, only 22 percent of similarly educated black Bermudians do; in other words, native whites are about 73 percent more likely than native blacks in Bermuda to obtain these types of positions.

But despite the solid evidence of ongoing white hegemony in Bermuda, many whites there seem to be on pins and needles, anxious about the way that political power—having been assumed recently by a black-dominated party—may tilt the balance against them. Despite the advantages they have obtained and continue to enjoy, many whites in Bermuda appear convinced that they are the targets of reverse discrimination and that their victimization, if not in evidence yet, is never too far around the corner. Many there speak of having become a "minority" (which is fascinating, since whites have *been* the minority since the 1830s, however much their power may have insulated them from realizing this fact), and worry that blacks will abuse their power in a way that would harm those of European descent.

While I was in Bermuda, in fact, a prime example of perceived white victimhood (and the extent to which said claims are so vacuous as to be nearly laughable) emerged. In the days leading up to my arrival, a controversy had exploded when the premier at that time, Alex Scott, fired off an angry e-mail regarding something said to him by a white conservative on the island, Tony Brannon. Brannon, who has a reputation for berating politicians (especially in the mostly black PLP) for what he perceives as their incompetence, corruption, and unwillingness to let go of the racial history of the island, had fired off an e-mail to the premier, in effect blaming him for Bermuda's sorry economic state and a decline in tourism. The premier, thinking he was sending a reply only to his close associates, apparently hit "reply all" to the e-mail, and let loose with the impolitic and offensive remark that he was tired of getting flak from "people who look like Tony Brannon."

Brannon, naturally, went to the press about the premier's remarks, and it became something of a mini-scandal by the time I arrived on the island that October. The premier, chastened by significant public backlash to his remarks, backpedaled, insisting that he hadn't mean the comment as a racial remark against Brannon or whites generally. Virtually no one believed him, because frankly, the claim of innocence was wholly unbelievable.

Since I was there at the time, talking about race, the local press sought my opinion on the matter, as did individuals, black and white, during my stay. To me there seemed to be a couple of key issues, both of which speak to the larger subject of institutional white privilege.

On the one hand, I made clear that I thought the premier's comments to be inappropriate and offensive. But that was the easy part. In a larger sense, whites in Bermuda desperately needed to try and place themselves in the position of the premier, especially as the head of a majority-black party.

After all, there has been a long history in Bermuda of whites verbalizing their doubts that blacks were capable of self-government. Sir Henry Tucker's racist comments, as mentioned previously, were hardly unique in the annals of Bermudian political history. During a mid-1990s debate over independence from Britain (favored by most blacks, and certainly by the PLP), it was common to hear whites express blatantly colonial rhetoric to the effect that independence, by removing Bermuda from the loving oversight of the mother country, would cause the island to descend into political and economic chaos.

So against that background noise, for a white man like Tony Brannon—who has regularly made comments to the effect that blacks need to get over the issue of racism and move on—to criticize the premier and call into question his competence, would naturally cause alarm bells to go off in the ears of virtually any black person hearing it. Though Brannon may well have meant nothing racial by his critique, for a black premier to have his competence questioned (which is different than a simple disagreement over a particular policy), is to trigger a litany of negative stereotypes and call into question the extent to which the white questioner may be offering the critique from behind the veil of those prejudiced beliefs about blacks as a group.

That whites wouldn't understand this is due almost entirely to privilege. If a white politician is criticized for being incompetent, or not intelligent enough to run a country, for example (and certainly one hears barbs regularly about George W. Bush's intellect), no white person would have to worry—just as that individual white politician wouldn't have to worry—that the critique was intended as a group slam against whites. We wouldn't have to wonder whether the individual white politician had somehow triggered by his or her actions a larger group stereotype about white intelligence as a whole, because there *is no such negative stereotype* when it comes to white intelligence. But stereotypes about black intelligence are commonplace and longstanding. So when a comment is made that could be perceived as stemming from that stereotypical view, it is quite understandable that a black person on the receiving end of that critique might react in a way that seems over the top and hypersensitive. The larger social context doesn't make the comment acceptable, but it does allow us—provided we as whites are willing to consider it—to understand the way privilege and its opposite work.

But even more significant than putting the comment in historical context, the most important aspect of the incident, to me at least, was Scott's apology and the fact that he had felt compelled to issue it. The very fact that Premier Scott felt compelled to backpedal after his remarks were made public is testimony to how little power he had, in effective terms. After all, if power truly resided in his hands, or the hands of other blacks such as himself, he (and they) would be able to regularly insult whites, say terrible things about them, and never have to apologize at all. Premier Scott would then have been in a position to say, in effect, "screw Tony Brannon" and everyone like him. But he can't, and that's the point. Deep, isn't it? A black man is forced to apologize to white people for a simple comment, while whites have still never had to apologize for the centuries-long crimes of slavery, segregation, and white institutional racism!

Alex Scott, despite holding political power in Bermuda, had essentially no power to effectuate his biases against whites. Even were we to grant that he was a vicious antiwhite bigot (and frankly, as unfortunate and inappropriate as his remarks were, this charge seems extreme), the fact would remain that he would have been utterly impotent to do anything with those biases. He couldn't have expelled whites from Bermuda, taken away their right to vote, or imposed discriminatory laws against them in terms of hiring and education. He couldn't have done any of the things that have been done to blacks in Bermuda over the years, political power notwithstanding. Totally dependent on tourist dollars—most of them spent by white tourists—and white-dominated corporate investments, to say nothing of ultimate British control of the island, black politicians in Bermuda could be as racist as they like, but to no effect, except insofar as they might be able to hurt white feelings. That's about it. So too with the newest premier, also from the PLP, Ewart Brown. Despite criticism that he too harbors ill will towards whites, the fact remains that with economic power so tightly controlled in Bermuda by white folks, black politicians are incapable of doing anything of substance to harm the interests of whites.

It is also worth noting that the very same whites who were so incensed by Premier Scott's remarks said nothing when the black premier of the more conservative (and white-dominated) party told blacks in 1989 to "lower their voices" regarding the issue of racism. In other words, telling black people to shut up is fine; telling white folks to do so makes you a racist.

And so whites in Bermuda, as with the United States, insist that racism is no longer a barrier for blacks—despite the evidence of widespread disparities that have virtually no alternative explanation but racial discrimination—but has become one for them: a charge that takes white denial to a pinnacle unrivaled in the annals of racial irrationality. To avoid dealing with the legacy of white supremacy, we will change the subject, blame the victims, *play* the victim, and generally do anything to avoid confronting the truth that rests just in front of our eyes.

WITH FRIENDS LIKE THESE: THE SPECIAL PROBLEM OF WHITE LIBERALS

UNFORTUNATELY, CONSERVATIVES ARE not the only ones in denial when it comes to racism. When it comes to recognizing and then committing to doing something about the problem, white liberals can be just as intransigent. In fact, white-liberal denial—though it isn't typically as purely dismissive as denial from the right, in that it feigns concern, even as it minimizes the extent of the problem—is in some ways worse. For people of color to be given short shrift by those on the right is at least to be expected. It isn't shocking when you receive little sympathy or concern from those who've never really pretended to care. It was conservatives of their day who opposed every piece of civil rights legislation ever passed, after all. But liberals and so-called progressives claim to be on the side of the angels when it comes to these kinds of things. To have self-proclaimed allies in the struggle minimize your concerns has to be almost more maddening.

White-liberal denial manifests in a number of ways, and although it usually is sugarcoated, relative to the denial of conservatives, it amounts to a brush off nonetheless.

The first time I went to Minnesota I got to see white-liberal denial up close. The year was 1995, and I had been brought in for an event at a college outside of the Twin Cities. Picked up at the airport by three very nice, very white, and very liberal (for what that was worth) students, we chatted on the way to my hotel, where I was to rest a while before the evening's event.

The students all expressed excitement about the program that night, and noted how glad they were that I was there for their "diversity day" event. Putting aside how patronizing the notion of a "diversity day" is—and of course, such an occasion pretty well lets you know what the other 364 days are going to be like—I thanked them and said that I too was glad to be there.

"So," I asked, "Are there any particular things about your campus that I should know before this evening?" It's a question I ask any time I go somewhere to speak, so that I can tailor my remarks to the greatest extent possible to whatever the local issues might be at a given time.

They began by giving me some very basic information, essentially the kinds of things I could have gotten from the school's Web site or catalog, about course offerings, number of students, and the racial demographic mix.

"I was thinking more along the lines of the campus climate, racially speaking," I sought to clarify. "You know, have there been any incidents I need to know about, any specific tensions, that kind of thing?"

They looked perplexed. "Oh no," one of the young women replied. Another of my hosts then piped up to explain, "We really don't have any racism on campus."

This seemed strange. After all, here I was, an *antiracism* activist and educator, and yet I was being told that there was really no racism at the school to which I had been invited, against which one might need to be active. Having heard before that there was "no racism" somewhere, only to find it in abundance upon closer examination, I asked them how they could be so sure.

"Well," one of the three began to explain, "it's sorta this thing we have here." Admittedly, I was lost, and my confusion showed. "Thing?" I asked, "What kind of thing?"

"Well," a second student chimed in, spookily able to finish the first young woman's thought, "it's just our culture up here. It's sorta hard to explain to someone who's not from here."

"*Really?*" I responded, barely trying to conceal my sarcasm. "Well by all means, what is this thing? Because I need to get some before next week. I'm going to Michigan, and I'm pretty sure they don't have any of it."

And here's the thing about Minnesotans. They are nothing if not earnest. And this earnestness apparently prevents one from detecting cynicism in the voice of another.

"Well, it's pretty much our state slogan. We call it Minnesota Nice."

The moment was not unlike something out of a Coen Brothers film, or worse, a Fellini flick. I didn't know whether to laugh, or to, well—laugh, that was pretty much the only option. Minnesota Nice, after all, was not a "thing." A bumper sticker, yes; a thing, not so much.

"What is *that*?" I asked, through a slight chuckle, almost scared at what the answer might be.

"Well, you know," one of the young women said. "It's like the Golden Rule: you know, do unto others, that kinda thing."

I sat in stunned silence, halfway expecting them to bust out laughing and admit that the whole thing had been a joke. I mean, the Golden Rule has been around since, like, forever, and hasn't done much of anything to get rid of racism. So what were the odds that in this one state, and given a unique upper-Midwestern, Scandinavian spin, it would suddenly prove capable of doing the trick?

Needless to say, I didn't buy it, but not wanting to offend, I let it drop, and resolved that once I got the chance, I would ask some folks of color about this Minnesota Nice thing. Something told me they would have a take that was a bit different.

So, when I was finally able to sit down with some black folks, some Latinos, some Asian Americans and some indigenous folks from the state, I did just that. "So tell me," I asked them, "what's up with Minnesota Nice?"

When I asked these questions of people of color, I did it in separate meetings, with folks in different parts of the state, who had never met one another. But once asked, they all said the very same thing, in the very same way, accompanied by the very same look of disgust and rolling of the eyes. Like it was rehearsed. Or more to the point, like they'd been waiting for a chance to say what they felt about Minnesota Nice for a long time.

"Minnesota Nice is *killing us.*" That is what they said, every last one.

"How so?" I asked

The answers I got back consisted of two main points. First, nice was in the eye of the beholder, and outward niceness (civility really) often merely masked underlying hostility. Having caught white folks who wore Minnesota Nice like a fancy overcoat, yet nonetheless engaged in the telling of racist jokes, or the making of highly inappropriate comments, people of color were quick to rename Minnesota Nice as something else altogether: namely, institutionalized passive-aggressive behavior.

Secondly, they explained, nice is often the enemy of agitation. In other words, if they are feeling marginalized or discriminated against in a particular space, and they raise their voice above a whisper to protest the mistreatment, *they* end up getting pegged as "not nice," which violates this overarching cultural imperative to which everyone is supposed to buy in.

So Minnesota Nice not only failed to eliminate racism, it actively contributed to it, by making it harder to raise the issue in a forthright manner in the hopes of making change.

It's an important point, and not only for those reading this book and who live in Minnesota. The truth is, every state has a version of this. And white folks all around the nation sometimes mistake being civil and kind and "nice" with actually doing something to end injustice. But just because you're nice to people, just because you chat around the water cooler, or whatever, doesn't mean that racism and inequity aren't present in the place where you work or go to school. White privilege exists with or without bigoted actions on the part of individual whites. And no matter how diverse an institution may be, the numbers alone can't ensure equity. On a recent trip to Stanford, for example, I was told by a group of Asian and Pacific Islander students that racism was rampant on the campus, even though students of color make up half the student body.

Liberals, by substituting personal kindness and a commitment to the "colorization of the room" for real equity and an eradication of racial hierarchy, do no one any favors. By minimizing the extent of the problem and failing to hear what people of color say about their own lives, white liberals can be every bit as much of a barrier to progress as any conservative. Until whites of whatever political stripe realize that the norms we take for granted—be they Minnesota Nice, or our preconceived notions of what makes a person qualified for college admissions, or the old-boy's network, which even in the absence of bigotry would perpetuate race and gender inequity—are the problems, we will merely contribute to the longevity of racism.

BUT ARE WE REALLY THAT NAÏVE?

AT SOME LEVEL, one has to wonder whether white folks are really in denial about the reality of racial subordination and our own privileges. Do we really believe that things are equal nowadays? Do we really believe that privilege is a thing of the past and that people of color, if anything, have it better than we do? That's certainly what we say, but is it really what we think?

A recent study on white perceptions of racism would suggest that the answer to the question is yes. The study sought to get at the extent to which whites understand the reality of black disadvantage, and did so by asking white college students how much money they would require as compensation, were they to be changed from white to black, and have to live as a black person for the rest of their lives. In keeping with the notion that whites are utterly clueless as to the experiences black folks face when it comes to racism, the average answer was only $10,000 per year. In other words, blackness was not seen as much of a disadvantage for most—perhaps a slight one, yes, but nothing to become too concerned about.

But then the students were given a different hypothetical. This time, they were asked how much compensation they would require if, living in a fictional land, they were to be made into members of a subordinated group there, with average income half the level of the dominant group, with poverty rates that were three times higher, with life expectancies that were far less, with one-tenth the average net worth as the dominant group, and all sorts of other disadvantages. The average response this time shot up to $1 million per year in required compensation. Of course, the conditions to which the whites would be subjected in this fictional land are precisely the conditions faced currently by blacks in this one, but by not mentioning race, and by allowing the respondents to believe they were talking about something else, whites demanded compensation and a lot of it—the very compensation they would view as unjustified if demanded by blacks in the United States today.

So on that level, it would appear that the problem with white folks is indeed denial, perhaps even simple ignorance, as to the conditions of life faced by people of color. Maybe if whites knew the truth—that the conditions in the hypothetical were really the conditions to which blacks are exposed every day—they would become more sympathetic.

Yet I wonder, and this is because of another experiment I do with students sometimes, during workshops, so as to gauge how much they really know, but are perhaps unwilling to let on. Rather than ask whites how much compensation they would require to become black, I ask them: if they knew that there was a pill they could take, that when taken would cause those they don't know already to perceive them as black, would they take it? To their friends, family, and all who knew them, they would still appear as they were, but to persons newly encountered, like police officers, bank officials, potential employers, or one's teachers in the coming year, one would appear black.

Would they take that pill, perhaps before their next job interview? Would they take that pill the next time they went to get a mortgage or business start-up loan? Would they take that pill before the first day of high school, or college, and every day thereafter, thereby allowing themselves to be seen by teachers as African Americans? Would they take the pill the next time they went shopping, or had to drive a long distance?

I have asked the question several hundred times. I have not had one white person answer affirmatively. Not one.

That speaks volumes. If being black, or perceived as such, paid such enormous dividends, there would be no reason *not* to take such a pill. After all, you wouldn't really look any different to people who already knew you. So the pill wouldn't require a total reworking of existing relationships, nor would it prompt any kind of schism with white family or lovers, for whom such a change would be dramatic. All the pill would do is alter your appearance to those with whom you had no prior connection. If being black were such a boon, whites would be *lining up* for a pill like this. That we are not, and would not—and that indeed there are virtually no whites who have ever tried to pass for black (except for John Howard Griffin, and he was trying to prove a point), while millions of blacks over the years sought to pass into whiteness—tells us all we need to know about which side of the bread the butter is on.

It is not, to put it mildly, on the rye.

RESISTANCE

"What societies really, ideally, want is a citizenry which will simply obey the rules of society. If a society succeeds in this, that society is about to perish. The obligation of anyone who thinks of himself as responsible is to examine society and try to change it and to fight it—at no matter what risk. This is the only hope society has. This is the only way societies change."

JAMES BALDWIN, "A TALK TO TEACHERS,"
Saturday Review, December 21, 1963

BUT WHAT IF we're not in denial? What about the white folks who "get it," at least at the intellectual level? What next for us? Once we begin to acknowledge our privileges as whites, we are immediately confronted with a challenge: what do we do with both the privilege and the knowledge of it? On the one hand, it would be easy to feel guilty, or to beat ourselves up over the system that benefits us, but that hardly seems helpful. After all, if unjust privileges stem from a system of unjust social arrangements, over which most of us have little control, there isn't much point in feeling guilty about them.

Yet one can decide to do something about those arrangements, since whether or not we are responsible for their creation, we clearly live with their consequences today. Regardless of our guilt, we can choose resistance. Just as we choose to correct environmental damage caused by pollution stretching back years—and which we aren't necessarily responsible for, at least directly—and just as we choose to pay down the national debt, even though its accumulation cannot be pinned on any one of us individually, so too we can opt to challenge racial inequality, even if it was brought about initially by someone else.

Make no mistake, resisting injustice is never easy. Sometimes we don't have the faintest idea where to begin, or how to fight injustice, especially when the source of that injustice is so systemic, so ingrained in the society that its gears, its engine, seem far from our immediate reach. Because resistance is difficult, and because we have so many other day-to-day concerns, many whites who care deeply about issues of racism and inequality will find ourselves paralyzed either by uncertainty, fear, or both; as such, our resistance will be rare, short lived, and often ineffective.

The fear often felt by whites when it comes to speaking out about racism is palpable. It is a fear of alienating family, friends, or colleagues who may not understand why we feel as we do—the fear, as James Baldwin explained, of "being turned away from the welcome table" of white society. Added to that fear is the very real possibility that our acts of resistance or rebellion might not pay off: our activism, or our efforts to educate others about the issues may not change things, and certainly won't do so quickly, given the time frame needed for most social transformations to occur.

Fighting injustice only to see injustice win, again and again, can be frustrating, especially to members of dominant and privileged groups. We, unlike those who have been systemically subordinated, can usually take for granted that our efforts will pay off, because that's how things tend to work when one is a member of a powerful group. So when we put our minds to resisting something like racism, sometimes we have the idea that the job will be no more difficult than anything else to which we might turn our attention, not recognizing how hard it can be to alter a fundamental social relationship that has existed for hundreds of years.

I'll never forget the young white woman I met a few years ago who came up to me after a speech I had given and said how much she appreciated it, and how much she agreed with everything I had said, and then added that she really wanted to "get busy on this racism thing, so I can still have time to save the rainforests before I have to sell out and get a real job."

Putting aside the self-evident absurdity of the sentiment, perhaps the bigger problem is that such a mindset implies that although racism is a problem to be tackled, it is one that is no more difficult to address than any other problem—just one of many areas of interest from which to choose on the cafeteria line we call life. Such a view is profoundly disrespectful of peoples of color, since it implies that although they haven't been able to end racism despite centuries of effort, certainly we as white folks can figure it out in a few years if we just put our minds to it.

No, it isn't going to be that easy. But it is possible. There are choices we can make, paths we can travel, and when we travel them we will not be alone. There are others making the same journey at the same time, and those who have made that journey in the past. What they have done and what they have learned along the way is a font of common knowledge—we need to tap a knowledge that has afforded us some vital lessons, assuming we're prepared to learn them.

TRADITION IS A CHOICE WE MAKE:
Connecting to Antiracist History

BEFORE WE CAN explore the *how* and *what* of resistance, it might do us well to examine what seems to be blocking us from resisting, or at least resisting effectively. There must be a reason why it's so hard to get whites—even those who espouse progressive views and claim to be antiracist—to get off the mark and really challenge racism, white supremacy, and white privilege.

On the one hand, the reason most whites don't join the struggle is fairly simple: white privilege provides immense advantages to us as a group, so in the most basic analysis, resisting that system would appear to be against the best interests of white people. Although, as we'll explore a bit later, the long-term (and frankly even short-term) consequences of indulging privilege and inequality can be catastrophic, even for those who benefit from the advantages provided, it should hardly surprise us that these costs might not be readily apparent to most.

But I am neither speaking nor thinking about typical white folks now, for whom resisting white supremacy is probably the last thing on their minds, and for whom we should hardly wait before engaging these issues in any event. I am thinking of the white folks who *do* care, who read this book and think that yes, white privilege and supremacy are wrong and need to be confronted, but who then, for one reason or another, freeze up, or falter at that place where the rubber meets the road, so to speak. What's going on with them?

One of the biggest problems in sustaining white resistance is the apparent lack of role models to whom we can look for inspiration, advice, and even lessons on what *not* to do. Growing up, we don't often see many whites taking up the banner of racial equity, fighting for an end to unjust privileges and institutional racism. Although there have always been whites who fought for these things, we typically don't learn of them in school nor from our parents.

Most people reading this book would have a hard time naming more than a handful of white antiracists, for example. In fact, when I ask audiences around the country to name a white antiracist, the most common reaction (other than total silence) is "Abraham Lincoln." Such an answer is stunning, given Lincoln's actual racial views and stated willingness to send black folks back to Africa, had he found it possible to do so; and yet the answer makes sense, given the way in which Lincoln is taught in American schools, and the degree to which real antiracist white allies are ignored.

Not knowing of white antiracist history, and not seeing many examples of the same in our own families, we sometimes can feel alone, even crazy, for thinking the way we do about racism and privilege, if we find these things enraging. And for whites in general, lacking a historical perspective on antiracist resistance makes it all the easier to go along with things "the way they are" and have long been.

During the spring semester of 2007, I went to the University of Illinois, in Champaign-Urbana, for a three-day residency. While there, I had the occasion to meet with a number of different groups: residence hall advisors, fraternity and sorority members, student life personnel, faculty, staff, and students of all types.

The timing of my visit couldn't have been better, or worse I suppose, depending on your perspective. For the previous year, Illinois, like many other schools, had been under intense pressure from the National Collegiate Athletic Association (NCAA) to no longer caricature American Indian peoples, by way of their team mascot: Chief Illiniwek. The chief had been a staple of U of I athletic events dating back over eighty years, at least thirty-five of which had witnessed protests of the mascot from indigenous students and their supporters. As with Indian mascots around the country, the chief had come under fire for making a mockery of Indian traditions, reducing Indian peoples to a stereotypical image of warriors or "noble savages," and papering over the very real oppression faced by indigenous persons, past and present in the United States.

In the case of Illiniwek, the chief had always been played by a white man (most recently a very blue-eyed, blonde-haired white man at that), and he wore an outfit that bore no resemblance to what actual Illini Indians would have worn prior to being driven off the land where the college now stood. Furthermore, the dance performed by Illiniwek at halftime shows, though touted as a traditional "fancy dance," was, in truth, a mix of inauthentic Indian dance moves and gymnastics.

The NCAA, in 2005, had announced that schools with Indian mascots would no longer be allowed to host basketball tournament games. Some schools complied and changed their mascot names while others, like Illinois, dug in and tried to challenge the NCAA in court. But by the time I arrived on campus in early 2007, the governing board of the university had decided to give in, realizing that continued legal opposition to the NCAA's move would likely prove fruitless, and concerned about the loss of revenue that would follow from enforcement of the new regulations.

A few weeks prior to my time at the U of I, the chief had done what was billed as his "final dance," during the halftime of the Illinois-Michigan basketball game. A somber, tight-lipped white man, in a regionally inappropriate headdress, covered in buckskin, gesticulated around the gym floor, on national television, while thousands of white Illinois fans wept openly in the stands.

The sight was nothing short of amazing; here were white people having an existential meltdown in front of millions of television viewers, all because a tradition *that wasn't even theirs* was being taken from them. They were going to be prevented from playing dress-up, and this fact was sending them into fits of apoplexy. It was as if someone had cut off the limb of a parent, or killed a small puppy in front of their eyes. Here were young women with Greek letters emblazoned across their chests and tears cascading down their cheeks, next to young men with backward baseball caps, and still more Greek letters, wearing looks of icy rage on their faces. These were people who had likely never spent one second of their lives crying over the fact that indigenous peoples lost some 90 million souls, their traditional cultures, religions, and almost all of their land to make way for folks like us, but who couldn't help but sob at the thought of losing a few seconds of entertainment. Deep.

Tradition. It was the word on the lips of just about everyone I met at Illinois. For those defending the chief, and who were beside themselves at the thought of losing him, tradition was being ripped apart and discarded, all for the sake of political correctness. Tradition, to these folks, was a noble and worthy thing, in need of being defended and carried on, although for reasons they could rarely articulate. To the opponents of the chief, tradition was also an important word, though one spoken with far less reverence, and not a small amount of contempt. Tradition, to these folks, was something used to oppress, to vilify, to spread racism, and to further marginalize students of color on the campus.

Yet, what neither group seemed to realize was that tradition is a choice we make. In other words, there are many traditions in our culture, and the ones we choose to venerate are not foregone conclusions but are the result of conscious and volitional acts, for which *we* have to be responsible. By ignoring this aspect of tradition—which ones we choose to discuss and remember, and which ones we discard—the rhetorical combatants at the University of Illinois fell into a trap from which extrication seems highly unlikely. If defenders of the chief feel as though there is only one tradition to which they can cleave—the tradition of impersonation, or what they like to call "honoring"

Indian peoples—and if the opponents feel that that, too, is the only thing meant by the term tradition, then both sides dig in, and the development of constructive resistance to racism becomes less likely. To abandon or preserve tradition becomes an all-or-nothing gambit for both sides in the debate.

But what if students understood that there was another tradition they could choose to uphold? What if they had been made aware long before, and during their time at the university, of the tradition of resistance—resistance to Indian genocide and racism, not only by people of color, but also whites?

What if they knew about, and had been encouraged to identify with, Europeans like Bartolomé de Las Casas, who wrote eloquently against the crimes of Columbus, having traveled with the "peerless explorer" and having witnessed his depraved treatment of the Taino on Hispaniola? What if they knew of and had been encouraged to identify with whites like Helen Hunt Jackson, Matilda Gage, or Catherine Weldon, all of whom spoke out forcibly against the mistreatment of indigenous persons in the mid-to-late 1800s? What if we were encouraged to follow the example set by Lydia Child, who not only demanded justice for Indian peoples but was also the first white person to write a book calling for the abolition of slavery? What if whites knew of and had been encouraged to emulate the bravery of Jeremiah Evarts, a white man who spearheaded opposition to Andrew Jackson's Indian Removal Act and the forcible expulsion of the Cherokee peoples from the Southeast?

But we haven't been taught these histories. We know nothing, by and large, of these alternative traditions. And so we are left, all of us, but especially white folks, with a prefabricated and utterly inaccurate understanding of what our options are. Whites like those at Illinois seem to feel as though the only or best way to "honor" Indian peoples (to the extent they honestly think that's what they're doing) is to portray them, to dress like them, to act as we assume they act, or once did.

Yet if the alternative tradition were the one to which we had been exposed, we might choose resistance, as other whites have done, and commit our schools to something more meaningful than symbolic representation by way of mascots. We might uphold that alternative tradition by pushing for the quadrupling or quintupling of indigenous students on our campuses, or by working towards the establishment of well-funded Native American studies programs. Even better, we could uphold tradition—the tradition of Jackson and Weldon and Evarts—by partnering with organizations that work with indigenous peoples, so as to improve the economic and educational opportunities available to such folks, on and off campus. And we could begin by stopping the celebration of Columbus Day.

Tradition is, after all, what we make it. The definition of the term is simply this: "a story, belief, custom or proverb handed down from generation to generation." There is nothing about the word that suggests tradition must be oppressive, or that it must necessarily serve to uphold the status quo. It is simply the narrative we tell ourselves, and as such, could just as easily involve resistance to oppression or injustice, as the perpetuation of the same. But if we aren't clear in articulating the alternative tradition, we can hardly be surprised when persons don't choose the direction in which it points, having never been appraised of its existence.

In the South, for instance, too many white folks cleave to the tradition of the Confederacy, and one of the battle flags most commonly associated with it. But that is not because the Confederacy *is* Southern history, or synonymous with the South. Rather, it is because of an ideological choice those white southerners are making to align themselves with that tradition as opposed to the other, equally southern traditions with which they could identify. White southerners who wave that flag are choosing to identify with a government whose leaders openly proclaimed that white supremacy was the "cornerstone" of their existence, and who over and over again made clear that the maintenance and extension of slavery into newly stolen territories to the west was the reason for secession from the Union.

But white southerners *could* choose to identify with and praise the 47,000 whites in Tennessee who voted against secession—almost one-third of eligible voters—or the whites in Georgia whose opposition to leaving the Union was so strong officials there had to commit election fraud in order to bring about secession at all. We could choose to remember and to celebrate abolitionists in the South like Kentuckian John Fee, a Presbyterian minister, who was removed from his position by the Presbyterian Synod for refusing to minister to slaveholders, so severe did he consider their sins to be.

Instead of venerating Jefferson Davis, the Confederate president, we could praise the brave women who marched on Richmond in 1863 to protest his government and the war, shouting, "Our children are starving while the rich roll in wealth," and who Davis then threatened to shoot in the streets if they didn't disperse. Instead of identifying with soldiers who perpetrated atrocities against black Union forces—like Nathan Bedford Forrest (for whom there is a garish statue a few miles from my home, and with whom one of my relatives fought, sadly, at the Battle of Sand Mountain)—we could proudly note the bravery of those one hundred thousand or more white Southern troops who deserted the Confederate forces, many because they had come to see the battle as unjust. Or the thirty thousand troops from Tennessee alone who not only deserted the Confederacy but went and joined the Union army, so changed did their beliefs become over time.

White southerners could choose to venerate the tradition of the civil rights movement, which rose from the South and lasted far longer than the confederacy. We could choose to valorize the tradition of Historically Black Colleges and Universities, which grew throughout the South as a form of institutionalized self-help because of the denial of educational opportunity to persons of African descent. We could choose to identify with the tradition of resistance to racism and white supremacy by black southerners to be sure— John Lewis, Ella Baker, Ed King, Amzie Moore, Unita Blackwell, Fannie Lou Hamer, or E. D. Nixon, to name a few—but also by *white* southerners: persons like Thomas Shreve Bailey, Robert Flournoy, Carolyn Daniels, Anne Braden, Bob Zellner, Mab Segrest, and hundreds, if not thousands of others throughout history.

That we are familiar with few of these names, if any, leaves our ability to resist compromised, and limits us to playing the role of oppressor, or at least quiet collaborator with that process. It is always harder to stand up for what's right if you think you're the only one doing it. But if we understood that there is a movement in history of which we might be a part, as allies to people of color, how much easier might it be to begin and sustain that process of resistance? For me, I know that such knowledge has been indispensable.

* * *

OVER THE YEARS I've had the occasion to drive through Mississippi—and particularly the route from Louisiana up through Hattiesburg and Meridian— probably thirty or forty times. Nothing against Mississippi, but it's a drive I would probably never have made if I hadn't gone to school in New Orleans. It's long, hot, and pretty forgettable as road trips go. But there was one trip I made to Mississippi that I know I will always remember.

It was June 21, 1989, the summer between my junior and senior years at Tulane, about a week before my grandfather died, during which time I was working as a canvasser (which is to say a glorified door-to-door salesperson) for Greenpeace, the environmental group.

For those well steeped in history, particularly that of the civil rights movement, you may recognize the importance of that date, June 21, especially as it relates to Mississippi. It was on that day in 1964, twenty-five years prior to the trip of which I'm speaking, that civil rights workers James Chaney, Michael Schwerner, and Andrew Goodman went missing in Nashoba County, never to be seen alive again. Their disappearance came at the outset of what would come to be known as Freedom Summer, the voter registration and community organizing initiative developed by a coalition of four civil rights groups, which brought hundreds of students, mostly white and from the North, into the heart of American apartheid. By working with local leaders and residents of color, the summer volunteers had hoped to begin the process of driving a stake through the heart of segregation, in that, the most difficult and intransigent of states.

For Chaney, Goodman, and Schwerner, however, the summer would end too soon, as would their lives, with bullets to the backs of their heads, fired from the guns of Philadelphia, Mississippi, law enforcement officials and their cohorts. Their bodies would be found in mid-July, buried in an earthen dam, with the black victim, James Chaney, having sustained head injuries consistent with a high-speed car accident.

My mother had been too young to volunteer for Freedom Summer, though her heart had been with the effort, much to the chagrin of her parents, who came from the "why do they have to go and stir things up" school of segregationists. In other words, they weren't bigots, not by a long shot. They just thought Dr. King and all the others should have left well enough alone. After all, in their world, everyone, white or black, had always gotten along so well.

In order to participate in Freedom Summer, you either had to be eighteen or have your parents' permission. My mother was six months too young, and in the wrong family for either of those things to work in her favor. Although she hadn't been raised by hateful types—and so in that sense avoided the fate of so many white southerners of the time—she had still had to deal with her family's indifference to what was going on in the country. She had still had to contend with their deafening silence in the midst of the nation's most epochal struggle. One can imagine that the silence, in some ways, might have been worse than open displays of racist contempt.

After all, to hear your parents cast aspersions upon Dr. King could be seen as almost pathetic, given the towering greatness of the latter and the rather ordinary mediocrity of the former. But to have his greatness and that of this movement met with blank stares, with *nothing*, had to have been worse. Unlike hatred, silence bespeaks an assumption of irrelevance, a ho-hum indifference. This indifference, especially regarding an issue of great magnitude, can hardly be less maddening than overt hostility. It's not unlike the difference between the person who seeks to openly justify the death of civilians in war time with bloodthirsty logic, on the one hand, and the person who blankly stares at the TV screen as it projects images of the death and destruction while not even blinking, on the other. The latter may not openly celebrate the carnage, but their refusal to show any emotion whatsoever is somehow more troubling.

At least the hater, the celebrant of death, is willing to demonstrate by virtue of his agitation that he is indeed alive and capable of feeling something, however grotesque. I have long thought I would prefer a land filled with angry and hateful people than one populated by spectators who watch the drama unfold, and no matter how bad it gets, never miss a single beat of their ordinary, predictable lives.

Kids dying in Mississippi? *Gotta remember to call Betty and make my hair appointment.*

Water cannons being turned on black people in Alabama? *Gotta pick up the dry cleaning and grab a few things at the grocery.*

Medgar Evers shot down in his driveway? *Did I remember to feed the cat?*

Acting as if nothing is happening, or at least nothing of real importance, has to be worse. It is the silence of the collaborator, the person who is unwilling or unable to see that they are in and of history, and that history has called on them to make a choice, not to passively observe and go with the flow. So far as I know, the only reaction my grandmother ever had to the civil rights movement was to express her concern about shopping downtown during the sit-ins, which hit Nashville in February of 1960. She truly feared that the completely nonviolent black and white kids who were sitting in at Kress or the Tic Toc restaurant might decide to riot. That the only folks threatening to riot were white segregationists, and that the only violence came from them as well, didn't occur to her I guess, nor did it alter her perceptions about who the good guys were and who the bad.

Even her concern—feeling put out at the limitations placed upon her ability to shop downtown—bespoke numbness. She didn't express openly contemptuous remarks about the protesters, so far as I know, but simply viewed the whole episode as an inconvenience. At one of the most important moments in the history of her country, she, like so many of her compatriots, whether in the South or the North, had no idea what was happening, nor did she particularly care.

But my mother did, and she had held it dear for years, and passed it on to me. And now, a quarter-century after that fateful day when Goodman, Chaney, and Schwerner met death at the hands of those whom—although they couldn't have seen it at the time—the three had been trying to save, she would finally make that trip to Mississippi.

We drove to Philadelphia for the anniversary gathering, organized by local civil rights leaders and movement veterans, which took place on the very site where once had stood the Mount Zion Baptist Church, the burning of which Schwerner had gone to investigate that day in 1964. It was that visit to Philadelphia that ultimately brought Schwerner and his comrades to the attention of Sheriff Rainey, Deputy Cecil Price, and their assorted Klan brothers.

The drive from Nashville takes about six hours, and we made it in almost complete silence as I recall. I can remember the miles ticking by as we headed south, and noticing, in ways I had missed in all of my previous trips, the ubiquity of the kudzu, consuming everything to the side of I-59: trees, shrubs, old highway signs, everything. Kudzu, for those who haven't spent much time in the South, is a particularly tenacious vine that is every bit as common in

Mississippi as the state flower, the magnolia. It is everywhere, thick, dense, and dark green. It spreads over the ditches and gulches and easements just off the shoulder of the roadway. If one falls asleep while driving and has the misfortune of hurtling one's car into a thicket of the stuff, there is a better-than-average chance that one might never be seen or heard from again.

Kudzu is more than a vine though, and it is no coincidence, I think, that it is to be found almost exclusively in the southern United States. It is the perfect vegetative metaphor for the way in which we southerners have so long sought to cover up our—crimes, crimes that are not ours alone but which we, in so many ways, perfected and turned into an art form. Lynchings happened in all parts of the country to be sure, but *Mississippi Goddam,* as Nina Simone would sing, was an entirely different geographic and, for that matter, historic species. It was the nerve center of white supremacy.

This was so much the case that later that year, when I was doing honors thesis research in the state, I would find black folks still afraid to talk about the events of 1964 for fear that they could even now disappear if word got back to the wrong people—people who were still there, and who knew exactly how those black bodies that would occasionally float to the surface of rivers and lakes had arrived at their final resting places; people who still knew the location of the deepest point in the Tallahatchie; people who had never forgotten, in all those years, how much weight was needed to keep a body submerged until it became impossible to identify it.

No, Mississippi was just plain different, and it still is.

We arrived in Philadelphia just in time for the beginning of the day's events and had to park well away from the site of the old church and walk the rest of the distance. It was unbearably hot, and there were a few thousand people there already, many from out of state, and many others from around the Philadelphia area, including those who had decided to capitalize on the day's events by marketing T-shirts to commemorate the festivities. Whether or not the locals had cared about Goodman, Chaney, and Schwerner twenty-five years earlier, it was clear that now, all seemed quick to wrap themselves in only the finest and most tightly-woven cloaks of racial ecumenism.

Among the highlights was a speech by Governor Ray Mabus, a white man so liberal by Mississippi standards, and perhaps even those of the South more broadly, that the fine white folks of that state must have wondered what in the hell had happened that last election day. Had they forgotten to vote, for God's sake? Had they gotten drunk and voted for *this* guy? To be sure, they wouldn't repeat the mistake, and since that brief respite have elected a gaggle of fools to the office, including such retread reactionaries as Haley Barbour, whose cozying up to old-line racists and segregationists actually helped him secure victory in 2004.

But the most important aspect of the day, and which more than compensated for the heat or the tacky commercial exploitation of the tragedy, was the presence of so many white movement veterans who had returned to Mississippi for the event.

I had never in my life been in the presence of so many white allies in one place, so many whites who had put their lives on the line for justice. Growing up in this country, one learns very little about the role played by such persons. Not only are the contributions of people of color to this nation's history minimized in favor of a narrative that prioritizes the things done by rich white men, but those whites who resisted and joined with black and brown folks to forge a better way are similarly ignored.

Growing up, and even attending one of the "good" schools in my community, in which I took Advanced Placement American History, I had learned nothing of these people among whom I now stood, and whose contribution to human freedom had been so dramatic, far more so than that of Andrew Carnegie, J. P. Morgan, or Andrew Jackson, for example, about whom I had learned plenty in the same class.

To have taught us about these people—and not merely the ones who had died, but the ones who had lived and continued the struggle—would have been dangerous. It would have signaled to those of us born in the years after the height of the movement that we had a choice to make. It would have dared those of us who were white to dream of different ways to live in this skin. It was no coincidence that school boards and principals and the lawmakers who make educational policy wanted no part of such an enterprise, and still don't.

To see this collection of people, this mass of black leaders and white allies, and to be in community that day with them was a source of great inspiration to me at twenty, as it appeared to be to my mother, there with me, at the age of forty-two. That she had been unable to participate in the battle we were that day celebrating was unfortunate. That she had raised a son to join that battle a quarter-century later had made her contribution every bit as vital.

SIMPLE TRUTHS, STATED SIMPLY

MY MOTHER'S OWN modeling for me, though not of the dramatic type provided by white activists in the civil rights movement, was nonetheless critical to my own development. As parents we often wonder if we're doing right by our kids, in lots of different areas. What we fail to realize is that many of the lessons we impart to our children don't come in the form of didactic, sit-'em-on-your-knee-and-give-'em-a-lecture moments. They come indirectly, almost imperceptibly. And so it was, with one of my earliest lessons about race, which just so happens to involve one of my earliest memories about anything as a child.

I couldn't have been more than two years old when it happened, "it" being the first time I ever saw a black person. I mean really saw a black person, and noticed the difference between the color of his skin and my own. I had probably seen black folks before, of course, but never until that day had I processed blackness, contrasted it with my own whiteness, and commented on the two. The opportunity came one morning, as I looked through the living room window of my family's apartment and saw "Tommy," as I came to know him: one of the maintenance crew at our complex.

It is testimony to just how entrenched racism was at that time, 1970, and in that place, Nashville, that this man who was at least in his forties would never be known to me or my parents by anything other than his first name. I, a mere infant, would enjoy the privilege of addressing this grown black man, with a family and full life history, only as Tommy, as if we were equals, or perhaps "Mister Tommy," as my mother would instruct me, since at least that sounded more respectful.

As I gazed out the window my attention was riveted to him and the darkness of his skin. He was quite dark, though not really black of course, which led me to ask of my mother: "Who is that brown man?"

Without hesitation she said it was Mr. Tommy, and that he wasn't brown, but rather black. Now even at two I had developed a penchant for argument, so just as naturally as I had previously asked the question I now replied to her answer with a matter-of-fact, "No he's not, he's brown." After all, I had mastered the names of all the crayons in my Crayola box, and knew that this man, Mr. Tommy, certainly didn't look like the crayon called "black." Burnt umber maybe, brown most definitely, but black? No way.

It was then that my mother explained something that, although it was hardly profound, was stated so clearly and directly that I would venture to guess it had much to do with how I came to view race and racism over the years. "Tim," she explained, "Mister Tommy may look brown, but people who look the way Mister Tommy does prefer to be called black."

And that was it—end of argument. Even at two, it seemed only fair that if someone wanted to call themselves black they had every right to do so, whether or not the label fit the actual color of the person's skin—mine, after all, wasn't really white either—and so it was none of my business.

This may not seem all that earth shattering, and perhaps it isn't. But think for a moment how important it can be to have someone plant that thought in your head at an early age—the thought that says people have a right to self-determination. They have a right to define their reality. And you have no right to impose your judgment *of* them, *on* them. That's deep, whether you're two or twenty-two when you first get hit with it. And it's especially deep when it comes to race because racism, by definition, is about denying the right of self-determination and the exercise of full autonomy to others. Racism, by definition, is about imposing your judgments of people, on those same people; it's about saying, "You're not black, you're colored," or, "You're not African American, you're an American—why can't we just drop the whole hyphen thing?" The answer of course is simple: because it isn't your hyphen to drop.

To be told in passive but clear terms, early on, that my perceptions weren't the only ones that mattered, and that what I *thought* I knew might not be right, and that there are perspectives other than my own, all of which need to be considered, was a powerful and lasting lesson. It was an antiracist lesson, a lesson in resistance. Because resistance, to be effective, requires that level of humility that can only come from listening to what others have to say. It comes from the modeling of that humility. I was very fortunate to have been exposed to that modeling, and I hope my wife and I can do it at least half as well for our children.

The power of resistance, after all, is to set an example. It often won't change the person with whom you disagree, and even less often will it fundamentally bring about great social transformation. But it can almost always serve to empower the one who is watching, like children always do, waiting to see what we're really all about. And to not seek to offer that direction, to fail to resist injustice, for whatever reason—and among these we can count fear, cynicism, or just plain fatigue—is to ensure they will learn a very different lesson, with potentially disastrous consequences. As Baldwin put it: "Children have never been very good at listening to their elders, but they have never failed to imitate them."

RESISTANCE REQUIRES PRACTICE AND CREATIVITY

LET'S NOT LIE to ourselves about the fear, though. It's real, whether we're challenging a family member, friend, colleague, or complete stranger. And sometimes we blow it.

Before I ever stood up and challenged a store clerk for racially profiling customers, there were dozens of times that I saw it and did nothing. For every time I interrupted someone for making a racist joke or comment, or responded forcefully to such a thing, there were dozens of times that I didn't, when I let things slide, with a nervous laugh but little else. There was even the time that I said nothing after listening to a guy who was the head of the volunteer literacy program at Tulane talk about one of the kids he was tutoring, noting that while he was a cute little eight-year-old now, by the time he was a teenager, he'd be "just another nigger." I said nothing to this, and the silence then (and at other times) haunts me, as it should.

The point is, resistance takes work, it takes practice, and it helps to have as much support as possible. We shouldn't be ashamed of the times we fall short, but resolve to develop strategies that make resistance easier and more likely to succeed. Because sometimes, whether we're prepared or not, we'll be put to the test. At times like that, cultivated creativity is among the most important weapons at our disposal.

Several years ago, I began to notice a disturbing tendency whenever issues of race would come up in a group of whites that really didn't know each other all that well but happened to be together at a party or other social event, or for that matter, in a pub, coffee shop, or pretty much anywhere else.

What I noticed, because it was hard to miss, was that in these situations it seemed almost inevitable that someone in the group—often several someones—would take the opportunity to make some kind of overtly racist comment, or tell a racist joke, as if it were perfectly acceptable to do so, and as if no one else in the group would mind. "White bonding" was what I called it, for lack of a better term.

At first I thought I was the only one having this experience so I kept it to myself, but then when I began to mention it to others they talked of having the same thing happen to them. In fact, I would later learn that others whom I had never met were actually using the same term I had chosen to describe it—white bonding. Given the frequency with which it seemed to be happening, it became apparent that I would need to develop some kind of interruption strategy. Of course, coming to realize the importance of such a method is one thing, while actually developing it and putting it into practice is quite another.

One thing I've learned and am confident of, however, is that when it comes to practicing antiracist resistance, we should strive to make people think more, not less. Our resistance, to the extent this is possible, should be engaging, not enraging.

Take racist jokes, for instance. The simple truth, for most of us, is that our typical responses just don't cut it.

First, too often we don't respond at all, but rather let the joke or comment slide, which obviously isn't a very good strategy. But even when we do respond, it's doubtful the response has much effect. You know the response I'm talking about: the one where we offer up something like "I'm really offended that you just said that, and I'd appreciate it if you wouldn't say those kinds of things around me again."

Though such a reply lets everyone know where we stand, it is almost guaranteed to make the offending party defensive, and to reply the only way a person in that situation can, which is to make *you* the problem—the one without a sense of humor, the one who needs to "loosen up," or understand that "it's just a joke." Not to mention that telling someone not to engage in

racist commentary in front of you isn't the same as getting them to stop practicing racism, period. It's self-serving, really. It amounts to seeking protection
for one's own ears, rather than trying to truly challenge the offending individual, and move them to a different place.

A few years ago, I started trying something different: a response to racist
jokes that would make clear where I stood, but would also engage the joke-
teller in a process of critical thinking, reflection, and even dialogue.

One night a few years back, I was out with a group of people, all of them
white, including several students who had brought me in for a presentation
at their school. As the evening went along, a few others who knew some of
the students at the table (but who were unaware of the purpose for my visit)
joined us. At some point in the evening, and for reasons I have long since forgotten, conversation turned to race, and I braced myself, knowing that things
could turn very bad, very quickly.

One of the young men who had joined the group late asked if we wanted to
hear a joke, and then, without waiting for a response, he simply launched into it.
As expected, it was every bit as racist as I had feared it would be when he began.

When he was done, most everyone remained quiet or rolled their eyes. A
few people laughed nervously and a few others said something to the effect
that the joke had been terrible, and that he "really shouldn't tell jokes like
that." I, on the other hand, laughed as though it had been the funniest joke
I'd ever heard, because I needed to gain his confidence, his trust, for the set-
up that was to come. Although my laughter had clearly confused my hosts for
the evening—after all, they had just paid me to come and give an antiracism
talk, and here I was laughing at racism—I saw my opening, and took it.

"Hey I've got one. Wanna hear it?" I asked. Naturally, he did.

I continued: "Did you hear the one about the white guy who told this
really racist joke because he assumed everyone he was hanging out with was
also white?"

"No, I haven't heard that one," he replied, clearly not seeing where this
was headed, and apparently expecting a genuine punch line, all the while
missing the fact that he was it.

"Actually there is no joke," I explained. "That was just my way of telling
you that I'm black. My mom is black."

Telling a lie of this magnitude, I should point out, takes practice. So
much so that I had actually rehearsed it for weeks before getting to try it out.
But here was the moment, and I had pulled it off, looking right into his eyes
and making him actually believe that I was black. Indeed, I could be black.
There are lots of African Americans lighter than myself, or folks with one
black parent who may *look* white but who would certainly have been classi-
fied as black back in the day, and who identify themselves as such now.

His response was as immediate as it was revealing.

"Oh my God," he demurred. "I'm so sorry. I didn't know."

It was at that point that I fessed up. I wasn't really black, I noted, but as white as him. Now his look of embarrassment turned to one of confusion. After all, whites don't normally claim to be black when we're not. There just isn't much in it for us.

"I'm not black," I said, "but I find it interesting that when you thought I was, you apologized. In other words, you know that joke was messed up, so that if you'd been around a black person knowingly, you never would have said it. So why did you feel comfortable saying it in front of us? Why do you think so little of white people?"

Now he was really confused. It was one thing to have someone imply that he didn't much like black folks—which fact he no doubt already knew—but to be told that he must have some kind of negative bias against whites, against his own group? That was a new one.

"What do you mean?" he asked.

"Well," I explained, "You must think all whites are racists, and specifically, that we're all the kind of racists who enjoy racist jokes. Otherwise you wouldn't take a chance making that kind of comment around white folks you don't even know. So tell me, why do you think so little of white people?"

He stammered for a few seconds, but instead of getting angry, instead of telling me to get a sense of humor, he began to actually engage, and we proceeded to have a conversation about race. There is no way we'd have had that talk had I chastised him in the traditional manner. But by engaging him in a process, a reflective process that called into question how he knew what he knew—how he knew we were white, and how he knew we would all approve of racist jokes—I was able to stretch out the dialogue and ultimately contribute to making it more productive than it otherwise would have been.

For whites to resist racism this way sends a message to other whites: they can't take anything for granted. They can't presume to know our views; they can't be too sure that we'll accept their efforts at white bonding. Far from merely providing a feel-good moment, planting those seeds of doubt in other whites is an important step in the process of resistance, because racism, especially of an institutional nature, requires the collusion of many persons; the lone bigot can't accomplish it. By throwing racists off balance, we increase the costs associated with acting out, with putting their racism into practice. In the case of joke tellers, they can never be too sure that the next stranger they try that with isn't one of *those* whites—the *black* white people, or the kind of white person who won't appreciate the commentary—and as such may actually dial back their tendency to act in racist ways.

Just as antiracism takes practice, so does racism. So if we can inject enough self-consciousness and doubt into the minds of those who engage in racist behavior, we make it harder for such persons to practice it. And without practicing their racism, they may just stop utilizing it altogether.

* * *

LIKEWISE, IF WHITES creatively challenge racism in institutional settings, we can raise the cost to those who might be perpetrating the injustice. I began thinking about this several years ago, after witnessing a blatant act of racial profiling at a local shopping mall. After purchasing a pair of shoes and a few other items at Dillards—the anchor store at the time for the mall close to where I'd grown up—I sat down on a bench inside the complex, but just outside the store, to rearrange and consolidate my bags. While seated, I happened to notice two young black men enter the store together, and walk to the shoe department.

As I sat lacing up the shoes I had just bought, I suddenly became aware of the sound of someone running in my direction. I looked to my left and noticed the police officer sprinting towards the store. There had been no alarm, and there were no obvious signs of trouble. Immediately curious, I watched as the officer slowed, out of breath, and walked into the shoe department. He conferred with the salesman who had just sold me my new shoes, all the while looking nervously in the direction of the two young black men, who were barely visible to me from my vantage point outside the store.

The sales clerk pointed in the young men's direction, at which point it became obvious what was happening. Although they were doing nothing inappropriate and were dressed far nicer than I, the white clerk had let his suspicions get the better of him and called for law enforcement.

Wanting to make sure that I wasn't seeing things, I decided to conduct a little test, so I quickly gathered up my bags and went back into the store. Assuming by their behavior that the clerk and officer were expecting the two young men to shoplift, I decided to begin to act suspiciously in an attempt to draw attention to myself, and away from them. After all, if theft was what they were on the lookout for, and not just black people, surely a white guy acting like he was going to steal something should generate some concern.

So I began taking clothes off the racks, stuffing them under my arms, and looking around the store nervously, with a half-crazed expression. I began darting up and down behind racks of clothes, clearing my throat loudly, even walking precariously near the store's exit with several hundred dollars worth of stuff, as if to bolt—anything just to get some attention. But their eyes remained fixed on the young black men. When the two finally drifted a bit too far away from the shoe department, the officer began to follow them.

Having seen enough, I went up to the clerk, told him exactly what I'd witnessed, and demanded my money back for the shoes I'd just purchased. He denied any wrongdoing of course, but I persisted, telling him that I was offended *as a white person* that he would think it appropriate to treat law-abiding shoppers that way. Trying to encourage a little self-help, as one white man to another, I suggested that he was perpetuating the stereotype of white men, and that it would be to the benefit of all of us if he'd stop. With that, I left the store. Shortly thereafter, the black men left, too, having neither bought, nor, it should be noted, stolen anything.

Now of course, my solitary act that day probably made no difference whatsoever in the greater scheme of things. The clerk probably went home, told his wife about the crazy white guy who had accused him of racial profiling, and got on about his life, with never a second thought to changing his behavior.

But what if we made it a habit of doing this kind of thing collectively? What if we went out in teams—call it "freedom shopping" (I know, it's an oxymoron, but play along)—and then one after another called out the behavior when we saw it? What if a half dozen white folks and half-a-dozen persons of color went to the mall together, dressed similarly and with similar demeanors, and then shopped, paying close attention to whether or not some of the testers were treated with suspicion, or simply given worse customer service by clerks? On a good day, perhaps we wouldn't see anything untoward. Great, we could go home with some new socks, underwear, a blouse, or whatever we happened to pick up. But if things went down as they so often do, that's when the white testers, each and every one, would go up to a different clerk, report what they had witnessed, return the merchandise they had either bought already or were about to purchase, and proclaim loudly enough to be heard by other customers that they would never shop in the store again.

And what if we did this not only once—in which case the store could perhaps convince itself that the whole thing had been just a one-time stunt or a sting operation—but several times, with different white folks and folks of color as testers? What if we did it the first time on a Monday, then waited two weeks and came back on a Wednesday, then waited three days and came back on Saturday, then did it again the next week?

After a while, would the clerks be able to glibly go about the process of racial profiling, or offering differential service? Would they be able to take for granted any longer that people like themselves would play along? What would it do to their behavior to know that every time they even *think* about treating folks of color differently, and worse, that the lady sifting through nightgowns in the lingerie department might be ready to pounce, and accuse them of racism?

What it would do is raise the costs of that behavior for white people. And since most whites who engage in racist behavior do so more to go along with what they've been told to do, rather than as a result of hardcore bigotry of their own—especially when the behavior is institutional, or on behalf of a larger structure, like a store, or a school, or a police department—raising the cost can have a profound impact. The clerk at a department store, after all, has very little personal investment in seeing black shoppers profiled. He or she is likely responding either to a latent bias, about which no thought is even being given at the moment, or is following the orders or suggestions of superiors, who have conveyed the message that certain people are to be considered more suspicious than others. Either way, if the emotional tax of engaging in racism is made sufficiently substantial, at least some amongst us may decide the price is too high, and refuse to play altogether.

THE POWER OF QUESTIONS:
Engagement as Resistance

FOR RESISTANCE TO be engaging and not enraging, it's almost always best to start by asking questions. This is true whether the target of the question is a family member, a friend, a boss, a student in your classroom, or pretty much anyone, really. We know this is true with kids, for example. Child development experts are big on getting parents and teachers to use questions so as to elicit from children the kinds of self-reflection that leads to proper behavior. To wit, asking your child, "So, remind me again what you should be doing right now to get ready for school?" rather than just straight up telling them to "get in your room, brush your teeth, and get dressed!"

Interestingly, this technique, which often proves so effective with children, actually works with adults as well, though adults, quick to spot condescension, require a bit more sophisticated version. The logic, whether with kids or grown-ups is pretty simple: the truth a person comes to on their own (even if they had a little help being led there) is always more lasting than the truth you transmit to them directly. Folks like to think they've figured things out themselves.

Coming to realize this hasn't been easy. As an activist, I cut my teeth on telling people what I wanted to tell them, in their faces, and not always caring much about what they thought. While there is still a time and a place for that kind of thing, more often than not our acts of resistance are not large, epic demonstrations or protests, but things we do in smaller groups: at school, on the job, in a place of worship or a community setting. In those places, lectures rarely work, but dialogue just might.

The first time I started to notice this was in the mid-nineties, while working for Agenda for Children, an advocacy group in New Orleans. Among the projects on our plate at that time, we were trying to drum up grassroots opposition to the welfare-reform bill that had come before Congress. We suffered under no illusions that the existing public assistance programs were working—though they had worked pretty well for about a decade, before benefit levels began falling behind the rate of inflation, starting in the early seventies—but we knew that the bill, as proposed, would likely do little to solve the problem of poverty, and could actually make things far worse for millions of people.

In the midst of the debate in Congress, I was asked to come on a local radio show to discuss the legislation and to explain why, despite its popularity, the public should pressure the Louisiana delegation to oppose the bill when it came up for a vote.

I came armed to the teeth with facts and figures. Data, written on dozens of index cards, lay spread out on the desk in the studio, on the soundboard, wherever I could find space. I had every intention of making sure that no matter what questions came my way, be they from the host (who was friendly to our position) or the listeners (who I had every reason to believe would not be), I would be ready.

The host walked me through about ten minutes of softball questions, allowing me to provide every bit of possible information one could need to realize how awful this legislation was. Then the phones began to light up. Once she began to field the questions, it became obvious that no matter how good the data had been, no matter how tight my facts, listeners didn't much care. And although we hadn't discussed race directly during the introduction, it was pretty obvious who the white callers were thinking of, every time they blasted families who were receiving one or another form of government aid.

The questions (or comments really), had to do with things I had just finished addressing, as if they hadn't been heard at all. So first, there was the caller who insisted that everyone on welfare has extra babies, just to get more money from the government; this, despite the information I had provided not five minutes before, demonstrating that the typical family receiving assistance was the same size as the typical nonrecipient family, and that the extra amount received in assistance for each additional child was so minimal—a couple hundred dollars a month in cash and food stamps—that no one would have a child just to collect such a paltry sum.

The next caller insisted that something needed to be done to get families off of welfare, since most of them had been on the system for generations; this, despite the data I had just offered up, indicating that eight in ten women who received assistance as a child *never* receive any form of welfare as an adult, and that the typical length of stay for someone who goes on the dole is about two years, not ten, twenty, or whatever intergenerational number the caller seemed to have in mind.

Then there was the caller who said folks on welfare had no incentive to look for jobs, since they could make more money "sitting around on their lazy butts" than they could by getting out and earning it for themselves. Although I had previously noted the average amount received by families on assistance in Louisiana—a whopping $385 per month in cash and food stamps *combined*, which was hardly sufficient to provide an incentive for laziness—the caller was undeterred.

The host, surprised that no one seemed to be paying much attention to the facts, asked the caller if he had heard the information I had shared previously. And if so, she asked, what did he have to say in response to it?

"Well," the caller explained. "There's an old saying: Figures always lie, and liars always figure."

Click. The line went dead.

And that was it. Lesson learned. Facts are insufficient when the person with whom you seek to share those facts is so dug in as to have a real and persistent *need* to ignore them, to revert back to their preconceived notions about whatever subject you're discussing. And when the subject is race, or touches on race in some way (as poverty and welfare issues clearly do, given the stereotypes so commonly held about who receives assistance and who doesn't), let us be clear about at least one thing: white people are *dug in*. We are hunkered down, behind fortifications built up over decades and centuries to keep us from having to face the truth.

About two weeks later, I had the chance to go back on the program. As with the previous engagement, I still offered some facts and figures to make the case against the welfare reform bill. But this time, I decided to try a different approach with the callers, one that would engage, and hopefully allow them to come to the place I wanted them to be, without hitting them over the head with a bunch of footnotes, jargon, and academic analysis. It was a strategy suggested by several women of color with whom I had been discussing the issue, who were, all of them, residents of public housing. Despite having less formal education than me—and maybe *because* of that fact—they were infinitely wiser when it came to knowing what might have a chance of moving the public to a different place on the issue

About fifteen minutes into the show, I got my chance.

"Ya know what galls me?" the caller asked. "It's going to my office every day and passing a bunch of black guys out on the corner, just sittin' around, drinkin' or whatever, not working, and then expecting the government to take care of 'em! And meanwhile, there's plenty of work to be done, and not enough people to do it."

There was much I could have said here. I could have pointed out that adult men are almost never eligible for welfare benefits like AFDC, and usually don't receive food stamps either, unless they are part of a family unit in which the income is low enough to qualify. But in any event, such men are usually not the same as the ones you see on the corner with a brown bag of malt liquor in their hands, presumably—in the eyes of people like the caller—up to no good.

But rather than getting into that, which really wouldn't have addressed his larger views about black folks as shiftless and unwilling to work—and studies have found it is *this* racially-prejudicial view that is the primary determiner of whether someone wants to "get tough" on welfare recipients—I asked him a question instead.

"Let me ask you something," I interjected, trying not to let my frustration with what I perceived as his racism come through in my comments.

"What do you do?" I asked.

"I'm a contractor," he replied. "We do roofing, siding, light construction, that kind of stuff."

"Cool," I shot back. "Now, let me ask you something else. Are you hiring right now? Taking on new employees or contract laborers?"

No matter how he answered this question, there would be a larger point to be made at the end of the process. If he said yes, then I would ask him whether or not he would hire any of the guys he mentioned, were they to walk into his business and ask for a job. Given his view of them as lazy, the odds are good he'd say no, in which case he would have admitted that no matter their own initiative at this point, they wouldn't be likely to find work—at least not with him, and one presumes a lot of other folks who held the same views. But I didn't want him to say yes, actually. Trapping him in a logical inconsistency might be fun, but it wouldn't likely do much to keep him thinking about the issues. I really wasn't looking for the gotcha moment, so much as hoping to get him someplace very particular, where he might begin to see the larger systemic issues at play when it comes to poverty, unemployment, and the economy.

"No, not right now, but I was earlier in the year, and every day I'd drive by and see these guys out there, drinking and carryin' on, and not doing a lick of work," he replied.

"So what changed between earlier in the year and now, which caused you to stop bringing new people on?" I asked, thinking that I might already know, but wanting him to say it.

"Well, I got a bit stretched financially ya know, borrowed all I could afford to expand the business, and had to slow down a bit," he explained.

What he hadn't said, but what I wanted to discuss with him, was *why* he had hit the borrowing limit. Why wasn't he able to afford to borrow any more?

Because the reasons were as clear as the headlines in the news: on seven different occasions in the previous year, the Federal Reserve Board, which controls the nation's credit and money supply, had raised interest rates on borrowers. After a while, they raised them just enough to make it tough if not impossible for lots of employers to keep hiring new people, because they either couldn't expand their operations or were going to have to pay so much more to borrow that they wouldn't be able to make additional payroll as a result. Either way, decisions made by a small group of economic elites (all but a few of which, historically, have been white), had made it so that the caller couldn't hire anyone, white, black, or otherwise, no matter how hard such folks might be looking for a job, and no matter what kind of workers they might be.

So I mentioned this, and asked him what it meant for folks on welfare, if people like himself couldn't even hire right now because of the interest rate hikes? If he can't hire, they can't work, and if they can't work, what are they supposed to do? In other words, what he was telling me—not what I was telling him but what he was telling *me* about the economy, and about unemployment—was making the case *against* punitive welfare reform. If people are out of work, in large part because of a monetary policy that requires a hiring slowdown (because, in the eyes of the Fed, too little unemployment might cause wages to rise, God forbid, and that would spark inflation), then poverty is no accident, and it's not due to laziness. It is the result of a deliberate policy.

I could tell by the sound of his voice after this exchange, that although he hadn't completely changed his views, his resistance to hearing a side other than his own had been lowered considerably. The only possible explanation for this development was that he himself had offered the answer that, if followed to its logical conclusion, breaks the back of his entire position. He wasn't ready to follow it all the way that night, nor had I expected him to do so. But he had moved a bit. And that's the first step in resistance: getting those who appear to be your adversaries to doubt themselves, to wonder, even if only for a second, whether they really know the world as well as they claim to. Questions will almost always get them to that point of doubt more quickly than answers.

* * *

SOMETIMES, IT'S BETTER to offer a little of both. Questions alone can be too passive perhaps, just as didactic and self-assured answers can be off-putting. But when the two combine, the results can be quite impressive.

If you've never seen the film *The Color of Fear*, you really should seek it out and watch it. A powerful documentary released in the mid-nineties, it features a group of eight men—two white, two African American, two Asian American, two Latino—and a Chinese American filmmaker, as they discuss race, and the way in which race has shaped their lives and their understanding of the world.

Filmed over a weekend, the distillation of material into roughly an hour or so couldn't have been easy. The honesty and candor with which the men spoke was refreshing, even when frustrating—even when maddeningly so—and really is a model for how these kinds of conversations should, but rarely ever, go.

One of the white men in the film, David Christensen, seems right out of central casting: a nice guy for sure, but one who has bought hook, line, and sinker, into the mythology of America. When the men of color discuss their feelings of marginalization as a result of racism, he clearly doesn't get it, and offers up platitudes about how "everyone stands on their own two feet," and how anyone can make it if they try, and how he feels that people of color often block their own progress by not taking advantage of all the opportunities available to them.

After several minutes of this agonizing display of white denial (hours really, while the filming was going on), one of the black men, Victor Lewis, whom I am honored to call a friend, lets it be known that he has had quite enough. Watching the film, the viewer could sense for a while that the tension was building up, not only in Victor, but in all the men of color. Vic's jaw tightened, his eyes rolled, his pupils seemed to dilate, and then, boom!

What follows is possibly the most poignant forty seconds or so of documentary film footage I have ever witnessed. It is also, for a lot of whites who watch the film, scary as hell. As Victor goes off—and make no mistake he goes *off*—whites in every audience seem to tense up, recoil, even lean back in their chairs, as if they think Vic might be coming out from behind the screen to snatch 'em up any second. As if David, and by extension, they, are in danger.

Victor schools David in a way that I won't even try to recapture here, by printing the dialogue. Honestly, the words on a page don't do justice to how righteous the scene really is. You have to see it. It is truth made flesh.

But what is important for our purposes here is what happens afterward. You can tell that the rhetorical blows dealt to him by Victor (and the other men of color, though perhaps without the same level of intensity) have weakened David. He's like the boxer who has just been hit with a solid right hook, dazed, but not yet down—staggering, but not quite ready to fall. Truth, raw, visceral, and unwavering, can do that.

It is at this point, or very shortly afterward, that the filmmaker, Lee Mun Wah, turns to David, and with skill, compassion, and very deliberate purpose, delivers the knockout punch, the follow-up to Victor's hook. It is a rhetorical uppercut, delivered so softly you don't even see what it's done to David until he is forced to respond, at which point you get to witness something rather amazing.

Mun Wah asks David, very simply, what it is that is keeping him from believing that what Victor says happens to him, as a black man, is really happening to him.

When David replies that he just doesn't "want to believe" that Victor's life is that difficult, Mun Wah punches again:

"So what would it mean David, then, if the life really was that harsh? What would it mean in your life, if it really were that harsh?"

To this, David responds, as his eyes literally begin to well with tears, that it would be "a travesty of life. You have here something that shouldn't exist."

And Mun Wah, lastly:

"And so what if it does? What if the world was not as you thought, that it is actually happening to lots of human beings on this earth? What if it actually were, and you didn't know about it? What would that mean to you?"

Understand the brilliance of these questions. The fact is, and Mun Wah well knows it, that those things *are* happening to the men of color in the room, including himself. They are real, and not the figments of overactive imaginations. But if he merely says that, if he merely snatches David up by the lapels, figuratively speaking, and demands that David wake up, there is little doubt that he will remain quite blissfully asleep. It is only because the comment is rephrased as a question, to which any rational human being would almost instantly realize there was only one conceivable answer, that David is stopped in his tracks.

And David says:

"Oh, that's very saddening. You don't want to believe that man can be so cruel to, to, himself and his own kind."

But you know in that moment that he *does* believe it now, that he knows it. And he knows it because he has come to that place, led there by the one-two punch of hard truths stated without apology or compromise, and a compassionate query, intended to bring him the rest of the way.

Victor knows it, too, for at this point he drops his hands from his face, his facial expression noticeably loosens, and he notes, speaking to David, "From here I can work with you."

For those who've seen the movie, but don't know the back-story, you might be interested to know that the experience had a profound effect on David

Christensen. His views have matured, his wisdom has deepened, and his willingness to hear the truth about racism has probably far surpassed most white men of his age. He has since gone on to challenge other whites when he witnesses their racism, and he makes a point to consciously treat people equitably (which is important since too often, people, thinking themselves good, rest on their goodness and see no need to consciously make the effort). And he credits all of that to the experiences he had during the filming of *The Color of Fear.*

There is a lesson in that for all of us.

UNCOVERING TRUTH IN EVERYDAY PLACES:
Raising Antiracist Children

FIGURING OUT HOW to resist racism requires that we first figure out how to notice it, even when it isn't obvious. It also helps to begin this process early on. As with anything, unless we exercise our brains and train them to spot certain things, and to analyze and think critically about what we see, the odds are good we'll miss a lot more than we catch.

Although it used to be believed that kids didn't see color, and although many I meet still believe that children are too young to think about or deal with issues of race and racism, all the available evidence seems to suggest that such beliefs are wrong. Sure, there are age-appropriate ways to introduce certain concepts to kids, but it is never too young to start the process. Research has shown that as early as preschool, children have begun to pick up cues about race and gender from popular culture, from parents and from peers, such that they begin to form hierarchies on the basis of those identities.

Unfortunately, most white parents haven't given much thought to how they might raise antiracist children. Parents of color typically know that they have to prepare their children for the possibility of racist rejection and mistreatment, even if they aren't always sure how to do this effectively. But white parents are usually ill-prepared to instill antiracist principles in their kids, even when they know it's important to do so. Beyond basic things, like teaching your children not to make judgments on the basis of skin color, or perhaps making sure your children have a mixed group of friends and associates, what else can we do?

One thing I've learned since becoming a parent is that talking about the "right way" to raise antiracist children is always easier when you don't have any. What I mean by this is that figuring out what to do with other people's kids is far less complicated than it is with our own. The first few years as a parent don't really make this clear to you. It takes a while.

For me, it took until the first time I watched a Disney film with the eyes of a parent. Suddenly, race, class, and gender all became frighteningly relevant. Even though it was obviously too early to really sit down and talk to my oldest daughter about what we were seeing from an antiracist perspective (I mean, she was all of two), it certainly wasn't too soon to think about what would need to be said to her as she got a little older.

And please, if you're one of those parents who's smirking right now, because, being appropriately liberal you refuse to allow your kid to watch Disney films, or TV, or partake in popular culture because it's "too commercial," or whatever, check in with me ten years from now, when your kid is the one who can't fashion an intelligible critique of mass media, precisely because you never allowed them to be exposed to it. In other words, sheltering your kids, whether for reasons of right-wing, faux-Christian morality, or left-wing, granola-crunchy purity, does nothing to create thinking and analytical human beings, let alone one capable of engaging the vital issues of the day. As someone who grew up playing Superman, even (God forbid) Lone Ranger, and nonetheless turned out militantly opposed to the notion of either one, let it suffice to say that one can raise progressive children, even if those children are exposed to all kinds of reactionary nonsense growing up, which, if they live for long in the United States, they will be. But it does take work.

As for Disney, it had been years since I had seen the films our oldest daughter was watching, among them the big three: *Cinderella, Sleeping Beauty,* and (ugh) *Snow White.* The formula is clear: white girl is in trouble; white girl falls asleep, or has an evil stepmother trying to do her in; and then, white girl gets saved by a tall, handsome, dark (but not *that* dark) white man.

What's the message here? Pretty simple: a) purity is white, and blonde (or in Snow's case, brunette, but they make up for it with whiter than eggshell skin); b) women are in need of male saviors, and c) princesses are good and royalty is good, never mind all the really evil things they had to do in order to procure all that wealth.

And now we also have Ariel, in *The Little Mermaid,* who falls in love with Prince Eric, who looks a lot like Prince Philip before him. And then there's Belle, from *Beauty and the Beast.* Although Belle can be read as a feminist character who refuses to be defined by male norms of either beauty or womanhood (she wears plain clothes and likes to read, as opposed to the other women of the village who swoon over Gaston, the bully hunter), and although the underlying message of Disney's *Beauty* is progressive—that it is wrong to judge people on the basis of appearance, whether it's the prince judging the old lady who gives him the rose, or the villagers judging Belle or her father, or Belle judging the Beast—it is frankly up to parents to make sure that those kinds of things come through for kids. The film alone, watched without a discussion afterward, likely won't do it.

But after I took our oldest to see the Broadway production of *Beauty* for her fourth birthday—and I should note, the social commentary about judgment came through much more clearly in the stage play than the animation—we were able to discuss the themes quite deeply: as deeply as a four year old is likely to get. She understood the message with just a little prompting.

Sometimes, Disney even makes our jobs easy, though likely without intending to do so. Take the Disney film *Pocahontas,* for example.

According to Disney, Pocahontas, whose real name was Matoaka, was a deeply-in-tune-with-nature young woman, who helped white people like Captain John Smith get closer to the earth. In reality, Matoaka was a teenager who was ultimately kidnapped by whites, forcibly converted to Christianity, and made into a virtual concubine for John Rolfe, who, as mentioned earlier, is the man responsible for bringing export tobacco to the Americas. After Rolfe whisks her away to England, her people are, within a short time, virtually wiped off the map, having received no assistance from the talking tree with the face like an old lady, who was apparently Pocahontas's friend and confidant.

As bad as the film may be, I urge you to buy it anyway. And when your kids are old enough to understand, I want you to play the bonus material on the DVD. Play the part where the chief illustrator jokes with a room full of corporate mouseketeers about how he altered his protagonist's appearance, to make her prettier. Note how he expresses his smarmy distaste for the real Pocahontas, who, needless to say, hardly resembled the version you see on the screen: the Europeanized or at least "Asianized" (in that formulaic, geisha kind of way) Indian, who despite her darker skin and somewhat elongated face, more or less appeals to European standards of beauty, and so remains acceptable to a mostly white viewing audience. And of course, she shows a lot of leg.

It is a stunning lesson in the way white supremacy works. And discussing it with a young person can allow all kinds of questions to come up: Why did the creators of the film feel the need, and feel as though they had the authority, to alter Pocahontas's looks and even her story so dramatically? What might have been the response to the film had it been more true to history, or to an accurate rendering of Matoaka's face? Would such a film, even if it took a few liberties for entertainment purposes (which are to be expected and perfectly understandable), have even been made? And if not, why not?

No, these questions aren't the kind you could likely put to a first grader. But when a child gets older and is beginning to notice certain things, films like this, which they may have watched with one set of eyes originally, can be revisited. You can even make it like a game, like uncovering a mystery—looking for all the things in the film that don't seem right, or which make the truth seem more palatable. It can become like a giant real-life version of "I

Spy," in which the child is encouraged to pick out lies, half-truths, and distortions. It can be educational and informative, even as it remains fun.

For teenagers, the process of discovery can be even more elaborate, because their ability to conduct research will have developed well beyond the capacity that existed for them as kids. Have them observe the way that gas costs more in poor black neighborhoods than in rich white ones. Go to groceries in white neighborhoods and then communities of color, and have them compare the quality of the merchandise, especially the fresh produce. Have them watch the news for two weeks and keep a journal of the differential ways in which whites and folks of color are portrayed. Drive around a white neighborhood, even one that is only middle class, and then drive through a mostly black or brown community, taking notes as to how many banks and ATM machines you see in the former, and how many pawn shops or check-cashing outlets you see in the latter. Ask why your child thinks there might be a difference.

Go shopping. Try on clothes. See how easy that normally is for whites—we aren't going to be followed around the store like potential shoplifters or looked at nearly as strangely as we head to the dressing room with a mountain of clothes on our arm—and then have a friend of color try the same thing. See how often it differs. And when it does, stand up, return merchandise, and demand to speak to the manager. Teach resistance by example.

Among the examples we could set:

- Refuse to accept jobs that come your way thanks to personal connections, unless those same connections are also open to persons of color.
- Refuse to use your alumni status at a school in order to get your kid into college, if you're white.
- Refuse to shop at institutions with a pattern or history of discrimination.
- Refer to white people with a racial designation when discussing them (just as we so often do with people of color) so as to stop normalizing whites as synonymous with human beings, people, or Americans.
- Refuse to attend a religious institution that insists on representing Jesus and/or God as white, or if you do attend such an institution, challenge the imagery.
- Spread the word to folks of color you know, on those occasions when you learn of job openings, and give them any inside knowledge you may have about the things the employer might be looking for in a candidate.

- Whenever someone slams affirmative action, speak up and talk honestly about the unearned advantages and "preferences" you've received as a white person over the years.

- If you move into a community with a large number of people of color (as with whites who are gentrifying several urban communities around the nation, thereby pushing up prices, property taxes, and often crowding out folks of color who have lived there for generations), find out who the grassroots leadership is, and subordinate your own agenda to theirs. Become part of the community and follow *its* lead, rather than coming in, imposing your own notions of what makes space "livable," and pushing harder for a coffee shop than an end to police brutality, failing schools, or a lack of jobs.

- Be radically color-conscious, by holding up every policy, practice or procedure at your place of employment or your school, and interrogating those policies, practices, and procedures, to see if they may be inadvertently perpetuating inequality on the basis of race.

- In schools, develop alternative admissions criteria that examine merit in the context of the opportunity structure, rather than as some abstract principle. After all, if two runners were competing in a five-lap race, and one runner started out three laps ahead of the other, we would expect the one with the head start to cross the finish line first. But so what? Should that runner be rewarded for having had an unfair advantage? Or should we consider how well the second runner performed, relative to where they started? In colleges, and for that matter selective private and independent K–12 institutions, merit should be completely redefined to take these kinds of considerations into account, with regard to test scores, for example, both for the purpose of fairness, but also for the purpose of a more accurate evaluation of an applicant's abilities.

The possibilities are as endless as our imaginations. But if the issue is important enough to us, we'll be willing to brainstorm, to lose sleep, and to never be satisfied that we've found the ultimate answer.

RESISTANCE REQUIRES ACCOUNTABILITY

IT ISN'T ENOUGH, however, for resistance to be creative and engaging. As important as those elements are, there is one more component of effective resistance that is crucial, but often overlooked: namely, accountability. This means that whites engaged in antiracist resistance need to be accountable for our actions, and especially accountable to the persons of color for whom the effects of racism are so great.

Although whites too often ignore the problem of racism, the opposite reaction—becoming indignant about it—can be equally problematic. Indignation can lead a person to react impulsively, without significant reflection as to what one is doing, or how they're doing it, and especially how those actions might affect people of color.

If folks of color ultimately pay the price for racism, we as whites have to think carefully about how we respond to the problem. If our actions make things worse, cause an even worse backlash against black and brown folks, or simply reinforce the marginalization of their voices, then we are collaborating with racism (more on this in the next chapter) rather than truly resisting it.

While the search for accountability should never be an excuse for paralysis and inaction—if anything it should serve as a template for praxis and constructive activism—it is a vital component of long-term resistance.

So what does accountability mean? What does it look like and how do we make sure we're taking it seriously? Though there is no single way to conceptualize the concept of antiracist accountability, there are a few principles that seem to be basic—necessary if not entirely sufficient to meeting the goal.

First, for whites to be accountable to folks of color, we need to listen more than talk and follow more than lead. This means relinquishing some of the power we receive when we begin to speak out against racism—power that we only receive because of our skin color.

To follow rather than lead doesn't mean that whites should never assume a leadership position, but that we have to be mindful of the ways in which our leadership can complicate things. When black activists in the Student Nonviolent Coordinating Committee (SNCC) voted to expel whites in 1967, they gave those whites the marching orders to go and work in the white community, to challenge whites as only they could. That was a form of leadership that whites were being asked to assume, but one that wouldn't impinge on the ability of persons of color to formulate strategies for the larger struggle and movement. Accountability, for whites who had been active in SNCC, meant following the lead of black and brown folks, going back home, so to speak, and applying what they had learned. Many were ill-prepared to take on this role. Others did so willingly and to great effect. But in either case, if we are serious about accountability, listening to and following even directives with which we might not instantly agree, it is part of the burden to be borne.

Accountability means, for whites, that we can't be setting the agenda for folks of color. It is not our role to say what the main issues are in communities of color, and to direct funding to those initiatives that we identify as the most important. To be accountable means prioritizing what those most impacted by racism say should be prioritized.

Learning this one was tough for me. I remember the first time I sat down and discussed community organizing with an activist in New Orleans, who worked for a grassroots group with a long history in the area. I asked him what the group was working on, only to learn that far from the "big issues" that I assumed would be at the forefront of the agenda, like police brutality, inadequate housing and jobs, health care, or unemployment, the community was focusing its efforts on getting a traffic light at one of the intersections in the neighborhood, where several kids had been struck by cars on their bikes, or crossing the street on foot.

I remember thinking that although a light would be nice, surely they had bigger fish to fry, so to speak. "Why a light?" I asked, with more than a little bit of foolish arrogance.

"Simple," the organizer responded. "We all know that getting that light won't change the world. But people who have been getting their asses kicked for years need to know that they can make a difference. They need to know that they *can* fight, and that occasionally they *can* win. If we went in there and told everybody that the goal of the campaign was to end institutional racism or economic inequality, everyone would be with us, but their enthusiasm wouldn't last long. They'd burn out, because let's face it, those goals, if we can get them to come at all, definitely aren't comin' any time soon. So you have to set small goals, attainable goals, that can give the community a sense of its own power, its own potential. That's what a good organizer does."

So accountability means prioritizing the agendas and concerns of people of color, even if you might think there are more important items on which we could be working.

It also means being prepared to do the unglamorous work, so as to empower folks of color to lead the charge.

A few years back, I met several antiracist white allies in Seattle who were trying really hard to get this part right. They had developed, over time, enough of a relationship with local activists of color so as to allow them to ask the folks of color how they could assist in furthering the work. This isn't always easy to do, because frankly folks of color get tired, exhausted even, by whites asking, "How can we help?" Not because allyship isn't valued, but because the question reeks of helplessness, and essentially asks black and brown folks to do all the thinking.

But because the relationship had been maturing over time, the white activists felt as though they could ask the question, and the folks of color were more than prepared to answer it. Their answer was simple: they didn't want the white folks to come to the next meeting where strategies would be discussed for ongoing antiracism work. They didn't want them to be in on those deliberations at all, in fact. What they *did* need, however, was for the white folks to provide child care for them, so *they* (the folks of color) would be able to make the meeting, and so that *they* could plan things themselves.

Although the request might have seemed strange at first, and it certainly wasn't asking the whites to work in a lead role, but rather as support, it didn't take long for the white would-be allies to recognize the importance of fulfilling the obligation. By freeing up the folks of color to do the planning and strategizing, and by facilitating their leadership by virtue of taking a huge obligation off of their shoulders, the white activists had acted in true ally fashion.

You can probably think of other examples where whites could provide support services, thereby making it easier for persons of color to lead. Whether it's child care, cooking the food for a meeting or gathering, making the phone calls to get people out, or something else that is frankly pretty unglamorous, but vital, whites can make a contribution and be accountable at the same time.

Accountability, of course, also means being open to criticism. More than that, it requires the creation whenever possible of a feedback loop, so as to make that criticism both more likely, and more helpful in the long run.

* * *

FOR PEOPLE IN different professions, this feedback loop may manifest quite differently. For teachers, social workers, or community organizers and activists, it may take one kind of shape, while for businesspersons, police, and bankers it may take another. For artists, writers (like myself), or entertainers, still other forms may emerge.

In my case, I try to make sure that my essays are accessible to instant feedback. I send them around to a list of about five hundred people, made up of folks of color and other white allies, in all kinds of professions and walks of life. I seek out feedback, even criticism, and when criticism is received (as it often is), I almost always make the changes necessary to reflect the insight offered to me. Sometimes I get criticism that the wording I've used is either too passive, or that I've used imagery that is inadvertently racist or sexist. I take those criticisms very seriously, usually find that the criticism is dead on, and correct the flaws.

Accountability also means being prepared to remove yourself from a setting, if and when your presence might be disruptive.

When I was a senior in college, I really wanted to take a class on feminist theory offered by the women's studies department at Tulane. I signed up for the class and was looking forward to the opportunity to learn more about the subject. Though I had long considered myself a feminist, I, like most twenty-one-year-old men, hadn't given much thought to what it really meant to think and view the world through a feminist frame.

Once the department received the list of students who were signed up for the class, I got a phone call from the professor who would be teaching it. She wanted to speak to me, and asked that I come over right away, before the end of the week, when the first meeting of the class would take place.

I went to her office, where I was asked, very kindly and graciously, not to take the class. At first I was hurt. Here I was, a feminist (at least in my own mind), wanting to take a class on feminism. Why shouldn't I take it? The professor explained, and her answer, though she hadn't used the term accountability, had been all about that.

"Tim," she said, "listen. You're the only man signed up for the class. You're a well-known activist on campus. Several of the women in the class are friends of yours, in fact. I can tell you, from all the research that's ever been done on this subject, and from my own personal experience, and from knowing you, and respecting your insight, that you will totally torpedo this class if you take it."

She continued: "You will talk, and not just a little, but a lot. And although you wouldn't mean to do it, you will talk over the women. And while many of them will push pack on you for doing it, others won't, I'm afraid. Some will defer to you, because that's what women in this culture are taught to do to strong-willed men, and *especially* when those men appear to be liberal and caring, and even feminist. I can't force you to drop the class, but for the sake of the values that I know you hold, would you please do it anyway?"

It wasn't easy to say yes. White men are not used to ever voluntarily removing ourselves from anywhere that we really want to be. But she was right, and I knew it. Women are the ones impacted by sexism. In this instance, they are the ones to whom my accountability was owed. But in order to be fully accountable, I still needed to ingest the material they'd be reading, so I asked the professor for the syllabus, which she gladly provided. I proceeded to buy the books at the bookstore anyway, and although I didn't read them in the timeline required by the class, I ultimately read them all. I needed the wisdom therein, far, far more than anyone in that classroom needed mine.

A few years ago, this concept of voluntarily removing oneself from a space, as a method of accountability, came up again. And this time, the subject was race.

I was speaking at Connecticut College, where there had been some recent conflict between students of color and LGBT students on the one hand, and their white and straight allies, on the other.

For years, they had all been working together and hanging out at a place called Unity House. Unity House had been the site where the group's members would organize, socialize, and plan strategies for educational campaigns and various forms of activism. It had been around since a major student move-ment in the 1980s had won the space as a concession from the administration, and was used by members of targeted groups and those from dominant groups who were fully allied with the movement for social justice.

By the time I arrived on campus, though (and at which point long-time antiracist legend Mab Segrest had just come on board as full-time faculty), things were beginning to turn a bit sour. The students of color and the LGBT students had requested their white and straight allies to leave Unity House. Ultimately, they were asking for Unity House to be theirs and theirs alone. They still loved and respected their allies, and were willing to work with them on shared projects. But they insisted that they needed some space where they could just chill, and frankly get away from those who—allies or not—couldn't really relate to their experiences.

Needless to say, the allies were hurt. They felt that the students of color and LGBT students were being separatist, that they were turning their backs on them, that they were saying allyship no longer mattered, and all manner of other things. The students asking for Unity House responded that the pressures of attending the college were so great, and their feelings of margin-alization were so strong, that if their allies couldn't or wouldn't go along with the request, several of the students of color and LGBT students might liter-ally leave college. They needed some space to themselves in order to continue as students.

It was painful to watch the back and forth. Mab and I were asked to come in and help facilitate a discussion with several dozen students, from both sides of the equation, and nothing about it was easy. But it was produc-tive. We talked about accountability. Mab offered her own house as a place for the ally students to come and chill, if they needed a place to talk—after all, she noted, they too needed to get together and discuss their goals and hopes for the work; *they too* needed an affinity group—and I mentioned all the examples I could think of (and there are several) where a refusal to do some intragroup work and to work on oneself without the presence of the "other" had really set back the cause of social justice.

At the end of the evening, we had attained no consensus. But I did go away, with the feeling that the ally students had been exposed to an impor-tant discussion about accountability, which, even if it didn't "take" right then and there, would likely follow them throughout their lives. And their activism would be the better for it.

Finally, accountability isn't something that whites who choose to fight racism owe only to people or color. We also need to strive for accountability with other whites, too. If it is whites we seek to change, we have to work to be compassionate and committed to our white brothers and sisters, just as with folks of color. We need to remember that we're not doing this work *for* people of color. We're doing it *with* them, hopefully, but ultimately as whites, we're doing it for us as much as anything. If this sounds strange, just stick with it for a second.

When I first went out on the lecture circuit, the very first place I visited was Northeastern Illinois University, in Chicago. I had been brought in by a sociology professor there to speak to a few classes in the department and, despite having a terrible case of the flu and a raging fever, I did the best I could.

After one of my talks, a young white woman in the front row raised her hand somewhat tentatively and asked me how I was received doing this work, as a white man, by black people specifically. I asked her why she was curious about this, trying to figure out the real substance behind her question, and she was only too happy to fill in the blanks.

"Well," she said, "I really agree with you, and would love to do the kind of work you do, but I'm afraid black people won't trust me, won't accept my contribution, and so I'm just wondering how you think blacks feel about you. Do you think they actually like you, or that they still don't really trust you?"

Although I was new to nationwide lecturing, I had been doing antiracism work at that point for several years, much of it in black communities, so I explained that based on my experience, I had never personally felt any hatred or resentment on the part of black folks. Of course there is going to be some mistrust up front, I noted, and in fact, I'd be worried about any person of color who *didn't* look at whites who choose to fight racism a bit suspiciously. They've been burned too many times to take it for granted that we're serious and in it for the long haul.

It was at this moment that I noticed a young black woman in the back row, who had her hand up and wanted desperately to talk. I had observed her facial expressions all throughout my speech, and could read her body language well enough to know that she simply wasn't buying anything I was selling. Thinking this might make for an interesting interaction, given the white woman's fears and concerns—not to mention that she wanted to be called on, so it was pretty much her turn—I pointed to her and asked her for her input. Her response was classic, and perfect for the situation.

"Make NO mistake," she insisted, "We do hate you and we don't trust you, not for one minute!"

I thought the white woman in the front was going to literally come unglued, as she began to palpitate and sweat, and bury her head in her hands, as if this only confirmed her worst fears.

"Well, I'm sorry to hear that," I said to the black woman who had issued the comment, "since after all, you don't know me. But that's fine, because I'm sure you haven't got much reason to trust me, and anyway, ultimately I'm not doing this for you.

"I mean no disrespect by saying that," I explained. "It's just that I don't view it as my job to fight racism so as to save you from it. That would be paternalistic and would imply that you aren't—or that black folks generally aren't—capable of liberating yourselves from white supremacy. I think you are, though it might be a bit easier with some internal resistance from whites like myself. But that's neither here nor there. I fight racism because racism is an evil to which I'd rather not contribute. It is a sickness in *my* community, and I'm trying to save myself from it."

It was at that point that I looked at the white woman and explained to her that if she wanted to do this work for black people, then of course they wouldn't trust her. White missionaries have rarely brought things of lasting value to peoples of color, after all. If, on the other hand, she wanted to do it because it was the right thing to do, and because she no longer wanted to collaborate with it by way of her silence, then what the woman in the back thought of her sincerity shouldn't matter. And anyway, if she really did the work and proved herself, black and brown folks—including the black woman who had made her so nervous that day—would likely recognize her seriousness and work with her gladly. Or not. But either way, why should it matter?

What whites must understand is that people of color owe us *nothing*. They don't owe us gratitude when we speak out against racism. They don't owe us a pat on the back. And if all they do is respond to our efforts with a terse "about time," then that's too bad. Get over it. Challenging racism and white supremacy is what we *should* be doing. Resistance is what we need to do for us. Although people of color have often thanked me for the work I do, and I always accept the thanks with as much grace as I can muster, it is a thanks that I am not owed, and whenever it's offered I make sure to repay the compliment. Accountability demands it.

While much discussion has been had recently about whether or not America should apologize for slavery—and I happen to think apologies are pretty empty absent substantive reparations and recompense—I think that perhaps before we focus so much on apologies, we could simply say thank you to people of color for pointing the way when it comes to resistance. We could say thank you for *refusing to die*. People of color owe us nothing, but we owe them at least that much, and a whole lot more.

COLLABORATION

"Indignation and goodwill are not enough to make the world better. Clarity is needed, as well as charity, however difficult this may be to imagine, much less sustain, toward the other side. Perhaps the worst thing that can be said about social indignation is that it so frequently leads to the death of personal humility. Once that has happened, one has ceased to live in that world of men which one is striving so mightily to make over. One has entered into a dialogue with that terrifying deity, sometimes called History, previously, and perhaps again, to be referred to as God, to which no sacrifice in human suffering is too great."

JAMES BALDWIN, "THE CRUSADE OF INDIGNATION,"
The Nation, July 7, 1956

IT WOULD BE much easier if one could forever and always remain on the side of the angels, but alas, it is not to be. Our world is far too complicated, and the opportunities for collaboration far too extensive, to allow for perfect—or even fairly consistent—resistance by any of us. This is all the more true for those who reap so many benefits from our status as members of dominant groups: whites, men, persons with money, or able-bodied heterosexual Christians.

It's important to be upfront about this, to own one's collaboration; this is so, not because one should labor to feel guilty about it—again, collaboration is inevitable in a social order such as this one on more occasions than not, and one can hardly be wracked with guilt for doing what is inevitable—but merely because doing so allows one to relinquish the guilt that our culture otherwise encourages and even promotes as a healthy alternative to committed action.

What I'm trying to say is that by owning our collaboration we can see our shortcomings, place them within the larger context of our culture's subsidizing of those shortcomings, and then commit ourselves to doing better next time. The most dangerous person is the one who refuses to admit that he contributes to injustice at least as often as, if not more than, he truly rebels against it. Such a person is capable of learning nothing, because he honestly perceives himself to be in such control of his beliefs and actions, that there is simply nothing anyone else can teach him, nothing on which he needs to work, and no point at which he too is part of the problem, at least sometimes.

Race and its role in our national life is so deeply entrenched that it is virtually impossible to avoid collaborating with the oppression of persons of color on occasion. Even the most liberal-minded and antiracist white person will have an extraordinarily tough time avoiding the process. In that regard, our innocence is something we almost automatically relinquish the minute we are born white in this land. We will not be innocent, but will instead be implicated in the suffering of others, merely because our skin demarcates us and signifies that we will be viewed (and treated) as superior. Under a system of institutionalized white supremacy, there are no "good whites" and "bad whites," in other words—there are merely whites and everyone else.

For example, even the parts of my family that didn't own slaves collaborated with the institution of slavery. This was true for most any family in the South, in fact. State authorities made sure of that, by passing laws that enlisted the lower-income and middling whites in the service of white supremacy. In 1753, Tennessee passed its Patrol Act, which required whites to search slave quarters four times each year for guns or other contraband. By the turn of the century, and at which time large parts of my own family had made the trek to the state, these searches had been made into monthly affairs. And by 1806, most all white men were serving on regular slave patrols, for which service they were paid a dollar per shift, and five dollars as a bonus for each runaway slave they managed to catch.

Throughout the period of my family's settling in middle Tennessee, laws required that *all whites*, without exception, check the passes of slaves they encountered to make sure they weren't runaways. Any white refusing to go along faced severe punishment. With no record of such racial apostasy having made it into our family lore—and surely such an example of brazen defiance would have been hard to keep quiet had it occurred—it seems safe to say that the McLeans, the Dean/Deanes, the Neelys and the Carters all went along, regardless of their direct financial stake in the maintenance of the chattel system.

Likewise, although whites were members of an impressive twenty-seven antislavery societies in Tennessee by 1827—so much, once again, for the old "all whites back then supported slavery" excuse—there is nothing to suggest that any of my family actively belonged to one. Nor is there anything to indicate that my kin objected to the uprooting of the Cherokee in the 1830s, even though many whites in the eastern part of the state did. And when Tennessee's free blacks were stripped of the right to vote in 1834, or when the first Jim Crow laws were passed, also in Tennessee, in 1881, there is once again nothing in our family history that would portend an objection of any kind. Tellingly, in reading over reams of family documents, handed-down stories, homilies, and tales of all kinds, it is nothing if not jarring to note that race is almost completely absent from their discussions at all. It simply never came up. Which is to say that for so many, white supremacy was so taken for granted as to be hardly worth a fleeting moment of consideration, let alone the raising of one's voice in objection.

Race was the backdrop for nearly everything that happened in this country in those days, and yet, it is as if the families from which I descend weren't even awake, such that they might notice the gathering storms. You can read their accounts of the time, and never know that you were reading about families in the United States: families living in a society of institutionalized racial terrorism, where there were lynchings of black men taking place monthly, where the bodies of these men would be not merely hung from trees but also mutilated, burned with blowtorches, the ears and fingers lopped off to be sold as souvenirs.

That was the way this country was when my family (and many of yours) were coming up. And most of them did nothing. Most of them said nothing. They knew exactly what was going on—lynchings were advertised openly in newspapers, as if they were no more unusual than the county fair—and yet the white voices raised in opposition to such festivals of gore, such orgiastic violence, were so rare as to be drowned out by those whose thirst for blood all but turned them into modern-day vampires

What collaboration sounds like is silence. And what it looks like is the averting of one's gaze, the turning of one's head. And what it smells like is the rotting of one's conscience—a smell that is not easily forgotten, for there is nothing else quite like it in the human experience.

Yet it is easy for us to condemn collaboration of this type: the collaboration of whites in the days of slavery, or Jim Crow. But what about now, and what about *us*?

BEING GOOD WHILE DOING HARM

EVEN WHEN WE enjoy a real and abiding closeness to people of color, that closeness will be complicated by our relationship to the larger institutional structures within which we find ourselves. It will be rendered at best a mixed bag, simply because of our ability to enjoy privilege, and even extend privilege, on the backs of others, no matter how much we may genuinely love and respect those others.

It was only a few years ago, during a workshop that I was attending (not as a facilitator but rather as a participant), that I really came to understand these issues. I mean, really understand them, at a deep and personal level.

During the session, we were all discussing our family histories. I mentioned a few of the things discussed earlier in this book, and happened to note, almost as an afterthought, that my comfort in and around communities of color likely stemmed from the fact that my paternal grandfather had owned and operated a business in the heart of Nashville's black community for many years, an establishment I would visit dozens of times growing up, from the time I was a very small child until I was a teenager.

Prepared to move on to another subject and wrap up my time to share, I was interrupted by a black man, older than myself, whose ears and eyes had quite visibly perked up when I had mentioned my grandfather and his business in North Nashville.

"I'm originally from North Nashville," he noted. "What kind of business did he have?"

"A liquor store," I responded. "My family owned liquor stores across town and my grandfather's was on Jefferson Street."

"Your grandfather was Leo Wise?" he replied, appearing to have known him well.

"Yes, yes he was," I answered, still not certain where all this was headed.

"He was a good man," the stranger shot back, "a very good man. But let me ask you something: have you ever thought about what it means that such a good man was, for all intents and purposes, a drug dealer in the ghetto?"

Time stood still for a second as I sought to recover from this serious body blow, right to the gut. I could feel myself getting defensive, and the look in my eyes no doubt portrayed my hurt and even anger at the question. After all, this was not how I had viewed my grandfather—as a drug dealer. He had been a businessman, I thought to myself. But even as I fumbled around for a reply, for a way to defend my grandfather's honor and good name, I began to realize that the man's statement had not been a condemnation of Leo Wise's humanity. It was not a curse upon the memory of the man to whom I had lovingly referred as Paw Paw all of my life. And anyway, he was right.

The fact is, my grandfather, who had spent several of his formative years living with his family on Jefferson Street, indeed made his living owning and operating a liquor store in the black community. Though the drug he sold was a legal one, it was a drug nonetheless, and to deny that fact, or to ignore its implications—that my grandfather put food on his family's table (and mine quite often) thanks to the addictions, or at least bad habits, of some of the city's most marginalized black folks—is to shirk the responsibility to own our collaboration. His collaboration hadn't made him a bad person, mind you, just as the black drug dealer in the same community is not necessarily a bad person. It simply meant that he had been complex, and ethically complicated, like all of us

We teased out the complexity as the workshop went along, using the example of my grandfather's business as a way to investigate this issue of collaboration even on the part of "good whites." As uncomfortable as the discussion was, it was necessary, for it is only in moments of discomfort that we find ourselves likely to grow.

The discussion led to the discovery and articulation of some difficult truths, truths that demonstrated how messy the whole business of racism can be, and how easy it is to both fight the monster, and yet still, on occasion, collaborate with it. On the one hand, my grandfather trafficked in a substance that could indeed bring death—a slow, often agonizing death that could destroy families long before it claimed the physical health or life of its abuser. On the other hand, he, unlike most white business owners who operate in the 'hood (any 'hood, anywhere in this country) left a lot of money behind in the community, refusing to simply abscond with it all to the white suburban home he had purchased in 1957, and in which he would live until his death in 1989—his wife living there an additional nine years until she too passed.

Even the man who had raised the issue of my grandfather's career as a legal drug dealer was quick to point out the other side: how he had seen and heard of Leo paying people's light bills and phone bills, hundreds of times, paying folks' rent hundreds more; how he paid to get people's cars fixed, or brought families food when they didn't have any; how he paid people under the table for hauling boxes away, moving liquor around, or delivering it somewhere, even when he could have done it himself, or gotten another store employee to do it. The man in the workshop remembered how my grandfather would slip $20 bills to people for no reason at all, just because he could. By all accounts, he noted, Leo had continued to feel an obligation and a love for the people of the Jefferson Street corridor, even long after he had moved away.

But what he had likely never really noticed, and what I had never really seen until that day, was that he and his commercial activity were among the forces that kept people trapped, too. Not the same way as institutional racism perhaps—and not the same way as the so-called urban renewal that plowed the interstate through the heart of North Nashville, destroying black-owned businesses and homes and cutting off of easy access from one part of the neighborhood to the next—but trapped nonetheless. He had not been a bad person, but he had been more complex than I had ever imagined. He had been a man who could count among his closest friends several black folks, a man who had supported in every respect the civil rights movement, a man whose proximity to the black community had probably done much for me, in terms of making me comfortable in nonwhite settings. But at the same time, he had been a man whose wealth—what there was of it—had been accumulated on the backs, or at least the livers, of black people.

His personal affections and friendships, and his political commitments, hadn't changed any of that.

Oh, and as a final note—one filled with irony and a healthy dose of poetic justice—the corner of Jefferson Street and Eighth Avenue, where my grandfather's liquor store once stood, is now the location of a soon-to-be-constructed African American History Museum. I have very little doubt that my grandfather would have liked that. He would have liked it a lot.

THE TROUBLE WITH FRIENDSHIP

A FEW YEARS ago, a young white woman named Jen sat crying during a conference on race relations, insisting to me that she went out of her way to make sure her daughter had black friends, Latino friends, and Asian friends, and that she would invite these friends over to play regularly, and she thought that was all she needed to do to fight racism. She was crying because someone during the conference had insisted friendships were not enough, and this had challenged her in a way that had made her uncomfortable.

After trying to reassure Jen that no one was saying she was a bad mom, or stupid, and that it was fine and even admirable that she saw the value of interracial friendships for her child, I asked her how she as a parent would try to see to it that those friendships were maintained even in the face of institutional racism. And what would she do about the institutional racism that would inevitably affect the lives of her daughter's friends?

She was stumped, and not for lack of trying to understand. What did I mean by institutional racism, she wanted to know, and how could that affect the friendships her child would have with these black and brown kids?

Instead of getting into a lengthy and overly intellectual discussion about what institutional racism means, which is never easy in any event, but is especially unhelpful to someone who is crying, I decided to tell her a story—a story about myself. It was a story that demonstrates the inadequacy of friendship as a tool for eliminating racism, and which shows how even the best intended can sometimes miss what's really going on.

I began by telling her that when I was two-and-a-half years old, my mother had enrolled me in preschool, just as most parents do with children that age. But unlike any of the white parents we knew, my mom had decided to enroll me in the early childhood program at Tennessee State University (TSU), a historically black college, located in North Nashville, about a fifteen minute drive from the apartments where we lived.

The decision was not a universally popular one with all family members, and probably seemed strange to many of my parents' white friends as well, but the decision was made nonetheless. Though it was not necessarily a decision made for overtly political reasons—indeed I am convinced she did it, at least subconsciously, to piss her folks off as much as for any more noble motive—there was also a part of her that recognized the value of exposing me to an environment in which I would not be in the majority.

Her commitment to an integrated environment for me (and more than that, an environment where whites would actually be the minority) was so strong that a few years later when one of Nashville's mostly black junior high schools closed—the one to which I would have been zoned, in fact—she, unlike pretty much every other white parent in the Nashville area it seemed, was actually upset.

At TSU, I would be one of only three white kids in a class of two dozen or so. The students were almost all black—many of them the children of teachers or TSU students. So I would come to have a cadre of friends that were almost all African American.

I continued to explain to Jen that the friendships I formed were every bit as real and heartfelt as the ones that I was sure her daughter was forging with her friends of color at that very moment. What's more, the mere fact that I had therefore been socialized in this non-dominant environment, and that I had been fortunate enough to identify with black kids early on, meant that once I started grade school I would also identify with, relate to, and get along famously with other black kids, even if I hadn't known them before at TSU. My peer group would be different, and this would serve me very well in the realm of interracial friendships throughout those years.

I told her of middle school, during which time my closeness to my black friends had translated into a remarkable ability to code-switch, meaning an ability, in this case, to shift between so-called "standard" English, and what some call "Black English," and to do it naturally, fluidly, without pretense.

I noted that during those years, my friendships deepened even further thanks to my early affinity for hip-hop. I had been the first person in my school, white or black, to memorize every word to the fourteen-minute version of

"Rapper's Delight," (the first major rap hit, though purists dispute the legitimacy of its pedigree and its performers, the Sugar Hill Gang). My friends and I would have rap battles—and by this I don't mean freestyle battles mind you (this was Nashville, after all, and we were eleven years old), but battles nonetheless—seeing who could get through the latest song without dropping a line.

Yet with all of my interpersonal stuff taken care of, so to speak, and with my "colorblind" credentials well established, I asked her what she thought had happened to those friendships over time. With how many of those friends of color was I still in contact? When I told her the answer was none, she seemed genuinely shocked, having presumed, I guess, that her daughter's black and brown friends at the age of six would follow her naturally into adulthood, perhaps taking part in her wedding and growing old together with her.

Make no mistake, I explained, it hadn't been as though I had changed my views about them or that they had changed their views about me. There had been no personal falling out, no blow up, nothing. Except, that is, for one thing over which we had no control, and that had made all the difference. And knowing the school system Jen's daughter and these friends of hers were going to be attending, I knew it most likely would happen to them as well.

I explained to her that irrespective of our personal connections to one another, the school system would, from the outset, separate us and sort us. The teachers would treat us differently. I would be tracked into the high track no matter how lousy my grades were, and my black friends would be stuck mostly in the remedial track, no matter how well they performed. After several years of this, despite our closeness, we would drift apart. Of course we would—why would anyone expect anything different? Our frames of reference would no longer be the same; our experiences would be so disparate it would be as if we were attending two entirely different schools. We'd see each other only on the playground or in the lunchroom, but not in class.

I told her of the way tracking had been done in my sixth-grade class, with Mrs. Belote waving her hand, silently but obviously about midway through fifth period, signaling to the white kids that it was time for our enrichment experience down the hall, in a different room. I mentioned how we would quietly rise and depart like a receding tide of pinkness, leaving a room filled with black kids who couldn't have missed what was happening, even though we did—never thought about it once at the time, friendships or no.

That, I tried to explain, was what I meant by institutional racism: the kind of racism that requires no bigotry on anyone's part to drive a wedge between people, to create hierarchies and systems of inequality. The interpersonal closeness, no matter how genuine, can still be ripped apart by something like that.

Sometimes, the friendship model of antiracism, into which Jen seemed to have bought for her daughter, and in which I too had once believed, could even lead one to think that standing up against-individual level biases—the kind that could so obviously injure one's friends—was sufficient, even when it wasn't.

So, on the one hand, I told her how my mother had successfully demanded the firing of one of my fifth-grade teachers because of a racist remark the teacher made during a parent-teacher conference. Mrs. Crownover, appalled by my close associations with the black kids, lashed out at my mom, insisting that "any white parent who sends their child to public schools since integration should have their heads examined."

My mother, of course, was livid. Standing up for my friendships, and her own principles, she took action. Within a matter of weeks, Mrs. Crownover mysteriously and quite unceremoniously disappeared, at first to be replaced by a series of substitute teachers, and finally, the next year, by someone else altogether. Early retirement, though not early enough, had been her fate.

But then I told her the rest of the story, the part that demonstrates once and for all the inadequacy of challenging personal-level racism, when there's a much bigger systemic evil to be addressed. It was the part about how, when I returned to class after Mrs. Crownover's removal, I was still attending a school system that was giving the message every day that blacks were inferior. The school had never needed Mrs. Crownover to impart that lesson; it was implicit in the way tracking had been going on for five years by then, and in the way it would continue for seven more. And neither my mother, nor I, with all those close friends, had said anything about *that* racism.

In other words, even as my mother stood up against the obvious bigot, she had dropped the ball, just like everyone else, when it came to confronting institutional racism. My closeness with black people hadn't protected them from that system, hadn't allowed me to see what was happening, let alone resolve to fix it, at least not at that time.

I told her how on the first day of junior high school, when I saw my old friend Bobby in the hall early that morning, and met him with a hearty "what's up?" he just looked at me and said, "I don't talk to white people anymore." Before she could interject to say how awful that was and how he shouldn't have said such a racist thing, I noted that he had apologized, but that what he'd been expressing wasn't really a bias against me as a white person anyway. Instead, he had been giving voice to the sense that often comes over kids of color around that age: the sense that they must now close ranks, draw into themselves for protection and bond together in a way they had never done before. After six years of unequal treatment, of daily assaults upon their dignity, their intelligence, even their humanity, they had to be careful—and sadly the same thing would happen, quite likely, to her daughter's friends.

She needed to know that. She needed to know that so long as institutional racism remained, and continued to drive a wedge, slowly but surely between her child and her child's black and brown friends, those friendships would likely not last; and what's more, they would flounder on the shoals of injustice, irrespective of her best intentions and efforts. Unless Jen was prepared to go well beyond merely encouraging interracial friendships, unless she was willing to see the system for what it was, and what it would seek to do to her child and to her child's black and brown friends, she was going to end up collaborating, just as my mom had, inadvertently, by not doing anything to alter the unjust structure of my schools, even while she knew to stand up to individual bigots.

Knowing that she wouldn't want that, I figured I could at least warn her. That my mother hadn't fully seen what was going on, and that Jen also hadn't, didn't make either of them bad people. But it did make them, and it does make us, considerably more complex than we may have at first imagined.

We could make our lives a lot easier, if we'd embrace the complexity and confront the contradictions, with our eyes and our hearts wide open, willing to celebrate our victories but also willing to learn from our failures.

* * *

IT WAS ONLY by being forced to confront my own failures, my own collaboration with racism, that I ever came to understand my privilege, and how easy it is to abuse it.

When people ask me if there was a particular "light bulb" moment where I suddenly understood the issues of racism and privilege, I always say no. Coming to understand either issue is a lifelong process—one that is far from complete as I write this. But having said that, there are individual experiences along the way, certain moments, if you will, when things become a bit clearer. Though no one of these moments is enough to allow a person to completely "get it," they can each contribute to the process of becoming a stronger antiracist white ally.

Perhaps the most significant of these, for me, came late in my senior year of college, but before I recount it, I should provide a little background information so as to set the scene.

When I began college in the fall of 1986, the primary outlets for campus activism were the Central American solidarity movement and the anti-apartheid movement. The first of these focused mostly on two issues:

opposing the Reagan administration's arming of the contras in Nicaragua, who were seeking to overthrow the Sandinista government (which in turn had booted out a U.S.-backed dictator, Anastasio Somoza, in 1979); and opposing military and economic assistance to right-wing governments (both of which were linked to paramilitary death squads) in El Salvador and Guatemala.

In the case of Guatemala, its dictator in the early eighties had been Efrain Rios Montt, a man who Ronald Reagan insisted had "gotten a bum rap on human rights," and was "dedicated to social justice" despite his policies of bombing peasant communities and other atrocities, which ultimately took the lives, in his term alone, of over seventy thousand Guatemalans.

At the same time that opposition was rising to the administration's policies in Latin America, so too was anger fomenting over its ongoing support for institutional racism in South Africa. Under apartheid, 26 million blacks in South Africa were denied the right to vote, and restricted in terms of where they could live, where they could work, and where they could be educated. The white minority government also routinely tortured antiapartheid activists and had engaged in military operations and subversion campaigns in surrounding black majority nations like Angola, Zimbabwe, and Mozambique.

All of this it had done with substantial economic and even military support from the United States government and multinational corporations. In the case of corporate support for apartheid, antiapartheid activists noted that not only did the presence of these companies in the country send a signal that apartheid was acceptable to them, it also resulted in the economic support of the racist state, and the transfer of technology and capital, both of which could and did help maintain the system.

In an attempt to pressure companies to leave South Africa, college activists had begun calling for their trustees to sell off stock in those firms, if and when such stock was held in the school's investment portfolio. By 1985, the divestment movement, as it came to be known, was in full swing on dozens of college and university campuses across the country.

But since Tulane has always been a little behind the times—New Orleans has always had a tendency to slow things down a bit—it wouldn't be until after I arrived, in 1986, that the stirrings of such a movement began there. Upon getting to Tulane, I first joined in with the Central American solidarity work, but by my sophomore year, had mostly thrown my attention and energy into the issue of South African apartheid and our school's support for it, by way of its investments.

Although Tulane was unwilling to expose its portfolio to public scrutiny, the administration acknowledged in 1987 that it continued to hold shares in approximately twenty five companies that were still doing business with the apartheid government. This, combined with the offer of an honorary degree to Archbishop Desmond Tutu, who had won the Nobel Peace Prize for his anti-apartheid efforts in 1984, was too much for some of us to stand. To offer a degree to Tutu, in effect making him part of the Tulane family, while we continued to turn profits from companies that were propping up the very system he had dedicated his life to ending, struck us as hypocritical, to say the least.

In March 1988, a coalition of organizations joined forces in a press conference to announce the formation of the Tulane Alliance Against Apartheid. The alliance took as its three principal concerns (at first intimately linked in the minds of all participants) divestment from companies doing business in South Africa, the restoration of an African American studies department at Tulane, and the intensification of affirmative action efforts, both for student recruitment and retention, as well as faculty hiring. The last of these was seen as especially necessary, since in the 1987–88 academic year there were no African American faculty members in the College of Arts and Sciences or Newcomb College, the two principal undergraduate schools.

In the days following the press conference, alliance members constructed makeshift shanties (reminiscent of the dilapidated housing in which millions of South African blacks lived) on the main quad in front of the University Center, so as to raise awareness of the issue and to pressure the Board of Administrators to divest. A few days after the beginning of the shantytown occupation, students demonstrated at the board's quarterly meeting to demand divestment and to decry the offer of an honorary degree to Tutu so long as the school remained invested in apartheid-complicit firms.

During this time we also sent the archbishop a packet of materials concerning Tulane's investments—what little information we had—and requested that he make a strong statement condemning the school's role in supporting, even if mostly symbolically, South Africa's racist system of government.

A few weeks later, a reporter from National Public Radio woke me up in my dorm room. What she had to say made clear that Tutu's statement would be far stronger than we could ever have anticipated.

"What do you think of the Archbishop's announcement in Canada today that he would be turning down the degree from Tulane because of the school's investments?" asked the reporter on the other end.

Having not heard the news until that moment, I was stunned, but pleased. The administration was shaken, as news spread worldwide of Tutu's boycott and, a few days later, his subsequent announcement that he would be returning all honorary degrees ever accepted from schools with investments in South Africa, unless they divested fully within one year.

Clearly, the university had been denied the moment they had hoped for—one in which Tutu would be honored by the school and thereby lend anti-apartheid cover for their otherwise morally indefensible investment practices. Although Tutu's boycott didn't change the board's mind about divestment, we all anticipated that, upon returning to campus in the fall, the movement would hit the ground running in full stride, having obtained such a high-profile victory in the spring of the previous year.

As it turned out, nothing could have been further from the truth. Summer sapped the energy of the movement considerably, and several of the key founders and movers within the group graduated. Although I returned as a junior, and there were others of the original membership back that next year, we struggled from the outset to replicate the success of the previous semester. Membership waned, and our direction seemed unclear. Although we continued to educate the university community about South Africa, and the role of corporations in propping up the apartheid system, we seemed stalled when it came to making any progress with the board.

Most importantly—and this will prove highly relevant to the moral of this story—the organization in that second year became almost entirely white, and the alliance between the mostly white activists and the black-led organizations that had created the movement in the first place fell apart entirely, in a quiet but noticeable fashion.

The lack of dynamism would remain a problem until the fall of 1989, when the alliance—now renamed Tulane Students Against Apartheid because of the University's threat to sue us if we continued to call ourselves the Tulane Alliance, thereby implying (supposedly) official university endorsement—once again took over a board meeting. Facing several hundred demonstrators, and with the divestment petition having grown to include the names of over thirty-five hundred people in the Tulane community, the trustees finally agreed to negotiations with the protestors.

At our first meeting to discuss divestment with the board, it became obvious that the university's wealthy white policymakers had no intention of taking the issue seriously. First, I mentioned that the university already had an ethical investment policy prohibiting it from investing in companies that contributed to human rights violations; as such, continued investment in the twenty-five corporations in South Africa was a violation of the board's own policy. Upon being issued this challenge, one of the board members—either Sybil Favrot or Virginia Roddy (their moral compasses being similarly off-kilter, and thus making them hard to distinguish from one another)—responded.

"Well, how do we know if those companies are actually contributing to human rights violations?"

Putting aside the argument that any corporate investment in South Africa would automatically bolster apartheid and thus amount to a contribution to human rights abuses, I posed a hypothetical.

"Imagine," I asked, "that we were invested in Shell Oil (which given the ubiquity of the petroleum industry in and around New Orleans seemed a reasonable likelihood, though it was unclear given the refusal to open the portfolio). "Since Shell recently called in South African security forces to shoot rubber bullets at striking workers, would that, in your mind, constitute a human rights violation sufficient to trigger the policy with regard to ethical investment?"

"Well," she replied. "I guess it would depend on why they were striking."

Such moral clarity is something about which I'm sure all Tulane alumni can be proud and proves, if anyone was still inclined to believe otherwise, that wealth and power bear no relationship to either intelligence or character development.

Fast forward to winter break. While at home for the holidays I stumbled upon a book detailing the connections between university investment and research on the one hand, and political and economic repression in South Africa and Central America on the other. In the book's index, the author provided a summary of several companies involved in human rights abuses, and the names of some of the schools that held stock in those companies, along with the number of shares held at the time of the book's writing. Tulane was listed several times, and was invested, apparently, in about a dozen companies that had contributed everything from oil-refining technology to the South Africans, to military helicopters to the dictatorships in Guatemala and El Salvador. It was the material we'd been looking for, and it was political dynamite.

Upon returning to campus in January, we called a press conference to release the list of Tulane's "dirty dozen" corporations and to demand that the school follow its own policy with regard to ethical investment by divesting itself of stock in those firms and any others about which we were unaware. The board, in response, announced they were breaking off negotiations with the antiapartheid group, because the release of the information had indicated we were acting in bad faith—this coming from people who needed to know why workers were on strike before they could say, definitively, that shooting them might be objectionable.

In the third week of March, we once again built shanties, but this time on the lawn in front of Gibson Hall (the administration building), facing the streetcar line on St. Charles Avenue. By bringing the protest to the exterior of the campus, in front of its most visible structure, we hoped to heighten the public's attention to the school's practices, and to force divestment, or at least the opening of the portfolio to full scrutiny. A week into the protest, when Jesse Jackson came to campus (for an unrelated speech) and called for the university to heed the protesters' demands, we figured we were on our way to victory. That evening, I announced that several of the group's members, including myself, would begin a hunger strike the following Monday if our key demands (short of divestment itself) were not met by that time. Needless to say they wouldn't be, and so the hunger strike started on schedule.

On the fourth day of the strike, we received word that the university had agreed to five of the ten demands, including those we had insisted upon in order for the action to end and for negotiations to resume. These included the opening of the portfolio and exploring the possibility of bringing in ethical investment experts to plan future directions for the management of the school's general fund.

Though we celebrated this outcome as a victory for the movement, deep down everyone knew there was something unsatisfying about it. Apartheid was, thankfully, in its waning days, as signaled by the release of Nelson Mandela early in 1990. As a result, the board had recognized that before it would really have to make any changes, the situation in South Africa would probably change dramatically, and with it, there would be no more need to clean out its portfolio. Tulane was going to hold out longer than the racists in Pretoria, it seemed, which was saying a lot.

The point here is not to wax sentimental about my role as a campus activist or to pat myself on the back for the work in which I was involved—quite the opposite, in fact.

In fact, the real point of the story is that the way in which the Tulane antiapartheid movement developed provided, in retrospect, clear and convincing evidence of how even in the midst of our resistance to racist structures we can reinforce racism and collaborate with the very forces we claim to be opposing. What's more, my own actions and inactions while an activist at Tulane demonstrated the extent of my own white privilege and how taking that privilege for granted harmed the movement itself.

Though I saw none of this for most of my time at Tulane, the closest I ever came to having one of those light bulb moments was during that period, on the second night of the hunger strike. It was on that evening, with only a few weeks left in my academic career at the school, that we had scheduled a debate on campus against representatives of the New Orleans Libertarian Party. The Libertarians would argue that investment in South Africa was a good thing for blacks because it provided them with jobs, however unequal those jobs might be, and that if the companies pulled out, black South Africans would be the ones to suffer most. It was an argument with which we had been contending from the outset, and which all of us in the antiapartheid movement knew how to pick apart. By the time the debate was over, it was obvious that virtually everyone in the crowd of three hundred or so was on the side of divestment.

Confident that we had made our point that evening, alliance member Eldann Chandler and I leaned back during the question-and-answer period, expecting to further drive home the moral imperative of divestment to the audience. Most of the questions were pretty routine and directed pointedly at our opponents, rather than us. Until the very end, that is. And then it happened. The moderator for the evening's festivities called on a young woman in the dead center of the small but packed auditorium, who as it turns out would get the last question of the night.

Because she was black, I assumed that she, too, would be on the side of divestment. She was, of course, but that wasn't what was on her mind. After identifying herself as a first-year student at Xavier University—the nation's only historically black Catholic college, located about two miles away—and prefacing her question by noting that as a New Orleanian she was embarrassed that Tulane was still invested in these companies, she got to what was on her mind, and in doing so, dropped the bomb that would, more than anything else in my life, alter the way I understood my own relationship to privilege.

"Tim," she asked. "How long have you lived here in New Orleans?"

"Four years," I replied.

"Okay," she continued. "Then tell me, in that four years, what one thing have you done to address apartheid in this city, since, after all, you benefit from that apartheid?"

She crossed her arms in front of her, and stood, and waited.

One Mississippi, two Mississippi. . . . The milliseconds crept by, each one pounding like a drill into my skull. By now, the air had been sucked out of the room entirely, she having asked the one question, and I mean the only question for which I had been unprepared—the only one I had never anticipated, and the only one that, at the end of the day, really mattered.

Three Mississippi, four Mississippi. . . . It seemed like hours since she had asked her question, and I briefly considered the possibility that we had been sitting there overnight waiting for my answer. I'm sure no more than a few seconds actually passed, but in those seconds, enough truth was revealed to last a lifetime.

I began to have the sensation that I was in my car, speeding down the I-10 away from town, and suddenly saw the blue lights flashing in my rear view mirror: the ones that say, "Gotcha! Oh you *thought* you were getting away with that move you just pulled, buzzing through here like no one would notice, like no one was watching you, like no one was waiting for you to screw up, but now we *got* your ass, so pull it over and start explaining."

Then I was snapped back to reality, and realized that unlike the last time I got a ticket, I wasn't going to have thirty seconds to come up with some story, some bullshit fable that could get me out of what gun drawn ever trouble I was in. The officer, this time, was at my window already, badge out, gun drawn, and it was now or never that I would offer an answer. So I did.

"Well," I said, clearing my throat before the now dead silent audience, "I mean, um, ya know, um, we all pick our battles."

Oh.

Shit.

No he didn't.

Oh, but I did. And as soon as it tumbled from my lips, lips I could not feel at that moment, I knew something significant, but also bad, had happened; more to the point, so did just about everyone else.

The young lady uncrossed her arms, and smiled a wicked, knowing smile, the expression on her face betraying a mix of satisfaction and disgust at how easy it had been to expose me as a fraud. It was *tight*.

A buzzing started behind my ears, coupled with a strange warmth that made me fear, just for a moment, that my head might explode, sorta like that guy on the stage in that sci-fi flick *Scanners*. I started having flashbacks to all those dreams—you know the ones I mean, I'm sure you've had them too—the ones where you suddenly find yourself completely naked in front of your third-grade class or at your prom or something like that.

An earthquake could have hit at that moment—thinking back to it, I probably wished that one would have, but lucky me, I had chosen to go to a school in one of the only states in the union without a fault line—and had it done so, I wouldn't even have noticed. I don't remember another thing from that night, so shaken was I by her question and my answer, not because I had a better answer that I had simply forgotten to offer, but because I had no answer at all. That had been it. I had told the brutal truth, and now had to confront what such disturbing honesty really meant for me.

Over the next few days, the administration would partially cave in to our demands, the shanties would come down, and the hunger strike would mercifully end. But even after I began to replenish my body with the nourishment I had been denying it, the pit in my stomach remained, because it had nothing to do with food.

I tried to put the whole thing behind me but couldn't. I kept coming back to the fact that I had been doing all of this work against racism half-a-world away, but frankly had done nothing to speak of in opposition to the racism in the town where I was living. I had done nothing in answer to the de facto apartheid conditions that existed in New Orleans—conditions that, as the young woman that night had pointed out, had benefited me, as a white man who could count on my privilege to insulate me from their impact.

I began to remember all the things I had ignored or downplayed as I focused on the racial oppression that was occurring on another continent:

Harry Lee and racial profiling in Jefferson Parish, for example, or Tulane's lack of recruiting in New Orleans schools, being two of the most obvious. And there was one more, even worse than those two, which had just transpired under our noses and about which we had said and done nothing. Namely, three days after our shanty siege had begun, New Orleans police had murdered a black man named Adolph Archie, suspected of killing a white police officer. When police caught him, beat him, and took him to the hospital, a lynch mob of cops had gathered, after broadcasting open death threats over their police scanners. Instead of entering the hospital with Archie, officers drove him to a precinct station and over several hours beat him so badly that every bone in his face had been broken. He would die at the hospital after police got tired of brutalizing him, and although his death would be ruled a homicide "by police intervention," no officers involved in his murder would ever be punished.

As Adolph Archie was being pulverized by New Orleans cops, my comrades and I were sleeping the sleep of the just, or at least of the self-righteous, uptown, in shacks of our own construction, and I should mention, protected by Tulane police, round the clock, for the entire two-week period of the protest. We had never even discussed the killing of Archie, never connected the all-too-obvious dots, never supposed that perhaps there might be something similar about the way police operated in New Orleans and the way they operated in Soweto. Remember, we all pick our battles.

The mistakes were starting to add up. Remember, when the alliance first formed it was just that, an *alliance*. If you look up the term in your dictionary you'll find it right between *alliaceous* and *allicin,* both of which have to do with garlic. This is strangely appropriate, because the smell of this alliance was starting to become just as strong and distracting. Now, if you read the definition, you'll notice that the word implies a multiplicity of forces—as in more than one, as in several—all bound together for some common purpose. In fact, it's right there—the second entry: "a close association for a common objective."

Yet by 1990 and really by the end of fall 1988, only nine months since the alliance had formed, it had ceased to operate as a collaborative effort. Although I had lamented the loss of the collaboration, as had everyone else still involved in the antiapartheid struggle, none of us were apparently ready to confront the reasons for its demise; just as none of us were prepared to deal with the truth of why the organization had gone from being about fifty-fifty black and white in terms of active members to almost entirely white, in a matter of less than a year. In fact, with the exception of Eldann, who as I mentioned before, was my debate partner on that evening, there were only perhaps three other black folks actively involved in the movement by the time of the second shanty siege.

Of course we came up with a convenient excuse for why black participation had fallen off. As one white member put it—getting no argument from me, sadly, in the process—the black students at Tulane were mostly "bougie," from upper-middle-class families, and didn't want to make waves. Aside from the fact that this was utterly untrue, who the hell were we to call anyone bougie? As if we were some hardscrabble working-class offspring of West Virginia coal miners or something.

Never did it occur to us that maybe black folks at Tulane were turned off by the way a handful of whites (especially me) were elevated to the status of leaders and spokespersons by the media, and how we weren't savvy enough to avoid the trap of our own minicelebrity status'. Maybe they were pissed because the original focus of the alliance—which you'll recall had been tripartite, involving not only South Africa but also black studies and affirmative action—was gone almost immediately, replaced with a single-minded focus on the one issue that was easiest for white Tulanians to swallow, and which would call for no sacrifice on our part, or alterations in the way the campus looked and felt. Maybe they fell away because we were so quick to jump to cavalier methods of protest like taking over board meetings, openly inviting arrest if necessary, or going on hunger strike, without consulting anyone, without discussing the privileged mindset that cavalierly treats going to jail or starving like just another rite of passage for students to experience.

Whatever the case, I had been blind to the way in which my own privilege and the privilege of whites generally had obscured our understanding of such issues as accountability, the need to link up struggles (like the connection between racism in New Orleans and that in South Africa), and the need to always have leadership of color in any antiracist struggle, however much that requires whites to step back, keep our mouths shut, and just listen for a while.

It's the same lesson still not learned by white activists in most cases, whether in the antisweatshop movement, the justice for Darfur movement, or the antiwar movement. Too often the same mistakes are made: mostly white radicals, who have the luxury of picking and choosing issues on which to get active (unlike people of color who also care about lots of issues but have to deal with racism as a matter of survival), refuse to connect the dots between the oppression taking place in another country, and the oppression going on down the block.

White leftists typically refuse to prioritize the daily issues of people of color and to show a commitment to working on those issues every bit as passionately as marching against a war on the other side of the globe; then they (we) put up signs announcing the next organizational meeting, and when the room ends up being pretty much all white, say in utter exasperation and with no sense of irony, "We advertised the meeting, and invited them, and they didn't come." And then the white progressives blame *them*, and naturally go on about our business, as if our self-righteous, sandal-wearing, tofu and tempeh-eating, no-car-driving, Nike-boycotting, coffee-ground-composting, macrobiotic-consuming, low-on-the-food-chain asses have done all they (we) can do. When we haven't—not even close.

And although we have to forgive ourselves for the mistakes we make, we must first acknowledge them. We must first face up to the fact that in our resistance we too often reinforce all the hierarchical nonsense we swear we oppose, much of it racist at its core. Only by being called out, as I was, can we learn this in most cases. Only by being exposed to our flaws, forced to deal with them, and to learn from them, can we move forward, can we strengthen our resistance in the future.

I wish it weren't true, but if there is one thing I've learned it is that we (white folks, and specifically white antiracists) will screw up, more times than we care to count, more times than we expected, and just as often as people of color already knew we would. It's as regular as rain, and you can set your clock by it in most cases. Saying this does not diminish us, it does not mean we shouldn't try, and it surely doesn't mean we don't have a role to play in the destruction of white supremacy. It just means that privilege carries a cost; in this case, it costs us the clarity of vision sometimes needed to see what we're really doing, and how even in our resistance, we sometimes play the collaborator.

This is the "twinness" with which whites live, to steal a concept from W.E.B. DuBois, and until we learn to confront the contradiction, it will sabotage even the most sincere efforts at white antiracism.

LOSS

"The price the white American paid for his ticket was to become white. . . . This incredibly limited not to say dimwitted ambition has choked many a human being to death here: and this, I contend, is because the white American has never accepted the real reasons for his journey. I know very well that my ancestors had no desire to come to this place: but neither did the ancestors of the people who became white and who require of my captivity a song. They require of me a song less to celebrate my captivity than to justify their own."

JAMES BALDWIN, *The Price of the Ticket,* 1985

SEVERAL YEARS AGO, after I had delivered a speech on white privilege to a mostly white audience, one of the few women of color in attendance stood to ask a question.

"You know, that was pretty good," she said. "I think any reasonable white person, hearing the things you just laid out, would have to agree that yes, white privilege is real, and they have it. But tell me something. Having come to accept that they have these privileges you talked about, why would any of these nice white folks want to give that up?"

It was a great question, to which I really didn't have much of an answer.

I said something appropriately liberal (and naïve), about how since most people are decent, once they saw the degree of their own implication in the suffering of others, surely they would seek to undo systemic injustice. To this, she smiled and laughed a bit, finally insisting that I should "keep working on that one," and get back to her when I'd figured something out.

She was right, of course. The problem wasn't that white people weren't mostly decent folks, but precisely that we *were*. Being basically decent had allowed us to ignore how implicated we actually were in the system of racism and racial subordination, or at least to smooth it over, downplay it, or insist that we were different. Our goodness had never been sufficient.

Her point was simple enough: people with an advantage are typically reluctant to give it up, because in a society rooted in cut-throat competition, if you aren't the one with the edge, you worry that someone else might get the jump on *you*. There's a reason parents used to tell their kids things like, "Eat all your food, there are children starving in China," rather than "Stop eating so much. We need to box up the food and send it to the kids who are starving in China." Likewise, when we are told to "count our blessings" we are rarely then admonished to give them away.

So why *would* whites want to join in a struggle for the eradication of a system that has afforded us so many advantages?

I thought about it for a long time, finally coming to recognize that there are some very good reasons why even those with privilege should seek to create a more equitable and just society, as counterintuitive as that may seem. The fact is, whites do pay a cost for the maintenance of the privileges and advantages we receive. Some of these are intensely personal—emotional and psychological costs, involving the warping of white perceptions, emotions, and even behaviors—while others are collective, as we'll see below. What they all mean, in the end, is that whites have an interest in change, and that that interest is not merely to satisfy some moral or altruistic impulse on our parts. Racism and white privilege are dangerous for us, even as they pay dividends—sort of like a precious gem that turns out to be toxic if held too close.

COLLATERAL DAMAGE:
White Privilege and the Conning of the Working Class

TO UNDERSTAND WHY whites should join the struggle against our own privileges, it might help to know some history—specifically, the history of how we became white in the first place, and for what purpose.

Contrary to popular belief, the white race is a quite modern creation, which only emerged as a term and concept to describe Europeans in the late 1600s and after, specifically in the colonies of what would become the United

States. Prior to that time, "whites" had been a collection of Europeans with little in common, and often long histories of conflict, bloodshed, and conquests of one another's lands and peoples. The English, for example, did not consider themselves to be of the same group as the Irish, Germans, Italians, or French. Indeed, even within a nation like Scotland, whence so much of my family had come, intragroup conflicts, such as those between Highlanders (like my family, the McLeans) and those down country, were common. While most Europeans by that time may have thought of themselves as Christians (and even then, the conflicts between Catholics and Protestants were legion) there is no evidence that they conceived of themselves as a race of people, with a common heritage or destiny.

But the notion of the white race found traction in the North American colonies, not because it described a clear scientific concept or some true historical bond between persons of European descent, but rather because the elites of the colonies (who were small in number but controlled the vast majority of colonial wealth) needed a way to secure their power. At the time, the wealthy landowners feared rebellions, in which poor European peasants might join with African slaves to overthrow aristocratic governance; after all, these poor Europeans were barely above the level of slaves themselves, especially if they worked as indentured servants.

As mentioned earlier, from the mid-1600s to the early 1700s a series of laws were promulgated in Virginia and elsewhere, which elevated all persons of European descent, no matter how lowly in economic terms, above all persons of African descent. The purpose of such measures was to provide poor Europeans (increasingly called whites) with a stake in the system, even though they were hardly benefiting in material terms from it. In other words, whiteness was a trick, and it worked marvelously, dampening down the push for rebellion by poor whites on the basis of class interest, and encouraging them to cast their lot with the elite, if only in aspirational terms. White skin became, for them, an alternative form of property to which they could cleave, in the absence of more tangible possessions.

This divide-and-conquer tactic would be extended and refined in future generations as well. During the Civil War era, Southern elites made it quite clear that their reason for secession from the Union was the desire to maintain and extend the institution of slavery and white supremacy, which institutions they felt were threatened by the rise of Lincoln and the Republican Party. One might think that seceding and going to war to defend slavery would hardly meet with the approval of poor white folks, who didn't own slaves. After all, if slaves can be made to work for free, any working-class white person who must charge for their labor will be undercut by slave labor and find it harder to make ends meet. Yet by convincing poor whites that their interests were racial, rather than economic, and that whites in the South had to band together to defend "their way of life," elites in the South conned these same lower-caste Europeans into joining a destructive war effort that cost hundreds of thousands of their own lives.

Then, during the growth of the labor union movement, white union workers barred blacks from apprenticeship programs and unions because of racism, with the encouragement of owners and bosses who would use workers of color to break white labor strikes for better wages and working conditions. By bringing in blacks and others of color to break strikes, bosses counted on white workers to turn on those who replaced them, rather than turning on the bosses themselves. And indeed, this is what happened time and again, further elevating whiteness above class interest in the minds of European Americans.

The effectiveness of racist propaganda to unite whites around race, even if it meant overlooking economic interests, has been stunning. And while it would be nice to think that this kind of shortsighted mentality were a thing of the past, it appears to still maintain a grip on an awful lot of whites in the present day as well.

Nothing could have demonstrated this more clearly than the electoral campaigns of neo-Nazi David Duke for U.S. Senate and governor of Louisiana in 1990 and 1991. In the first of these, 60 percent of whites in the state voted for Duke, knowing full well of his racist affiliations and beliefs. In the latter, 55 percent did the same. Only record-high turnout by the African American community prevented Duke from winning in those races. And overwhelmingly, the whites who supported Duke were working class. Although white elites were no less racist, their desire to project a more enlightened image—and it's tough to claim enlightenment while voting for someone who just ten years earlier had been the head of the largest Klan group in America—led them to oppose Duke, even if they agreed with many of his policy ideas.

The people who propelled Duke forward were the same working-class and lower-income whites who would later line the streets of Mardi Gras parades in 1993 to protest an ordinance banning Krewes that discriminated on the basis of race and gender from parading during the city-subsidized festivities. That was fascinating and instructive, too: watching the tin-roof and trailer crowd with their signs, proclaiming "Hands off Mardi Gras," and inviting the author of the proposal, black councilwoman Dorothy Mae Taylor, to take a slow boat back to the motherland. Here were a bunch of struggling white folks, defending the racist prerogatives of elite social clubs, despite the rather obvious fact that the clubs in question would no more have let *them* join than they would have any black person. It didn't matter. The clubs were standing up for white people in their minds, just as Duke had been, and since they were white, that meant *them,* it meant their team.

Never mind the class warfare being waged at that very moment by the kinds of whites who populated the Mardi Gras elite: folks who sought to break what little union strength working people in the state could rely on, and who received one tax break after another for themselves and their corporations while pushing the tax burden increasingly onto the shoulders of the very working-class whites who now rallied to their sides.

Never mind that Duke—the political mouthpiece for so many of these folks—proposed to maintain and even strengthen regressive tax policies that fell most heavily on the working class, or that he had no plan for job creation. What mattered was that he didn't like *niggers,* and was willing to blame *niggers* for welfare fraud, taking white jobs, ruining public schools, and making the streets unsafe. That's all that low, and moderate-income white folks needed to hear: an answer for why their lives had turned out to be so miserable; an answer with a brown face, that lived somewhere in New Orleans—in the part of the city that whites in St. Bernard Parish, and even neighboring Jefferson Parish, increasingly avoided, so sure were they that some Mandingo would accost them, rape their wives, and slow roast their children on a spit after stuffing apples in their mouths.

The whole process, the unfolding of that election season, was a lesson in how damaged whites are because of racism and how easy it has been to manipulate otherwise good people and lead them away from not only what is decent and right, but even from that which is in their own interest and the interests of their families.

So you had white working-class folks running to the polls to vote for a guy who promised to make people on welfare work off their support checks, despite the fact that such a plan would inevitably undercut the wages of workers. After all, those on public assistance would have been forced to work up to forty hours a week to receive their AFDC checks under Duke's plan— checks that came out to only a few hundred dollars a month, which was far less than nonwelfare workers would have been paid for the same jobs. So "workfare," as Duke termed it, would have only undermined the employment status of working-class folks— people of color *and* whites—yet it pushed the right buttons, so it worked.

Indeed, the racial resentments were so deep, so unresolved, that one Jewish woman in Metairie even told a friend of mine, who was doing thesis research on Duke, that she would be voting for him. No matter his views about Jews, she explained, he was "going to get rid of the *shvartzes*" (a Yiddish slur for blacks), and that was all that mattered.

That kind of thing illuminates the damage to whites from racism and privilege quite clearly. If whiteness can come to mean so much that whites won't even care about the economy, the job market, or their own real well-being, something has gone terribly wrong.

A few years later, I'd get to see just how distorted white thinking has become, thanks to racism, during an online exchange with a young white college student from South Carolina. He had been agitated by an article I had written criticizing the continued flying of the Confederate flag. We'd gone round and round over the course of two days, he insisting that the flag was an honorable symbol of the South, and I trying to explain why it wasn't.

After I pointed out to him the way the South—the region in which we both lived and that we both loved—had been harmed by racist thinking, and how our economic vitality had long been sapped by white supremacy, with wages being held down due to opposition to unions—opposition that was predicated on a fear of racial wage equality—he replied just as matter-of-factly as he could, "I'd be willing to work for $1 an hour if we could just go back to segregation."

If that doesn't suggest that whites have been damaged by racism and the mentality of privilege that comes from it, I'm not sure what else could.

That said, there is more.

WHITE PRIVILEGE AND THE DANGER OF FRUSTRATED EXPECTATIONS

SOMETIMES THE THINGS that *don't* get said are the things that are really important. Case in point: the media discussion a few years ago, when a young white man named Kip Kinkel killed his parents and shot up his high school in Springfield, Oregon.

I remember watching MSNBC's coverage of the event, and shaking my head every time a new "expert" would come on to pontificate about what had gone wrong in the young man's life. Why had this happened? That was the question on everyone's mind, which itself was telling. When poor black kids in the inner city kill someone, no one asks why? because we think we already know: those are bad kids, in bad families, with no values or respect for human life. Maybe they're even inherently violent! But when an upper-middle-class white boy does something wrong, confusion gives way to shock, which leads to a parade of theories meant to explain how otherwise "good" kids could go so tragically wrong.

I wrote down every explanation offered by commentators for what Kinkel had done. There were dozens thrown out before the list was completed: everything from violent video games, to violent movies, to rap music (because if we can manage to blame black people or culture for white wrongdoing we will), to sugary snacks, to antidepressant medications, to mental illness, to cold and unfeeling parents, to the removal of prayer from schools, to the "culture of death" brought on by abortion, among others.

But no matter the excuse, what was telling was what went unspoken: that there had been several mass-murder shootings in the years before Kinkel's rampage (and there would be several more in years to come, including Columbine), and in almost every case the shooter had been white and from a middle-class or upper-middle-class home. Though such incidents were rare, to be sure, they did seem to happen in precisely the places where no one thought they would, which seems the very embodiment of irony.

No one thought to ask what it was about the cultures in which these young men found themselves that might produce dysfunction. That's the kind of thing we might ask if a perpetrator of violence is black and from the 'hood, but which we never ask when whites are the authors of the mayhem. Their rage is inexplicable, it seems.

But what if it's not? What if the explanation is privilege?

What if the culture of privilege itself creates the risk of this sort of thing, by generating a set of expectations in the minds of the privileged, which, when frustrated (as they sometimes are) leads them to lash out, unable to cope with setback? And not just school shooters, but workplace murderers too, who are overwhelmingly white, almost always male, and usually solidly middle class?

Before dismissing such a thing, keep in mind the now-accepted sociological explanation for why urban rebellions and riots occurred in the midsixties and not the midfifties. After all, one could argue that the midfifties were worse in absolute terms for black folks, and that by the sixties, various legislative changes due to the civil rights movement were beginning to create hope where little had previously existed: so why would rebellions happen *then* as opposed to the days when things had been more bleak? Simple, according to the literature on the subject, when expectations start to rise, but the fulfillment of those expectations proceeds far slower than the aspirations, frustration builds up and can result in an explosion. So it was precisely because things were getting better that rebellions took place, since the pace of change was much less rapid than many hoped and believed it would be.

But if frustrating the expectations of folks who've never had very many can lead those on the bottom to lash out, why couldn't the same happen—and in a particularly extreme fashion—when the expectations of the privileged (which have always been high) get frustrated as well—when they lose their jobs, lose millions in the stock market, or in the case of school shooters have a relationship go sour, or get teased mercilessly? Remember, when the stock market crashed in 1929, it wasn't poor people who jumped out of windows and killed themselves, unable to deal with being broke. They had been broke the week before and the week before the so-called depression. It was rich folks, white ones to be sure, who couldn't stand the thought of having nothing.

So too it seems to be whites who engage disproportionately in a wide range of strange pathologies, all of which are about control and domination, either of others or even oneself. Whites, for example, are more likely than blacks or Latinos to binge drink or use drugs excessively (contrary to stereotype). Whites are more likely than blacks or Latinos to commit suicide. Whites are more likely than blacks or Latinos to develop eating disorders or to self-mutilate. Whites are a disproportionate percentage of serial killers and mass murderers (even as regular homicide is disproportionately the work of black males), as well as sexual sadism killers. None of this is because of some genetic predisposition to these things, nor because white culture per se generates such tendencies. But because these pathologies are all about one thing—the need to assert and exercise control, of others, or one's body, or one's pain—it raises the question: which kind of people would be most likely to manifest a control pathology? Would it be those who have never been in control, or those who always had been (or felt they were supposed to be), but who found something about their lives to be very much out of control, and were unable to cope with that reality?

Consider the woman who called in to a radio show I was doing in Minnesota several years ago, on which the host and I had been talking about the negative consequences of privilege for those who have it. The caller, an affluent white woman from a Minneapolis suburb, explained that she had recently come to see this exact problem, in the form of her son's drug addiction.

As she explained it, her son had always been a good student who seemed to have very few problems. However, a few years earlier, things had begun to change: a girlfriend dumped him, he got a bad grade in a class for the first time, and suddenly it was as if his life were spiraling downward. He began to lash out in rages at his family, began to use and abuse drugs and to drink—all of them ways of coping with the setbacks in his personal life.

Luckily, she said, her family had the resources to get their son into a top-notch treatment program, and so he was on the road to recovery. One day, after picking her son up after a therapy session, he began to discuss the substance of what he and his therapist had talked about that day. "I never realized how messed up it could be, being a white male," he said.

She confessed that she had been confused when he said this, turning to him, almost incredulous, and asking, "What does that mean? What does any of this have to do with being a white male? What does it mean to you to be a white male?"

"It means I was raised to always see myself as being in control, in charge, stable, together," he shot back. "That's how white men are portrayed, and that's the stuff I was being fed from the time I was a kid. It wasn't your fault," he was quick to point out. "It's just the constant message I got growing up:

always be in control, always win. Then when a few things went wrong I couldn't deal with it, *because I'd never had to cope with anything before.*"

Privilege breeds thin skin, in other words. Most of the time it won't matter, perhaps. Most of the time it all works out alright, because privilege insulates those who have it from catastrophe most of the time. But when it doesn't, the mess can be substantial.

LIVING AND DYING IN THE WHITE BUBBLE

A SYSTEM OF privilege also carries risks because it creates, for those of us who have it, a bubble of unreality, inside of which we need not think about the way the world really operates. So the fine folks of Littleton, Colorado, assumed they were safe because they had moved to the 'burbs, away from the city, where danger lived. Once they allowed themselves to think that, they let down their guard to the dysfunction that existed in their sanitized, seemingly sanguine space.

In other words, in some cases—admittedly extreme though they may be—privilege can be dangerous because it leads to expectations and a mentality of entitlement that makes it much more difficult to view the world accurately.

And sometimes the privilege of being treated differently and better than others might just be the very thing that gets you killed.

So consider the meaning of an e-mail I received several years ago after I'd written a piece about the school shooting phenomenon, which came from a guy who had actually been on the SWAT team at Columbine on that awful day back in April 1999.

When law enforcement arrived on the scene, he explained, they had been ready to take the building. That was the purpose for which they'd been trained, after all. There they sat, guns ready, body armor ready, listening as the gunfire continued to echo through the building, up from the cafeteria to the library. Waiting, and waiting. And just as they steeled themselves to take the building, to perhaps save the lives of some of these privileged (and almost entirely white) people who were pinned down inside the school, they received the word from their commanding officer to stand down. They were told to wait.

Confused, several of them asked why—why were they being told to hold back? And then the answer came: these were "white people, with money, and nice cars," they were told. And if they stormed the building, and in the process killed anyone, those same people would sue them blind.

In other words, it was the whiteness along with the class status of those in Littleton that at the end of the day would require law enforcement officials to treat them better than they would have treated other folks. And ironically, it was this preferential treatment that, at the end of the same day, would cause them to die. The SWAT team held back and eventually the shots stopped. Although there is no way to know if quicker action might have saved lives at Columbine High, what we can say for certain is that the failure to act, solely because of the privileged status of the persons living in the community where this tragedy occurred, made stopping the carnage impossible.

On any of the other 364 days of the year, the elevated status of the mostly white, affluent suburbanites in Littleton would serve them well: it would provide them with advantages in terms of jobs, education, housing, and anything else we can imagine. But on that one day—which was the only day that mattered in the end—it had let them down. More than that, it had worked against them; it had possibly been the thing that had sealed their fate. Having others defer to your status and power is always a good thing—until it's not, that is, as this suburban Denver community found out, albeit a dozen or so children too late.

Today, evidence of the dangers that come from living in the bubble continues to pour forth. While people of color have always had to know what others think of them—not doing so, after all, can get you killed—whites have had the luxury (or thought we did) of not knowing or caring. When you have the power, the feelings of the powerless, or simply those who aren't in your club, can be routinely ignored. But on 9/11 that bubble was burst, and perhaps whites would have been better off, and safer, having known a bit about other folks, and the way they viewed our nation, after all. Because privilege didn't keep us secure.

After 9/11, whites and only whites seemed stunned that anyone would hate the United States "Why do they hate us?" was a common mantra from the mouths of white folks, but rarely if ever heard from people of color, for reasons that are as obvious as they are illuminating. Privileged people had never had to know or care. Privilege allowed us to think that no one could mess with us. Now, of course, we know better, though sadly, we seem to have learned little. The war in which we find ourselves currently embroiled after all, also stems from a mentality of privilege: in this case, the privilege of believing that you can throw your muscle around and dictate the course of world affairs (and that you're entitled to do so)—a notion that those without privilege know better than to indulge.

As soldiers continue to die, and families continue to welcome home flag-draped caskets, let us at least be honest enough to face the consequences of privilege, entitlement, and what the Greeks called hubris. For those are things at the heart of our folly in Iraq. They harm not only those among the marginalized, but indeed, are perfectly capable of ending the lives of the privileged as well. This is a deadly game, for all of us.

BECOMING SOMETHING WE'RE NOT:
Racism and the Loss of White Humanity

JUST IN CASE the harm to whites from a system of privilege mentioned thus far seem too abstract, let us personalize things a bit.

The perverse thing about growing up amidst racism is that no matter your own views, no matter your own commitment to resisting it, you inhale it anyway; you ingest it as surely as you ingest the oxygen without which you could not live. Having inhaled it, you are then always at risk of coughing it back up, of vomiting it back into the world whence it came.

Sometimes all it takes is the right situation to bring it out.

I've already noted many times over how important the civil rights movement and the cause of racial equity were and are to my mother. And yet, even she was capable of conjuring up the language of racism when she needed to, when she was upset, or insecure. With the right circumstances, and just enough stress, even she was capable of going to that place that every other day she would have fought as though it were the very gates of hell. But not *that* day, not that summer day, not that day just a few weeks before her only son was about to head off to college.

My mom, like a lot of mothers who have kids about to go off to school, was sliding into a deep depression. For her, the notion of an empty nest was of no small concern. She was on her own now, my father having left the year before, after attempting to commit suicide when his latest extramarital affair ended and was exposed.

During the summer, I had prepared for my move to New Orleans and on this particular day had gone with my best friend, Albert, to the Nashville Peace Fair: a festival with music, and crafts, and dozens of informational booths set up by various nonprofit organizations from throughout the state and mid-South region.

Upon returning to the apartment that I was preparing to leave for the first time, having never lived anywhere else but the maternity ward on the first and second days of my life, I found my mother drinking. Actually, I found her blind-running drunk, and this was alarming because although my mother occasionally drank too much, it was very unlike her to initiate the festivities in the daytime.

When I realized she was in no condition to talk, even though I really wanted to tell her about all the Peace Fair, I thought it best to just keep it to myself for the time being. This was so even though I figured she'd like to hear what I had to say. After all, she shared my views on pretty much everything so far as I knew, but it just didn't seem to be the time.

My mother unfortunately felt otherwise, and not only did she want to discuss the Peace Fair, and politics, she was itching to pick a fight with me: something she had never done before, and has never done since, which is probably among the reasons I remember it so clearly. It started slowly, with her asking me about the event, and though I tried to brush it off, she seemed genuinely interested at first, so I began to tell her about some of the information I had picked up: information about U.S. foreign policy in Central America, and about apartheid in South Africa and how American corporations were helping to prop up the racist regime there.

I am not sure exactly how the discussion descended into the chaotic mess it would become. The whole episode was so bizarre, so out of the ordinary that I think I was too shocked to take it all in. What I recall, without any doubt, is that at some point, and for some reason we got on the subject of welfare and welfare recipients. And when one speaks of welfare in this country, whether one wishes to acknowledge it or not, one is almost always speaking of black people, not because black people are the only folks receiving state aid (indeed more whites receive benefits from the myriad social programs than do blacks) but because that is the image we have been encouraged to have when we hear the term. And that image has become implanted in the minds of Americans, especially white Americans, to such an extent that it is almost automatic, and it allows politicians to criticize "welfare" and "welfare recipients" without ever mentioning race, knowing all along that their constituents get the message.

However we got on the subject, it was obvious that my mom, angry at me for preparing to leave her nest, was going to use this issue—the one that she knew would injure me, because antiracism had been such an undercurrent in our home for so long—as a way to lash out. The next thing I knew, she was rambling on, spewing out one after another nonsensical statement about lazy black welfare recipients and their illegitimate children, and then launching into some extemporaneous diatribe about a particular black woman with whom she had worked (and with whom I always thought she had gotten along pretty well) who now, in today's white zinfandel-induced haze, had become incompetent, pushy, a bigot.

In other words, we had gone from talking about a Peace Fair to talking about welfare to talking about a colleague of hers in a matter of a few minutes, and now things were getting heated, and I was firing back, which is exactly what she wanted. I was watching her use racism in a way that would have sickened her in her sober moments, as a tool to express some totally unrelated angst—as a way to work out the existential crisis she was experiencing at that moment. It was ugly, and not really understanding what was going on—in fact at one point I contemplated that my mother was either having a total nervous breakdown, or had been a fraud all of my life when it came to race—I lit into her, and told her never to speak that way in front of me again.

It was finally at the point where she began to utter the word, the word that was the only word I knew, growing up, never to say, that I exploded, not allowing her to finish it.

"Goddamn n-" she started.

"Shut the fuck UP!" I screamed.

And that's when she swung at me, for the first time in my life, but slow, not as though she really wanted to hit me. Her right arm came up sadly and began the arc toward my cheek, palm open, face contorted in pain—a pain deeper than any I had seen there before, at any time, even as she had stood over my father's hospital bed on the night of his suicide attempt. The look that night had been a look of exhaustion, of resignation to the not-so-fairy-tale ending of her marriage. But this was not resignation to anything. She was imploding, and in the process burning away all illusions. She was going to make me hurt—not physically, as she surely knew I would stop her arm long before her hand could make contact with the side of my head, but at the core of who I was, by making me question who *she* was.

For that experience I thank her, because without it, I may never have really seen how utterly distorted white people could be as a result of racism. My mom, after all, had been my model when it came to things political. She had been consistent, she had been clear, and had never given me any reason to doubt her.

But that confidence, that faith in her perfection, was unhealthy; it was downright dangerous, because that is not the real world. That world of bedrock principle and never-wavering resistance in the face of social conditioning is not the world in which real people reside, and certainly not the one in which white people have ever lived.

Racism, even if it is not your own, but merely circulates in the air, *changes you,* allows you to think things and feel things that make you less than you were meant to be. It steals that part of our humanity that is the most precious: the part that allows us to see the image of God (however defined or conceptualized) and the goodness of creation in all humankind. And our unwillingness to see that, and more than to see it, to really feel it, deep in the marrow of our bones, is what allows us, and even sometimes compels us, to slaughter one another, in the name of the same God whose image we wouldn't recognize if our lives depended on it. Which, come to think of it, they probably do.

So my mother, by way of proving her own weakness, of exhibiting her own conditioning, taught me that one can never be too careful, that one can never enjoy the luxury of smugness, of believing oneself to be so hip, so together, so liberal, so radical, so *down* with the cause of human liberation that it becomes impossible to be sucked in, to be transformed, beyond your wildest imaginations. We may only do it once, or perhaps twice, but it can happen, and so long as that is true, we mustn't romanticize our resistance, but fight to maintain its presence in our lives, recognizing that it could easily vanish in a moment of weakness, a moment of anger, a moment of insecurity, a moment of fear.

Those moments are the ones that matter, after all. People never hurt others in moments of personal strength and bravery, when they are feeling good about themselves, when they are strong and confident. If we spent all of our waking moments in *that* place, then fighting for social justice would be redundant; we would simply have social justice and be done with it, and we could all go swimming, or fishing, or bowling, or dancing, or whatever people do. But it is because we spend so much of our time in that other place, that place of diminished capacity, of wavering and flaccid commitment, that we have to be careful. And it is for that reason that we need these reminders, however ugly they may be, of our own frailty, and of how much has been stolen from us by a society that has desperately and for a long time needed us to step right up and take this sucker punch square on the chin.

Though my anger that day, and even my fear for my mother's sanity, kept me from really internalizing the lesson of the afternoon's events for several more years, I would file it away, in the back of my subconscious, where it would linger until another episode in my life would bring it back around again—an episode that would clarify, beyond all hope of continued innocence, the harm that racism does to the white psyche, the way in which it robs us of our best selves.

* * *

MY FATHER'S MOTHER, Mabel Ruth (McKinney) Wise, was a central figure in my life. She was the person to whom I would often turn for emotional support whenever things got too chaotic in the home of her son and my mother. Whenever things turned especially volatile, it was to her house (hers and Leo's) that I would flee and spend the night until things blew over.

Maw Maw and Paw Paw, as I called them, were the politically liberal grandparents, counterpoised to the conservatives on the McLean side of the family. As with most American Jews of his generation, my grandfather was committed to civil rights, and both he and Maw Maw moved comfortably in and out of the black community where he worked.

When Leo died, in the summer of 1989, my grandmother began to disintegrate. Her slow descent was noticeable almost immediately, far more than what would have been expected as a normal part of the grieving process. When I arrived at the hospital shortly after he had passed and first saw her, in the arms of one of his doctors, it was as if even then her system had begun to shut down—as if part of her had died, and it was only a matter of time before her own heart would stop beating as well.

As it turned out, she would live another nine years, though only a few of them would be of much quality. A year after Paw Paw's death, while I was at home following college graduation, she had a car accident. It was nothing serious, but when I got the call to head to the scene, just a half-mile or so from our apartment, it was obvious that the fender bender had shaken her up, mentally if not physically. She seemed disoriented—not in shock, mind you, but just in a haze. As the years went by, it became obvious that she was in the early stages of Alzheimer's, and had probably begun succumbing to the disease at the time of that accident.

We would watch as her grip on reality slowly slipped away. It was a process that, in its early years, is hard to really categorize because a certain amount of mental slippage is inevitable as we get older. Since there are still plenty of moments of crystal clarity, there are times when you're inclined to think there really isn't anything all that serious going on. But then you see the person on one of their cloudy days and you're snapped back into reality, unable to run from the truth that your loved one is dying, and it's not going to be a fast or pretty thing to watch.

By the midnineties Mabel was still able to live on her own, in the house she and Leo had purchased four decades earlier, but she needed considerable help during the day. For the last two or three years of her life she would have a couple of different nurses who would stay with her for several hours, make her lunches, clean up after her, and near the end bathe her as well. We always worried that after the nurses left she would burn the house down because she was a smoker, and in the depths of her growing dementia could easily have fallen asleep, cigarette in hand, and that would have been the end of her.

In 1996, when I moved back to Nashville and was looking for a place to live, I spent a few weeks with her, sleeping in my father's old room, and witnessed the deterioration up close. She would, at any given moment, have as many as two dozen open Diet Coke cans in the refrigerator, having opened them, put them back in the fridge after a few sips, and then opened another one, forgetting about the first. Then she would repeat this process until she ran out of shelf space, or until someone—myself or a nurse, or another visiting relative—would pour them out. At night, she would forget that I was in the back room, and if she heard me moving around it would scare her, so she would come to investigate the source of the noise, and I would have to remind her, several times a night, that it was just me. A few mornings, when

I came into the den to see her, she would be startled, having forgotten yet again that I was staying with her.

By 1998, her deterioration had accelerated to breakneck speed. Seemingly at once she began to forget who people were, confusing me with my father regularly or even calling me Leo on occasion. In July, she came down with some kind of infection and had to be hospitalized. During her stay at the hospital it became obvious to her family and doctors that she could never return home. Upon her release, her mind barely functioning, she was placed in a nursing home, on the Alzheimer's ward. She would live for a little less than a month, dying two weeks before Kristy and I were married.

But what, you might ask, does any of this have to do with race? What does a little old lady with Alzheimer's tell us about whiteness in America? The truth is, it has everything to do with race, as a number of events around this time would make clear.

But before you can fully appreciate why this is so, there's some background context you'll need first. What you must know about my grandmother is that Mabel Wise was no ordinary white woman. She was not only married to an antiracist white man, but was herself an antiracist white woman. Though not an activist, she very deliberately instilled in her children, and by extension in me (as her oldest grandchild and the one with whom she spent the most time), a deep and abiding contempt for bigotry, for racism, of any form. She was very proud of what I had chosen to do with my life, and although her antiracism was of a liberal sort that likely didn't involve an amazingly deep understanding of the way that institutional injustice operates—it was, in other words, an interpersonal level at which she tended to think of these issues—it was nonetheless quite real.

That she saw racism and rebelling against it as a personal issue made sense actually, because it was at that level that she had learned to deal with it so many years before. You see, her father had been in the Klan, while working as a mechanic in Detroit in the early 1930s, and then after moving back home to Tennessee shortly thereafter. All of which would become a bit of a problem down the line when, at the age of fifteen, my grandmother would meet and eventually fall in love with Leo Wise, a Jew. Around the age of seventeen, she could no longer abide her father's racism, and that, combined with his anti-Semitism, which she now took very personally, led her finally to confront him.

More then merely confront him, she actually told him in no uncertain terms that either he was going to burn his Klan robes, or she was going to do it for him. I can't even begin to imagine the kind of strength, the fortitude it would have taken to issue such a challenge in 1937, especially since he was a large man, given to anger, and hardly used to being accosted in such a way by a young girl, or any woman. And it worked. My great-grandfather, having been given an ultimatum, burned his robes, quit the Klan, changed his life, and would later accept the man who would become my grandfather into his family.

From that experience, I guess, Mabel decided that standing up to racism wasn't so tough after all, and so she would do it again many times in her life. Among the most prominent examples would be the time she told a real-estate agent, who had proudly announced that the house he was showing to my grandfather and her was desirable because it was a restricted neighborhood, so there wouldn't be any of "those people" living around them, that he had best get in his car and leave, or else she would be forced to run him over in hers.

So that's who she was, and had always been, so long as any of us could recall. Which now brings us to the rest of the story, the part about the Alzheimer's, and the part that provides dramatic evidence of the way in which racism is capable of diminishing even the strongest of us, even the ones who have made a point of resistance.

If you've ever had a loved one who was suffering with Alzheimer's, you know that the loss of memories is among the more benign symptoms of the disease. The others are far worse: the paranoia, the anger—even rage—that accompanies the slippage of one's mental faculties; the persistent insecurity and helplessness which feeds both the paranoia and the rage, in a perpetual loop, right up until death. Maw Maw went through all of those stages: insecurity, fear, anger, and as we know, we are often not our best selves when gripped by any of those three emotional states.

So it came to pass that as she went through these stages of the illness that would ultimately contribute to her death, she began to work out the contours of her deepening crisis upon the nurses whose job it had been to take care of her—black nurses, to be specific.

Think hard now. Ask yourself, how might a white person treat a black person when they're angry, or frightened, or both? Oh yes, like *that*. And what might they call those black persons in a moment of anger or insecurity, or both? Oh yes, *that*.

Resisting socialization requires the ability to *choose*. But near the end of my grandmother's life, as her body and mind began to shut down, this consciousness—the soundness of mind which had led her to fight the pressures to accept racism—began to vanish. Her awareness of who she had been disappeared, such that in those moments of anger and fear she would think nothing of referring to her nurses by the term Malcolm X said was the first word newcomers learned when they came to this country: *nigger*. Though I'm not sure when white folks first learn the word, Maw Maw made clear a more important point: that having learned it, we will never, ever forget it.

It was a word she would never have uttered from conscious thought, but one that remained locked away in her subconscious despite her best intentions and lifelong commitment to standing strong against racism, a word that would have made her ill even to think it, a word that would make her violent if she heard it said, a word that, for her to utter it herself, would make her another person altogether. But there it was, as ugly, bitter, and no doubt fluently expressed as it ever had been by her father.

Here was a woman who no longer could recognize her own children, a woman who had no idea who her husband had been, who had no clue where she was, what her name was, what year it was, and yet knew what she had been taught at a very early age to call black people. Once she was no longer capable of resisting this demon, tucked away like a ticking time bomb in the far corners of her mind, it would reassert itself and explode with a vengeance. She could not remember how to feed herself. She could not go to the bathroom by herself. She could not recognize a glass of water for what it was. But she could recognize *a nigger*. America had seen to that, and no disease would strip her of that memory. Indeed, it would be one of the last words I would hear her say, before finally she stopped talking at all.

And no, it wasn't some free-floating word bouncing around in her diseased brain, which she was throwing around as if with no larger meaning. After all, she didn't call any of her family by that word, even though we were the recipients of plenty of her anger and fear as well. She would call her white daughters "bitches" and me an asshole once or twice; she even had some choice words for her white doctors, none of which I can recall now, but also none of which, I am certain, included *that* word. She knew exactly what she was saying, and to whom.

Given this woman's entire life and the circumstances surrounding her slow demise, her utterance of a word even as hateful as this one says little about her. But it speaks volumes about her country, about the seeds planted in every one of us by our culture—seeds that, so long as we are of sound mind and commitment, we can choose not to water, but also seeds that show a remarkable propensity to sprout of their own accord. It speaks volumes about how whites, even those truly committed to living in antiracist ways and passing down that commitment to their children, have been infected with a dangerous pathogen, which may or may not ever emerge to destroy the antiracist who carries it inside, but which just might, and therein lies the problem.

That someone like Mabel Wise could fall prey to such a sickness tells me all I need to know about the costs of racism to white people. Maybe this is why I tire of white folks who insist "I don't have a racist bone in my body" or "I never notice color." Maw Maw would have said that too, and she would have meant well. And she would have been wrong.

What was interesting about watching this unfold was seeing how the rest of my family dealt with it, which was as predictable as it was unfortunate.

Whenever Maw Maw would say the word, and either of her two daughters heard it, they would be quick to reassure the nurses that she didn't mean anything by it—which was patently untrue—and that it was just the illness talking, which the nurses already understood, far better than my aunts, in fact.

While apologizing for racial epithets is nice I suppose, far nicer would be the ability to learn something from this gift my grandmother was giving us. And it was a gift; her final way of saying *look at this, see what is happening here, do something about this.* Because ultimately, what those women at my grandmother's nursing home need and deserve, much more than sincere but irrelevant apologies from embarrassed family members, is for me to say what I'm saying right now, and to encourage everyone to say the same thing. They deserve an end to this vicious system of racial caste and the conditioning it provides to us all.

Those nurses knew, and so do I, why my grandmother could no longer fight. For the rest of us, there is no similar excuse available. We do not have Alzheimer's—not yet at least—and yet we all go through our moments of fear, anger, and insecurity. It doesn't take this awful disease to place any of us in those states of mind from time to time, and so we are all at risk, all vulnerable to acting out, to acting on the basis of something we *know* is wrong, but which is there, ready to be used if the chips are down, or merely if we aren't paying enough attention to the details.

If you still don't believe me, perhaps one more story will do it.

* * *

IN APRIL 2003, I boarded a plane bound for St. Louis. From there I would fly to Des Moines, Iowa, for a conference. Prior to that day, I had flown on a thousand or so individual flights in my life, but on that day things would be different. As I walked down the jet bridge to board the 737, I glanced into the cockpit, as I do with most flights just by habit, and there I saw something I had never seen before, in all the years I had been flying: not one, but *two* black pilots at the controls of the plane—a rare sight for any air traveler given the small percentage of commercial pilots who are African American.

In case you've forgotten what book you're reading, let me refresh your memory. This is a book by a white guy who makes his living fighting racism, speaking out against racism, researching and responding to racism, challenging racism, in thought, action, and policy. It's a book by a guy who was *raised* to be antiracist, who has been actively antiracist since he was a child, and who has studied enough about racism to know why it is not only evil but ignorant, based on illogical premises, the result of flawed thinking, albeit the kind of thinking that is often cultivated and even rewarded in our culture.

But despite my upbringing and whatever wisdom I possess on these issues, what do you suppose my *first* thought was, upon seeing who was going to be flying me to St. Louis that morning? Let's make it multiple choice, just for fun. Was my first reaction a) *Free at last, free at last, thank God almighty we are free at last! I am so happy to have not one but two black pilots. I can't wait to tell all of my friends?* Or was it b) *Oh my God, can these guys fly this plane?* If you actually have to think about it before answering, then you really haven't been paying attention.

Now don't get me wrong. Almost as quickly as the thought (it was "b" by the way) came into my head, I was able to stifle it, to beat it back, to wrestle it to the ground of my conscious mind. I knew instantly that such a thought was absurd; after all, given the history of racism, I had every reason to think that these two guys were probably among the very best pilots that the airline had—had they not been, they would never have made it this far. They would have been required to show not only that they could fly, but that they could do so over and above the prejudices and stereotypes that black folks have to overcome in any job they do.

I also knew, intellectually, that in the weeks before this flight, several white pilots had been hauled off planes because they had been too drunk to fly them, or because, in the case of two Southwest flyboys, they had decided to strip down to their underwear as a practical joke they would seek to play on the flight attendants. So intellectually speaking, I should have been damn glad to see anyone *but* a white pilot on my plane that day. But we don't always react to things on the basis of intellect, on the basis of what we know to be true. Rather, we sometimes operate on the basis of what we feel, something over which we don't have nearly as much control as we might like to think. We react on the basis of conditioning, on the basis of a lot of subconscious stuff: stuff we don't even see coming (that's why they call it *sub*conscious, after all), and that's what I had done.

Because no matter what I know to be true, I am also conditioned like all whites to see people of color and immediately wonder if they're really qualified for the job—to automatically assume they aren't as good as a white person. The fact that I'm lucky enough to have been working on my conditioning, and therefore could get a grip on my own nonsense is nice, but beside the point. The point is, it happened and could happen again. And maybe it wouldn't happen every time, and maybe it wouldn't happen to you (though don't be so sure; until it happened to me, I might have denied it too) but the fact is it could. All it takes is a situation that calls forth the conditioning, prompts the stereotype, and then cues up the response.

And I resent it, deeply, to the core of my being, speaking now of the fact that such conditioning had done a number on me, too. I resent it not for myself but for our daughters, because just as I was raised to know better, and just as our girls will be, too, the sad truth of what happened to me that day is that no matter how we raise them, no matter what we teach them, they will pick up the bullshit anyway. They'll get it from the media; they'll get it from friends; they'll internalize it and always be vulnerable to the possibility of having it transform them.

How much longer will we act as though it's not there, pretend we don't see it, or that it's only a problem for others? How long will we turn away from the mirror whose reflection we cannot bear? And how long before our refusal to face the truth makes it impossible for us to change, having so much invested in sustaining the lie of our innocence? I for one don't intend to find out by denying it a second longer. But then again, as I sat there in 12D, shaking at the visceral recognition of my own distorted humanity, it's not exactly as if I had much of a choice any longer.

NOTHING FOR SOMETHING:
Whiteness and the Loss of Culture

THE WEEK BEFORE Paw Paw died, I visited him, and brought him a folder with every article I had ever written up to that point—mostly from the school paper and the underground rag I was writing for in New Orleans. It was Father's Day weekend, and I thought it would be nice to give him a gift that would really mean something to him. He had been a journalist while in college, too, and because he so appreciated my politics, I figured it would mean a lot more to him than just another pair of socks.

We had no idea that he would never see another Sunday, though I think, in retrospect, that he knew. I had expected him to put the folder aside and read it later, perhaps in a week or so, after returning from the hospital, where he was going in a few days to undergo prostate surgery. Though he wasn't in good shape—he had been on dialysis at that point for several months—there was nothing to indicate that this would be anything other than a routine operation.

He read the entire folder, right then and there, methodically consuming a few dozen short pieces, leaving my mom, Maw Maw, and me to talk and visit with one another. It was as if he knew that if he didn't read them then, he wouldn't get a chance.

Looking back, I should have known something was up. A few weeks earlier I had been staying at Leo and Mabel's house—I still liked to go and spend the night there sometimes when I was home from college, to take advantage of the peace and quiet of living out a bit from the city—and had had a conversation with him unlike any I had ever had before.

I remember him, for the first time, beginning to speak of his father. He was trying to tell me stories of what his father had experienced in Russia, and about his journey to America (a story we only knew little bits and pieces of, principally the ones I shared with you earlier). But every time he started to tell a story, to actually provide me with a specific piece of information, his voice would trail off, and then he would start again, usually in a totally different place, and on some totally different subject.

He repeated the process a few times, until it became obvious that he wasn't going to get much out. It wasn't that his mind was going, or that his memories were fading. Though his body was at the end of a journey, his mind was strong. The problem was that he literally didn't have any stories to tell—not complete ones at least. And the reason he didn't have any stories, though he likely didn't realize it, as I didn't at the time, was because stories about the old country and a connection to that immigrant past were always the first casualties of whiteness, the first things that had to be sacrificed on the alter of assimilation.

To hold on to those stories, let alone to pass them down, would be to remain stuck, one was told; it would stifle one from becoming fully American (which, let's face it, meant white American at the time of entry for European ethnics); and so one had to begin the process of transformation: Don't seem too Jewish; don't teach your children the language of their forbears, nor the customs. Don't talk about the old country. Put all that behind and become a new man—a white man.

Only by giving up one's past, and one's family's connection to it, could a person like Jacob Wise win a future for his children, or so he was led to believe. Only in that way could he make others comfortable enough with his presence, with his accent, and with his way of praying, that they might welcome him and his brood into the American fold.

It had begun innocently enough of course, or so it seemed, there on Ellis Island, being told by some surly immigration official that they couldn't understand the thick Yiddish coming off your tongue, and so it would be necessary to give you a new name, to simply make one up. What was that, after all, which you were garbling? Shuckleman, Sheckman, Shuckman, Shankman? Ah, to hell with it, you name is now Wise. Not Weiss, but Wise, like the Virginia Catholics, whitened and sanitized for your protection, with all due apologies to Alex Haley, a Jewish Toby.

Had the name been the only thing lost, perhaps it wouldn't have mattered. What's in a name, after all? Well nothing, nothing except one's past, of course. Nothing except the intergenerational fiber that has kept your people together for generations. Nothing except the story of how you survived.

Nothing but that.

So the process of whitening had begun, and now it was culminating in the inability of my grandfather, Jacob's son, to pass down any story, any fable, *anything* at all about his father, his mother, his grandparents, or the place from which we come. Because to know those stories would first have required that he had been taught them. And for him to be taught them would have required that Jacob had been willing to do so. And for his father to be willing would have meant that he had been able to resist the pull and lure of whiteness. And to do that had been unthinkable.

So my grandfather joined our ancestors, about whom neither I nor, oddly enough, even he knew much of anything. With him went my connection to the past, leaving me—and now my daughters as well—with nothing other than one-half of a set of gold candlesticks, the only items smuggled out of Russia on that ship Papa boarded so many years ago. I don't even know the story that goes with the candlestick, but sadly it is all I have left.

All, that is, except for my white skin. And though that skin provides me with innumerable benefits, it is hardly better than the candle in the candlestick at keeping me warm at night. Because I know its true price: I know how much my family paid for it, and for my name. I know, because I saw in Paw Paw's eyes that day what the cost of white privilege had been for my people, what it had exacted of my kinfolk as they hit the reset button on the game of life, and stifled their traditions and cultures so they might find a place in this land.

I know the cost incurred and the penalty paid by those who had to give up who they were and become something they were not—white. I know because I saw the bill of sale, saw it in the silence between my grandfather and myself: a silence louder than any scream I had ever heard.

* * *

SEVERAL YEARS LATER, the magnitude of this loss was brought home in stark relief, as I sat in an training session on how to undo racism, facilitated by the People's Institute for Survival and Beyond, in New Orleans. For years I had known of the institute and its core trainers: people like Ron Chisom, Diana Dunn, David Billings, and Barbara Major. I had also been cautioned (by people who had actually never gone through an institute training) that the group's modus operandi was to attack white people and make them feel bad for their "inherent" racism. As it turns out, nothing could have been further from the truth.

From the beginning it was clear that the institute viewed racism as something that was anything *but* inherent. Rather, they explained it as a socially constructed power imbalance at the institutional level, which then tends to foster individual-level biases and racism.

What stuck with me most about the institute's analysis was how clear the trainers were about the damage done to whites in the process of internalizing white supremacy, and accepting racial privilege. One of the most telling moments came when Ron Chisom asked the participants in the three-day session what we liked about being whatever it is that we were, racially speaking. What did black folks, for instance, like about being black? And what did whites like about being white?

For most whites, it was a question to which we had never given much thought. Looks of confusion spread across most of our faces as we struggled to find an answer worthy of the occasion. Meanwhile, people of color came up with a formidable list almost immediately: they said they liked the strength of their families, the camaraderie, the soul, the music, the culture, the rhythms, the customs, even their color. And of course, they mentioned prominently the perseverance of their ancestors in the face of great odds.

When it was our turn we came up, finally, with a predictable list. It is the same one, in fact, offered pretty much every time I ask the question to white folks around the country. We like not being followed around in stores on suspicion of being shoplifters; we like the fact that we're not presumed out of place on a college campus or in a high-ranking professional position; we like the fact that we don't have to constantly overcome negative stereotypes about our intelligence, morality, honesty, or work ethic, the way people of color often do.

Once finished, we began to examine the lists offered by both sides. The contrast was striking. Looking at the items mentioned by people of color, one couldn't miss the fact that all of the attributes listed were actually about personal strength or personal qualities, actually possessed by the participants, and in which they could (and did) take pride. The list was tangible and meaningful.

The white list was quite different. Staring at the entries, it was impossible not to notice that *none* of what we liked about being white had anything to do with *us*. None of it had to do with internal qualities of character or fortitude. Rather, every response had to do less with what we liked about being white than what we liked about *not being a person of color.* We were defining ourselves by a negative, providing ourselves with an identity rooted in the external— rooted in the relative oppression of others, without which we would have had *nothing to say.* Without a system of racial domination and subordination, we would have been able to offer no meaningful response to the question.

As became clear in that moment, inequality and privilege were the only real components of whiteness. Without racial privilege there is no whiteness, and without whiteness, there is no racial privilege. Being white only means to be advantaged relative to everyone else.

Our answers had been honest, and devastatingly so. They had laid bare the truth about white privilege: that in order to access it, one first had to give up all the meaningful cultural, personal, and communal attributes that once kept our peoples alive in Europe and during our journeys here. After all, we had come from families that once had the kinds of qualities we now were seeing listed before us by people of color. We had had customs, traditions, music, and culture, and style—things to be celebrated, cultivated, and passed down to future generations. Even more, we had come from *resistance* cultures—most Europeans who came were the losers of their respective societies since the winners rarely felt the need to hop on a boat and leave where they were—and these resistance cultures had been steeped in the notion of resisting injustice, and of achieving solidarity.

But to become white required that those things be sublimated to a new social reality in which resistance was not the point, indeed quite the opposite. To become the power structure was to view the tradition of resistance with suspicion and contempt.

So while the folks of color in the room—and make no mistake about this—would have dearly loved to be able to claim for themselves the privileges filling the white folks's page on the flipchart, *we* would have just as dearly loved to be able to claim for ourselves even *one* of the meaningful qualities mentioned by people of color. But we couldn't.

To define yourself, ultimately, by what you're not, is a pathetic and heartbreaking thing. It is to stand denuded before a culture that has stolen your birthright, or rather, convinced you to give it up. And the costs are formidable, beginning with the emptiness whites so often feel when confronted by multiculturalism and the connectedness of people of color to their various heritages. That emptiness then gets filled up by the privileges and ultimately forces us to become dependent on them.

It's hard to deny that at the end of the day, this self-imposed cultural genocide has cost us more, in the long run, than it's worth.

REDEMPTION

> "Life is tragic simply because the earth turns and the sun inexorably rises and sets, and one day, for each of us, the sun will go down for the last, last time. Perhaps the whole root of our trouble, the human trouble is that we will sacrifice all the beauty of our lives, will imprison ourselves in totems, taboos, crosses, blood sacrifices, steeples, mosques, races, armies, flags, nations, in order to deny the fact of death, which is the only fact we have. It seems to me that one ought to rejoice in the fact of death—ought to decide, indeed, to earn one's death by confronting with passion the conundrum of life. One is responsible to life: It is the small beacon in that terrifying darkness from which we come and to which we shall return. One must negotiate this passage as nobly as possible, for the sake of those who are coming after us."
>
> **JAMES BALDWIN,** *The Fire Next Time*, 1963

AS I WAS writing this book, I stopped to read a few of the stories to my wife, Kristy, some of which she had heard me speak of before, but several of which she had not. Kristy, I should point out, shares my values on these and other matters, but—and this is no criticism, just an observation of fact—fighting racism is not where she chooses to place her energy. She supports my work, however, in many ways, not least of which is by doing the primary childrearing with our daughters, and as such makes it possible for me to do what I need to do, and what I literally couldn't do without her love and assistance.

Once I finished reading a few of the vignettes in the Loss section to her, she seemed genuinely upset, noting that the ways in which racism was so obviously ingrained in us made her wonder if perhaps it was impossible to ever really end it, to change things substantially. Though some might view this pessimistic assessment as cause for alarm—and for her it seemed alarming to be sure—I must say that for me it was not the least bit disturbing, though it did prompt me to add this section to the book, since I wouldn't want folks to come away from it with a defeated feeling.

I would have liked to be able to tell her not to worry; that good people have done great things, and changed the world before; that committed movements of committed people can shift mountains; and that the evidence for this kind of transformation was all around us. But in truth, I couldn't say that, not because it wasn't true, at least in part, but because it wasn't the point.

Several years back, when legal scholar Derrick Bell wrote *Faces at the Bottom of the Well*, in which he suggested that racism may indeed be a permanent feature of American life, never to be fully and finally undone, I remember the uproar it caused in many a white liberal circle, and among white liberal students who were often assigned to read it in class. White liberals, and radicals for that matter, place a huge amount of faith in the inevitability of justice being done, of right winning in the end, of the triumph of all that is good and true. And they take even the smallest victories—which are sometimes what we have to settle for—as evidence that in just a few more years, and with a little more work, we'll arrive at that place of peace and goodwill. Bell was challenging that faith, at least as it applied to race, and white folks didn't like what they were hearing.

When you're a member of the privileged group, you don't take kindly to someone telling you that you can't do something, whether that something is making a lot of money or ending racism. What do you mean racism is permanent? What do you mean we'll never have justice? How dare anyone imply that there might be some problems too large for the determined will, or should we say determined white will, since obviously the determined wills of black and brown folks haven't been able to do it yet?

But Bell's assessment, at least for me, was a liberating tract—no cause for pessimism but rather cause for recommitment to the purpose and mission at hand. This may seem counterintuitive, since for some, committing to fighting a battle you may never win seems futile. But fighting that battle is what people of color have always done and will continue to do, no matter the outcome. Is it appropriate then for me to say that if the fight wouldn't end in victory there was no purpose, that it is indeed futile? What would that kind of attitude say to black and brown folks who have always fought injustice as if ending it were possible, but who always knew they might well never see change come about?

What whites have rarely had to think about—because as the dominant group we are so used to having our will be done, with a little effort at least— is that maybe the point is not victory, however much we all wish to see justice attained and injustice routed. Maybe our redemption comes from the struggle itself. Maybe it is in the effort, the striving for equality and freedom that we become human.

Kristy's pessimism, understandable, perhaps, given the magnitude of the challenge, took me back to a letter I had received many years ago from Archbishop Tutu, during the divestment battle at Tulane.

It was almost as if he were reading our minds, or at least mine, knowing that I was doubting the relevance of our efforts. After all, it wasn't looking as though we were going to be able to force the board to capitulate to our ultimate demand, and even if we (and every other college) did obtain divestment, would things really change in South Africa as a result?

His letter was brief, but in its brevity offered an obvious yet profound rationale for the work of any freedom fighter: "You do not do the things you do because others will necessarily join you in the doing of them," he explained, "nor because they will ultimately prove successful. You do the things you do because the things you are doing are right."

There's much to be said for such simplicity, as it's usually a lack of complication that allows people to feel, to remain in touch with their humanity— a humanity that can sometimes be distorted by too many layers of analysis and theory. There is redemption in struggle.

If you ask those who believe in God—any God, any creative force from which we come and to whom (or to which) they think we are accountable— whether they can *prove* the existence of that God, they will likely say no. Most will tell you that such matters are matters of faith, and that they live their lives, or try to, on the basis of that faith. Believers do this, even though they could be wrong. All I am suggesting here is that we should live our lives as if justice were possible, too, but whether or not it is, treat it no differently than one treats one's perceived obligations before God. Indeed, if there were such a being, such a force, surely struggling to do justice would be one of those obligations, would it not? And surely one wouldn't be relieved from this merely because justice was not finally obtainable.

And let's just be honest: there is no such place called "justice," if by that we envision a finish line, or a point at which the battle is won and the need to continue the struggle is over. After all, even when you succeed in obtaining a measure of justice, you're always forced to mobilize to defend that which you've won. There is no looming vacation. But there is redemption in struggle.

Of course, that there is redemption in struggle, and that victory is only one reason for fighting, only seems to come as a surprise, or rather, as a source of discomfort to white folks. Invariably, it seems it is we in the white community who obsess over our own efficacy and fail to recognize the value of commitment, irrespective of outcome.

People of color, on the other hand, never having been burdened with the illusion that the world was their oyster and thus anything they touched could and should turn to gold, usually take a more reserved, and I would say healthier view of the world and the prospects for change. They know (as indeed they must) that the thing being fought for, at least if it's worth having, will require more than a part-time effort, and will not likely come in the life-times of those presently fighting for it. And it is that knowledge that allows a strength and a resolve that few members of the dominant majority will ever, can ever, know.

This is not to sentimentalize suffering or the strength often born from it. In fact, this last statement should be taken less as a comment about the strength of persons of color than as an observation about the weakness of those without it. For it is true, at least in my experience, that whites, having been largely convinced of our ability, indeed entitlement, to affect the world around us and mold it to our liking, are very much like children when we discover that at least for some things—like fundamentally altering the system of privilege and domination that first invested us with such optimism—it will take more than good intentions, determined will, and that old stand-by we euphemistically call "elbow grease."

Regardless, there is something to be said for confronting the inevitable choice one must make in this life between collaborating with or resisting injustice, and choosing the latter. Indeed, it is among the most important choices we will ever be asked to make as humans, and it is a burden uniquely ours.

I have no idea when, or if, racism will be eradicated. I have no idea whether anything I say, do, or write will make the least bit of difference in the world. But I say it, do it, and write it anyway, because as uncertain as the outcome of our resistance may be, the outcome of our silence and inaction is anything but. We know exactly what will happen if we don't do the work: *nothing*. And given that choice, between certainty and promise, in which territory one finds the measure of our resolve and humanity, I will opt for hope.

Letting go of the obsession with outcome, even while one fervently fights for victory, can in the end only make us more effective and stronger in our resistance—healthier even. After all, if one is constantly looking for the payoff, but the payoff is slow in coming (as is pretty much always the case), burnout is never too far around the corner. But if we are committed to the struggle because we know that our very humanity depends on it, that the fight for human liberation is among the things that give life meaning, then burnout is far less of a threat. We do the work to save our lives morally and ethically, if not physically.

A few years ago, the first time I spoke at the University of Oregon, I gave a workshop in the Ben Linder room of the student center—a room named for a man who, in April 1987, in Nicaragua, was murdered by contra forces armed and trained by my government and his, killed for the crime of helping bring running water to rural villagers. And as I sat there, inspired by a painting of the village where Ben died, and the tribute to his work that greets visitors to this room, I reflected on how I'd felt as a college freshman upon hearing of his assassination. I remembered why both he and the revolution of which he was a part ultimately had to be crushed. They both posed, as we used to say, the threat of a good example.

That's when I realized that Ben Linder's life and death sum up, as well as anything I could say, why I do what I do, and what I have come to believe is required of us. And what is required is that we be prepared to die for our principles if need be, but even more so, to be unafraid to live for them.

So let us begin.

EPILOGUE

AN OPEN LETTER TO WHITE AMERICA
ABOUT WHITE PRIVILEGE AND HURRICANE KATRINA

Dear White America,

Please step away from the remote control.

You are far too quick to reach for it. Far too quick to change the channel, to turn away from that upon which you can no longer bear to gaze.

I know this all too well for I am one of you, and I have done it myself before.

But no longer.

Unless you have lived in the city of New Orleans, as I did for ten years, you likely have no idea the magnitude of that which has been lost since the early days of September 2005. Unless you have lived there, you can't possibly appreciate the national catastrophe wrought by Hurricane Katrina, or more to the point, the failing of levees in the hurricane's wake.

And though you may wish to change the channel now—indeed, may already have done so and moved on to the next big story—I implore you to stay put for just a while longer, so that we may examine this thing together, you and I.

As I was saying, unless you have lived there, you just won't understand.

It isn't enough that you may have come to Mardi Gras, gotten drunk on Bourbon Street, eaten beignets at Café du Monde, shown your breasts to a stranger for some beads, or perhaps pissed in an alley somewhere, too busy to search out a bathroom and thereby interrupt your good time.

Much more than that was lost. In fact, that stuff wasn't about New Orleans so much as it was about you. New Orleans was always more than that, however little you may have known it.

New Orleans was a literal and metaphorical gumbo the likes of which the nation has never seen before, and now, sadly, may never see again. It was the crossroads of culture, and color, and ethnicity, and heritage: the birthplace of jazz and so much more. It was a place where I knew I wanted to be, ever since my first day in the city, in the late summer of 1986—the day that a little eleven-year old boy hustled me for a dollar in the French Quarter, betting me that he could tell me "where I got dem shoes." I took the bait, assuming he meant that he could tell me where I had bought them, and feeling confident that he could do no such thing. But he had been speaking literally, and knew exactly where I "got em," as in, at that moment, which was "on Royal Street." My money was his, and my heart belonged to the city. You have to appreciate any town where you can get hustled in such fashion by a child, and not even feel bad about it.

But when you looked at New Orleans, too often you didn't see what I saw. If you really saw the people, you saw in them only bad things: you saw the poverty, and yes it was real. You saw the crime, and yes, that was real too. You saw the political corruption (and Lord knows that was no hallucination), and for many of you, these things led you to conclude that the emptying of that great city by floodwaters several feet high was, however tragic, something of a blessing as well.

I heard many of you say this in fact, after Katrina. I heard many of you say that perhaps now the city could rebuild without certain people messing it all up. And I knew who you meant. It's who you always mean when you speak that way. Or even worse, for some of you, you suggested that perhaps it shouldn't be rebuilt at all. And no, I didn't believe you when you swore that this callousness had nothing to do with the racial and class demographic of the place affected. You swore it was just unwise to rebuild in a hurricane zone like that, in a place that is so likely to be hit again by a disaster at some point in the future. But you never say that when little Midwestern farm towns or rural map specks in the South get blown away by tornadoes, as happens from time to time. And you aren't telling all the old white retirees in Florida to pack up and move, all because they've chosen to live in a place that is equally impacted by named storms on a pretty regular basis. No, you save your heartlessness for this place, and we all know why.

In some ways, it's hard to blame you. After all, to watch the way in which the national media covered the inundation of the city two years ago, you'd almost think the flooding had been a good thing. With non-stop images of looters and constant rhetoric about thugs raping and killing evacuees in the Superdome and Convention Center, who can blame you for thinking the worst about the residents there?

Actually I can. But only because I've lived there and I know them. Before I had the opportunity to really get to know the folks there, I would probably have thought many of the same things about them that you think today.

That you could be so easily led to believe the worst about black folks who are poor, even when you have not met them, says a lot about the nation in which you live and the propaganda to which you and I have both been subjected. It says a lot about white privilege too: in this case, the privilege of never having to worry that you (that we) will be viewed through the prism of a negative group stereotype, just because some of our number do bad things from time to time.

And when you consider that all those reports about mass violence in the evacuation centers turned out to be false—there were no murders or molestations, and far fewer sexual assaults than were committed by white kids at Woodstock '99, according to multiple investigations—what does it say that you were so quick to believe them? See, I'm betting that if a storm took out Nantucket next summer, and someone was running around insisting that white people were raping and slaughtering children at the closest Episcopal Church, no one would actually report such a thing without evidence, without bodies, without proof. But in this country you can say anything about black people, no matter how absurd, and folks will believe it. Yes, that says a lot about privilege, and the consequences of its absence in the lives of others.

And so do the following things, about which I'd like you to think a bit.

During the flooding of New Orleans you got to see the same clips of the same looters—the same dozen or so people, shown over and over again in fact—

but you didn't see the white tourists, in the back of the Quarter, busting out the windows of the Walgreen's drug store, in search of sustenance. It happened, but the cameras weren't there to show it to you.

You didn't see the white sheriff's deputies in Gretna, on the West Bank of the Mississippi river, pointing their guns at New Orleanians—mostly black— seeking to cross the bridge to safety as the waters rose. This act of cruelty, of institutional barbarism and venal race and class bias happened, but was not captured on film for you to see, once and then twice, and then three, four, five times. Instead, you got to see the woman with the Huggies wipes, and the guy with the big screen TV: all the better for reinforcing negative stereotypes of what criminality looks like.

You didn't see the members of the National Guard, mostly white, aiming their guns at the folks at the Convention Center who were trying to get to the food in a locked pantry, so as to feed the multitudes. You didn't hear them tell the hungry to get away from the food or they would blow their "fucking heads off." That happened, because property is always more important than lives in this country, but you didn't see it. The media was too busy showing you footage of the looted and ransacked Wal-Mart.

You didn't see the prisoners at the Orleans Parish Prison, most of them non-violent offenders, and many of them awaiting trial, who had been convicted of nothing yet, who in the first days of the flooding were abandoned by the guards there, left to drown, so little value was placed on their lives. The TV didn't show you that—another act of structural neglect and cruelty that was deemed less important than stories of drug addicts raiding hospitals in search of a fix (which stories turned out to be almost entirely false by the way).

And you didn't see the police officers going into the crowds at the Superdome, or to the hotels downtown, and plucking out white folks—especially European tourists—and moving them to the front of the evacuation lines for buses. It happened, over and over again, but there were no cameras showing you this callous provision of blatant privilege, and the subsequent neglect of black folks made to wait.

And one more thing I know you didn't see, because almost no one has. Because the media—that institution you often think is so liberal—has refused to tell you about it. You haven't seen the satellite photos of New Orleans public school buses, leaving the city's bus barn, and driving to pick white people up in neighboring St. Bernard Parish, and drive *them* to safety, even as blacks were left by the tens of thousands to fend for themselves downtown. I've seen them though. More to the point, I have them in my possession if you'd care to see them.

You see this really was about race, though I know you'd love to think otherwise.

I know this because I saw the poll and how y'all answered it, back in December of '05, just a couple of months after the storm had passed. It was the one where you were asked whether Katrina and its aftermath held out any lessons for our nation when it came to race. And you said no. No lessons at all. Let's move on.

And you wonder why folks of color sometimes think we're insane? Heartless? Even straight up racists?

But how can you believe that Katrina wasn't about race?

Is it because the President said that "the hurricane didn't discriminate," and you believed him?

Maybe that was it. But see, what happened to New Orleans had very little to do with a hurricane at all. The storm did almost nothing to the city. What occurred there was no natural disaster. What happened was a man-made tragedy, the result of human decisions not to build adequate levees, not to reinforce those levees when the opportunity was there to do so, to divert money for that purpose to other causes, and to merely hope and pray that nothing too horrible would transpire. If the Corps of Engineers had done its job; had the federal, state and local governments done their jobs—in other words, had our priorities been different all the way around, and had they included protecting mostly poor people from disaster—things would have been different.

But things weren't different, because those poor black folks were nobody's priority. They never are. And so it was, indeed, the poor and the black who bore the brunt of the chaos. It was they who were most likely to be uprooted, to have their property destroyed. And it is they who are the ones receiving the least assistance when it comes to getting home. According to a study from Brown University, which you must have missed because it didn't make the news, race was more predictive of property damage in New Orleans than any other factor, including economic status.

Oh, and please note, for those among you who call yourselves "liberals," this wasn't about George W. Bush either. Nor was it about his FEMA chief, or about the administration's incompetence, however legion it may be.

This was about all levels of government, and about both parties, failing to prioritize certain lives, and choosing instead to focus on other things and spend money elsewhere.

This was about systemic neglect, about the dependence of a city on low-wage employment in the tourist industry, which left folks vulnerable and unable to escape. It's about the consequences of allowing vital wetlands, which can reduce the storm surge from a hurricane substantially, to be destroyed, all for the sake of oil exploration or shipping interests.

It's about a political system so dominated by white elites that Ray Nagin, the Mayor of New Orleans, had to pander to them in order to be elected the first time out. He ran on a platform to run the city like a business (which he did, seeing as how business is "sink or swim"), because to do otherwise—to suggest, for example, that his administration might seek to empower black people in Central City, the Ninth Ward, or the Treme—would be to alienate the white power structure. So he said no such things, and was rewarded with nearly ninety percent of the white vote, while receiving less than forty-five percent of the black vote. Black folks voted for his opponent, who was the chief of police. Do you have any idea what it takes for black folks in a city like New Orleans, with a history of police brutality, to vote for the *cop*?

And what does it say about us, white America, that we were more likely to get angry at Nagin when he made the remarks about New Orleans once again being a Chocolate City (which was nothing more than his attempt to signal, however half-assed, that black folks were wanted back and that the black-dominated culture of the city would be restored), than we were to get angry at the white elites who at that very moment had been scheming to make New Orleans considerably more vanilla than it had been? In other words, if a black man says black folks are welcome back, and that the city will retain its pre-storm demographic, whites allege racism of the reverse kind, but if whites draw up plans to let black neighborhoods revert to swampland, or convert them to parks, thereby whitening the city's racial mix, we say nothing, or even applaud the foresight of "rebuilding smarter" than before.

Anyway, and back to the point: what happened to New Orleans was not about Republicans or Democrats, but institutional white supremacy and a class system that operates for the benefit of a few, and ultimately says, to hell with the rest. It's a system that is even now throwing up obstacles to black folks' getting back to the city: waiting over a year before offering any assistance to rebuild rental units, and even now offering little or nothing to renters themselves—which means the majority of pre-flood black folks—so as to facilitate their moving back to New Orleans. A system that still has done next to nothing to get the city's public health infrastructure back up and running, meaning that there are tens of thousands of people with post-traumatic stress, who have nowhere to turn for mental health services, to say nothing of the physical health needs that a traumatized people also require.

And here's the even bigger truth: one that many have missed. What happened in the wake of Katrina was *not* a "system failure." That phrase has been uttered many times, and not only by white liberals. Even Spike Lee has used that terminology. But this was no failure.

Failure implies that in normal circumstances, things are different. It implies that something has gone wrong, which otherwise would have gone right. But in order to believe that what happened to New Orleans was a system failure, you'd have to believe that the system had been set up to serve the needs and interests of black folks and poor folks in the first place. And surely you can't believe that.

I was in New Orleans in the mid-nineties when Bill Clinton signed into law the welfare reform bill passed by the Congress. And I saw what that legislation did to poor communities: it didn't reduce their poverty, and it didn't alter their suffering. It did however, take away one of their means for support and survival. That was a Democratic and Republican shame.

And I was there during a period when state Democrats and Republicans both bowed to big business, giving away billions of dollars in property tax breaks to some of the wealthiest corporations on the planet. And this they did, even as those companies regularly failed to provide jobs, and pumped hundreds of millions of pounds of toxic chemicals into the air and water in low income and disproportionately black communities along the river from Baton Rouge to New Orleans. That was normal operating procedure.

And although I wasn't there, I can read the history—and hear it from the folks who lived it—about how the black community was devastated by the construction of Interstate-10 in the sixties. It plowed through the Treme (pronounced truh-may—the oldest free black community in the United States), and the Seventh Ward, uprooting thousands of residents, hundreds of businesses, and the public green space that was over a mile long, on which locals had long gathered and recreated, along Claiborne Avenue.

Even the Superdome, which became the symbol of such suffering during the flood, was not a latecomer in terms of its contribution to black pain. On that land where now stands this architectural monstrosity—a venue for professional and college football, not to mention arena rock concerts—once was a neighborhood. People lived and worked there, and were moved out beginning in 1971 when white elites decided they had a better use for it. For many black folks, their first return to the spot where the community once stood may well have been as evacuees. Ironic, but true.

What happened in September 2005 was not new. So when some of you sat slack-jawed, staring at the televisions, asking yourselves "how could this happen in America?" what you didn't understand was that it has happened many times before. The history of this country is the history of folks of color being uprooted, displaced, and moved around. And almost always for the benefit of us.

In the fifties and sixties, hundreds of thousands of dwellings lived in by black and brown peoples were destroyed to make way for those interstates, and office parks, and malls, and parking lots, all in the name of urban renewal and progress. No water, no wind, no storms, just people, deciding that the fate of the affected communities was unimportant. And it wasn't just New Orleans. It happened with a vengeance in St. Louis, the South Bronx, Montgomery, Columbia, Camden, Birmingham, Kansas Caity, Charlotte, Pittsburgh, St. Paul, Indianapolis, Los Angeles, Pasadena, Tampa, St. Petersburg, Jacksonville, Orlando, Miami, Milwaukee, Cleveland, Chicago and Atlanta, among others. And it was allowed and even encouraged by Democrats and Republicans alike.

And as black and brown housing was being destroyed, the government was subsidizing white housing in the suburbs, with FHA and VA loans that, in practice, were all but off limits to folks of color. Indeed, the interstates that replaced black communities served as conveyor belts for those whites who still worked in town but lived in those suburbs, allowing them to get back and forth more quickly. Meanwhile, those left behind had to crowd into dilapidated public housing or tiny apartments, unable to hustle it to the hinterlands themselves, their mobility limited by both economics and racial discrimination of a most profound sort. And this, too, was allowed by Democrats and Republicans alike.

No, this was no failure. It was the system operating exactly as intended: take care of the haves and to the rest, good damned luck. In systemic terms, this thing here was what we call, success.

How, after all, can this catastrophe be seen as a failure, or the result of incompetence, when the government—at the state and federal levels through the Office of Homeland Security—ordered the Red Cross not to provide relief to those in need? What's that you say? You hadn't heard that? Well of course not. But it's true: there was a relief blockade acknowledged by the Red Cross on their own website and elsewhere by various officials, within the first few days of the suffering. According to the Red Cross at the time, "The Department of Homeland Security continues to request that the American Red Cross not come back into New Orleans following the Hurricane. Our presence would keep people from evacuating and encourage others to come into the city." So, government officials, more desirous of evacuating the city than helping the sick and dying, told the premier relief group on the planet to stand down and to do nothing within the city of New Orleans. Nowhere else in the hurricane zone was this order given, but it was there. I will leave it to you to determine why, and what the answer suggests about the priorities of officialdom.

In truth, the entire frame through which most of you were encouraged to view the tragedy of Katrina was distorted from the get go.

First, there was the white obliviousness to how folks of color have been living for a long time; obliviousness so profound that we found it truly shocking that people could be left behind that way. David Brooks, who is one of our people—and a prototypical one at that—wrote incredulously in the New York Times, for example, about how "the first rule of the social fabric—that in times of crisis you protect the vulnerable—was trampled." But what kind of fantasy world could allow one to believe that? For some, including poor black folks in New Orleans or elsewhere, every day is a time of crisis, and they are never protected from it. So whatever social fabric dear Mr. Brooks may be referring to, it clearly has never meant much to millions of people whom he appears just now to have discovered.

Brooks went on to say that because of the government's "failure" in Katrina, "confidence in out civic institutions is plummeting." But confidence can only plummet when one has confidence to begin with. And who was saddled with such an affliction of naïveté, after all? Surely not the black folks of New Orleans, and surely not the poor anywhere. Only middle class and above white folks have the luxury of believing in the system and being totally amazed when it doesn't seem to work as they expected. That too is about privilege: the privilege of being stone cold stupid, and having no idea whatsoever about how your society actually operates.

Then there was the frame—pun very much intended—provided by the right-wing blowhards who hold forth on talk radio. I know some of y'all are as disgusted by these guys (and they are mostly guys) as I am. But an awful lot of you hang on their every word. You keep them in business, in fact. And you believe what they say, no matter how utterly counterfactual their verbal emissions tend to be.

So one after another lined up to sing the same tired song: the one that blamed the victims left behind for their predicament. The first verse of the song blames their laziness, while the second verse explains their laziness as a function of the welfare state, which has presumably sapped their initiative to do for themselves. In other words, as the chorus to the song suggests, it's all the fault of big government and liberalism.

But even five minutes of research could have dispelled such nonsense, had they or you cared to do it. You could have learned, with a simple Google search, and by following the links provided therein to the Census Bureau and elsewhere, that at the time of the storm there were only 4600 households in the entire city receiving cash welfare: this, out of 130,000 black households alone, which means that even if every welfare recipient in New Orleans had been black (and they weren't), still, less than four percent of such households would have qualified for your derision. And of those few receiving such benefits, the average *annual* amount received—that's right, annual amount—was a mere $2800 per household, hardly enough to make anyone lazy.

In the lower ninth ward, one of the hardest hit communities, and a place about which so much was said (and so much of it inaccurate), only eight percent of the income received by persons living there came from government assistance, while seventy-one percent of it came from paid employment. In other words, folks in New Orleans were by and large poor in spite of their work ethic. Forty percent of employed folks in the Lower 9 worked full-time and had average commutes to and from work of forty-five minutes a day. But the media didn't tell you that, and the right-wing commentators flatly lied about it.

And so with the people of that city fully demonized as criminal and lazy welfare cheats, the frame had been set, allowing so many of you to call for the shooting of looters—as was demanded repeatedly on chat room bulletin boards, and on national television by Reagan speechwriter, Peggy Noonan. Compassion is the first and most glaring casualty of racism and class contempt.

And so now what, white America? As rents are up seventy percent across the city, as schools remain closed, or converted to charter schools, inadequate to the task of welcoming back all the children emptied from the city? As health care remains spotty at best, and only one-fourth of the child care centers and bus lines are up and running? As the nation's attention has shifted to other issues, so much so that the candidates for President speak almost none at all about the tragedy that befell this great town only twenty-six months ago as I write this?

When are you (are we) going to wake up and demand better, of ourselves and others? When are we going to make the cessation of ethnic cleansing a priority, not only when it happens in some other place on the globe, but in our own backyard? When are we going to recognize the commonality of interests we have with those who are always the first and worst victims of these kinds of injustices?

Because that's really the point we've failed to appreciate up to now.

If you don't believe me, take a look next door to New Orleans, at St. Bernard Parish, and places like Chalmette. Chalmette is right across the canal from the Lower 9. And as with the Lower 9, it was populated before the storm mostly by working class folks. But unlike the Lower 9, it was almost exclusively white. And the white folks there, despite their class status, felt decidedly superior to the black folks across the way. That's why seventy percent of them voted for David Duke in 1991 when he ran for Governor. And that's why they would do it again were he to appear on a ballot in the future.

And yet, what does it say about the system of white privilege that those whites—who had the luxury of believing themselves superior—ended up in the same boat as the poor blacks whom they feared and despised, in the wake of Katrina? What does it say that while whites in "da Parish," as it's known, railed against black folks (to whom they referred in a decidedly more hostile manner, to be sure), they were missing the sad and tragic fact that the same elites who didn't give a crap about those in the Lower 9, or New Orleans East (a black and mostly middle class community devastated by the flooding as well), didn't much care about them either? The levees that failed, failed them all.

Perhaps if whites weren't so used to scapegoating black and brown folks for our own misfortunes, whites in St. Bernard might have extended their hand to blacks in the Lower 9, and together they could have marched on the Corps of Engineers, on Baton Rouge, on Washington. Anything. But no. And now they all ended up with their stuff jacked, so to speak.

But did they learn? Did you? As for St. Bernard, the answer seems to be no, sadly. The first thing the Parish leaders did upon returning home was pass an ordinance (since rescinded due to legal threats), which would have prohibited anyone from renting property to someone that wasn't a blood relative of the landlord—a pretty transparent way to limit entry to whites without saying that was your intent. So they still haven't learned very much it seems.

And what of you? What have you learned in the midst of this catastrophe? What are you prepared to do, to demand of your leaders? Of yourself? For it isn't enough to write a check, no matter how big, for relief efforts. That's charity, which is nice, but solidarity would be nicer and more meaningful. That means that it isn't enough to support the building of houses—or even to help build them yourselves with groups like Habitat for Humanity or whomever—unless you also begin asking the larger questions about why there is a housing crisis in this country in the first place, and why affordable housing is so hard to come by, not only in New Orleans post-Katrina, but across the country, including several of the places where you live. And you'd best care about this, because a lack of affordable housing ultimately creates the kind of real estate bubble which even now is bursting all across the country: prices keep going up, up, up, with no apparent end in sight, and then pretty soon even the so-called middle-class can't swing the mortgage any longer. Oops.

And it isn't enough to go down to New Orleans with your church group, or with others from your school, and "help" the suffering masses. You and I must do more. We must see our fates as linked to theirs. We must see them as family. We must demand that their needs be prioritized at all levels of government, and we must refuse to lend our support to candidates who fail to do so. We must listen to the leaders of the affected communities, and hear what *they* say they need, rather than assuming that we know what is best for them. If we go to New Orleans, let us do so to learn as much as to help; to learn what we need to know for the larger struggle back home—the struggle for justice and equity. For that is the battle in which your enlistment is so sorely needed now.

New Orleans as we knew it has died. What it will yet become is up to us. This is the legacy we will leave to our children. And I sincerely hope that you and I—that all of us—are up to the task.

I guess we'll see.

Venerates
p69

Oprah Effect